Getting Started with WAP and WML

Huw Evans
Paul Ashworth

SYBEX®

San Francisco • Paris • Düsseldorf • Soest • London

Associate Publisher: Richard Mills
Contracts and Licensing Manager: Kristine O'Callaghan
Acquisitions Editor: Brenda Frink
Developmental Editor: Tracy Brown
Editors: Ronn Jost, Julie Sakaue
Production Editor: Kylie Johnston
Contributing Technical Reviewer: Steve Potts
Lead Technical Editor: Steve Potts
Technical Editors: Steve Cook, Shayne Micchia
Book Designer: Kris Warrenburg
Graphic Illustrator: Tony Jonick
Electronic Publishing Specialist: Judy Fung
Proofreaders: Laurie O'Connell, Laura A. Ryan
Indexer: Nancy Guenther
CD Technician: Keith McNeil
CD Coordinators: Kara Schwartz, Erica Yee
Cover Designer: Design Site
Cover Illustrator: Jack D. Myers, Design Site

Copyright © 2001 SYBEX Inc., 1151 Marina Village Parkway, Alameda, CA 94501. World rights reserved. The authors created reusable code in this publication expressly for reuse by readers. Sybex grants readers permission to reuse for any purpose the code found in this publication or its accompanying CD-ROM so long as authors are attributed in any application containing the reusable code and the code itself is never distri-buted, posted online by electronic transmission, sold, or commercially exploited as a stand-alone product. Aside from this specific exception concerning reusable code, no part of this publication may be stored in a retrieval system, transmitted, or reproduced in any way, including but not limited to photocopy, photograph, magnetic, or other record, without the prior agreement and written permission of the publisher.

Library of Congress Card Number: 2001087088

ISBN: 0-7821-2870-X

SYBEX and the SYBEX logo are trademarks of SYBEX Inc. in the USA and other countries.

The CD interface was created using Macromedia Director, COPYRIGHT 1994, 1997–1999 Macromedia Inc. For more information on Macromedia and Macromedia Director, visit http://www.macromedia.com.

TRADEMARKS: SYBEX has attempted throughout this book to distinguish proprietary trademarks from descriptive terms by following the capitalization style used by the manufacturer.

The author and publisher have made their best efforts to prepare this book, and the content is based upon final release software whenever possible. Portions of the manuscript may be based upon pre-release versions supplied by software manufacturer(s). The author and the publisher make no representation or warranties of any kind with regard to the completeness or accuracy of the contents herein and accept no liability of any kind including but not limited to performance, merchantability, fitness for any particular purpose, or any losses or damages of any kind caused or alleged to be caused directly or indirectly from this book.

Manufactured in the United States of America

10 9 8 7 6 5 4 3 2 1

Getting Started with WAP and WML

Terms and Conditions

The media and/or any online materials accompanying this book that are available now or in the future contain programs and/or text files (the "Software") to be used in connection with the book. SYBEX hereby grants to you a license to use the Software, subject to the terms that follow. Your purchase, acceptance, or use of the Software will constitute your acceptance of such terms.

The Software compilation is the property of SYBEX unless otherwise indicated and is protected by copyright to SYBEX or other copyright owner(s) as indicated in the media files (the "Owner(s)"). You are hereby granted a single-user license to use the Software for your personal, noncommercial use only. You may not reproduce, sell, distribute, publish, circulate, or commercially exploit the Software, or any portion thereof, without the written consent of SYBEX and the specific copyright owner(s) of any component software included on this media.

In the event that the Software or components include specific license requirements or end-user agreements, statements of condition, disclaimers, limitations or warranties ("End-User License"), those End-User Licenses supersede the terms and conditions herein as to that particular Software component. Your purchase, acceptance, or use of the Software will constitute your acceptance of such End-User Licenses.

By purchase, use or acceptance of the Software you further agree to comply with all export laws and regulations of the United States as such laws and regulations may exist from time to time.

Reusable Code in This Book

The authors created reusable code in this publication expressly for reuse for readers. Sybex grants readers permission to reuse for any purpose the code found in this publication or its accompanying CD-ROM so long as all authors are attributed in any application containing the reusable code, and the code itself is never sold or commercially exploited as a stand-alone product.

Software Support

Components of the supplemental Software and any offers associated with them may be supported by the specific Owner(s) of that material but they are not supported by SYBEX. Information regarding any available support may be obtained from the Owner(s) using the information provided in the appropriate read.me files or listed elsewhere on the media.

Should the manufacturer(s) or other Owner(s) cease to offer support or decline to honor any offer, SYBEX bears no responsibility. This notice concerning support for the Software is provided for your information only. SYBEX is not the agent or principal of the Owner(s), and SYBEX is in no way responsible for providing any support for the Software, nor is it liable or responsible for any support provided, or not provided, by the Owner(s).

Warranty

SYBEX warrants the enclosed media to be free of physical defects for a period of ninety (90) days after purchase. The Software is not available from SYBEX in any other form or media than that enclosed herein or posted to www.sybex.com. If you discover a defect in the media during this warranty period, you may obtain a replacement of identical format at no charge by sending the defective media, postage prepaid, with proof of purchase to:

SYBEX Inc.
Customer Service Department
1151 Marina Village Parkway
Alameda, CA 94501
(510) 523-8233
Fax: (510) 523-2373
e-mail: info@sybex.com
WEB: WWW.SYBEX.COM

After the 90-day period, you can obtain replacement media of identical format by sending us the defective disk, proof of purchase, and a check or money order for $10, payable to SYBEX.

Disclaimer

SYBEX makes no warranty or representation, either expressed or implied, with respect to the Software or its contents, quality, performance, merchantability, or fitness for a particular purpose. In no event will SYBEX, its distributors, or dealers be liable to you or any other party for direct, indirect, special, incidental, consequential, or other damages arising out of the use of or inability to use the Software or its contents even if advised of the possibility of such damage. In the event that the Software includes an online update feature, SYBEX further disclaims any obligation to provide this feature for any specific duration other than the initial posting.

The exclusion of implied warranties is not permitted by some states. Therefore, the above exclusion may not apply to you. This warranty provides you with specific legal rights; there may be other rights that you may have that vary from state to state. The pricing of the book with the Software by SYBEX reflects the allocation of risk and limitations on liability contained in this agreement of Terms and Conditions.

Shareware Distribution

This Software may contain various programs that are distributed as shareware. Copyright laws apply to both shareware and ordinary commercial software, and the copyright Owner(s) retains all rights. If you try a shareware program and continue using it, you are expected to register it. Individual programs differ on details of trial periods, registration, and payment. Please observe the requirements stated in appropriate files.

Copy Protection

The Software in whole or in part may or may not be copy-protected or encrypted. However, in all cases, reselling or redistributing these files without authorization is expressly forbidden except as specifically provided for by the Owner(s) therein.

This book is dedicated to all those brave pioneers in the world of the wireless Internet, who like ourselves can see the limitless opportunities created by enabling anyone to connect to a server from wherever they are. We think it will have an even more profound effect on the way we live and do business than the Internet has already had. By reading this book, you become a pioneer in the world of the wireless Internet, too, and we invite you to learn about the main wireless Internet–enabling technology—WAP—and find out just how easily our vision can be turned into reality.

ACKNOWLEDGMENTS

Writing this book was one of the most difficult tasks we've both ever taken on in our lives. We both come from a computer consultancy background, and figured that if we can learn and assimilate new technologies, then use them to resolve our clients' problems, it would be relatively easy to learn and assimilate a technology and write a book about it. Not at all! First, we wanted to develop an example WAP application that we could use as an ongoing example throughout the book, in an attempt to make the learning experience as close to real life as possible. This became much more difficult than you would ever imagine, as the application developed from a few static WML cards to a fully functional WAP service with WML cards being served up by Java servlets. But what fun it was learning how to program using Java servlets, then having the satisfaction of seeing our own WML pages being generated by a Web server!

We both also went through big personal changes while writing this book. My second son, Hugo, was born in October 2000, roughly halfway through writing the book. This made the task twice as hard as it would have been, as suddenly I was holding a colicky baby during the evenings, instead of writing this book! At the same time, my co-author, Huw Evans, changed jobs and found himself ramping up in a new role at the same time as writing this book!

And through all this, the team at Sybex did a fantastic job of guiding us through our first book. Tracy Brown got us up and running, and Kylie Johnston did a great job of coordinating the project, as well as keeping the schedule on track when we both started getting bogged down with events in our personal lives. There were also complete editing and production teams involved in the creation of this book, whose care and diligence will ensure this book meets Sybex's high quality standards. Finally, just as we were running out of time, Steve Potts of Geoworks came in and helped us immeasurably by completing the unfinished parts of the book, as well as tying the loose ends together and generally making sure that the content of the book was coherent. Thanks to Steve for his enthusiasm and technical contributions in the writing of this book. A big thank you to you all.

—Paul Ashworth

CONTENTS AT A GLANCE

Introduction	*xv*
Chapter 1: Introducing WAP and WML	1
Chapter 2: Getting Started	21
Chapter 3: Your First WML Pages	45
Chapter 4: Spicing It Up	65
Chapter 5: Adding Intelligence with WMLScript	87
Chapter 6: Tuning Your Service	129
Chapter 7: Making Your Service Dynamic	153
Chapter 8: Internationalizing Your WAP Service	183
Appendix A: WML Elements	221
Appendix B: WMLScript Reference	259
Appendix C: ISO 639 Two-Letter Language Codes	311
Appendix D: ISO 3166 Two-Letter Country Codes	327
Index	*348*

CONTENTS

Introduction	*xv*
1 Introducing WAP and WML	**1**
What Is WAP?	2
What Is WML?	4
What Is WMLScript?	6
The WAP Architecture	9
The WAP Protocol	12
WAP Standards	15
WAP Devices	16
The Future	18
2 Getting Started	**21**
WML Structure	22
Cards and Decks	22
Elements	24
Attributes	26
Comments	27
Variables	27
The Deck Structure	28
Installing an SDK	29
WAP SDKs	30
WAP Emulators	32
A Simple WML Program	35
The Example Application	39
The First Steps	39
Performing Some Validations with WMLScript	40
The Server Side Programming	41
3 Your First WML Pages	**45**
Getting Started	46
Formatting Text	48
Adding Images to WML Cards	50

Moving Around	52
Navigating with User Agent Buttons	52
Navigating with Lists	54

4 Spicing It Up   65

Letting Users Input Data	66
Letting Users Enter Text	66
Letting Users Enter Options from a List	68
Using Variables	71
Displaying Variable Values	71
Setting Variable Values	72
Passing Variable Values to Other Applications	72
Referencing Variables in the Example Application	73
Acting on Variables Set by the User	74
Variable Escaping	77
Using WML Events	78
Intrinsic Events	78
User Events	82

5 Adding Intelligence with WMLScript   87

WMLScript Characteristics	88
WMLScript Interpreter Architecture	89
Error Handling	90
Debugging WMLScript	90
WMLScript Overview	91
Lexical Structure	91
Literals	92
WMLScript Variables	94
Data Types	95
WMLScript Operators	96
WMLScript Type Conversions	101
WMLScript Statements	101
Reserved Words	105
Pragmas	106
WMLScript Libraries	106
Connecting WML and WMLScript	107
Calling a WMLScript Function	108
Using Variables in WMLScript	111
Validating Data	118

	WMLScript Functions	119
	The Full Compilation Unit	121

6 Tuning Your Service — 129

HTTP Overview	130
HTTP Methods	132
Caching in HTTP 1.1	136
Some HTTP Caching Features	137
Caching in WAP	139
The WAP Caching Model	139
Data Quantities Using GET and POST	145
The WML <meta> Element	146
Using Multipart Messages to Enhance Responses	146
Minimizing WML Security Risks	147
WAP and Java	149
WAP and Java Servlets	149
WAP and JSP	150

7 Making Your Service Dynamic — 153

Basic Information about Java Servlets	155
Importing the Classes	155
Back to Importing the Classes	156
Declaring the Global Variables	156
Handling User Agent Interaction	157
Outputting WML Code	157
The Example Servlet	158
Logging On	159
Listing the Movies	165
Displaying the Movie Details	167
Reserving the Tickets	169
Calculating the Cost of the Reserved Tickets	170
The Complete Servlet	173

8 Internationalizing Your WAP Service — 183

Delivering Multilingual Content	185
HTTP Languages	187
Quality Value	188
Delivering Content Based on the Accept-Language Header	188
The Content-Language Header	193

	Text Direction	194
	Character Sets	196
	Transfer Encodings	197
	Tailoring Multilingual Content	205
A	**WML Elements**	**221**
B	**WMLScript Reference**	**259**
C	**ISO 639 Two-Letter Language Codes**	**311**
D	**ISO 3166 Two-Letter Country Codes**	**327**
	Index	*348*

INTRODUCTION

The Wireless Application Protocol (WAP) is a new technology linking the Internet to wireless portable devices. It marks the dawning of the new age of wireless commerce, a means of communicating and performing wireless transactions that will represent a major change in the way we live and do business.

WAP bridges the gap between the Internet and the wireless world, offering the potential for an unlimited range of value-added services to be delivered to users irrespective of the network or device they're using. This convergence of the Internet and cellular telephony, two of the fastest growing technologies of the last decade, will allow the transformation of information on the Internet to a form that can be displayed on the restricted screen sizes associated with cellular phones and other portable devices such as personal digital assistants (PDAs).

WAP is the essential link between the Internet viewed through a PC browser and the increasing capabilities of cellular phones and other wireless devices. It provides a single, industry-standard mechanism for wireless application interoperability called the Wireless Markup Language (WML), developed from the earlier Handheld Devices Markup Language (HDML). WML provides a clear way for application developers and content providers to create a range of services via WAP browsers installed on the new generation of wireless devices. WML is supported by a scripting language called WMLScript, which brings procedural logic to client services.

Wireless devices use WML and WMLScript to produce content, and they make optimum use of small displays and are designed to allow one-handed navigation. This WAP content is scalable from a two-line text display all the way up to the more sophisticated full-graphics-capability screens on the next generation of smart wireless devices.

The Next Internet Explosion

The Internet has changed the way people perceive and use the power of the computer. It has led to a revolution in the way we communicate and do business. And just as the revolution is beginning to influence the lives of the mainstream populations of most developed countries, the Internet is itself on the verge of an even more explosive revolution in the way we access it. Within the next couple of years, our ability to access the power of the Internet through wireless devices will start to become second nature as new WAP-enabled cellular phones and computing devices start to become commonplace.

A wireless device's screen can display only a few characters, its bandwidth is extremely limited, and entering text is awkward. However, the success of WAP-enabled cellular phones will be driven by the facts that users will be able to access WAP applications wherever they are and built-in billing mechanisms will allow service providers to automatically charge the device's owner for accessing services.

At the moment, European countries are leading the way in the adoption of cellular telephony. The huge increase in the use of WAP has been in Europe, where countries like Germany and Finland are setting the trends for the U.S. and the rest of the world to follow.

This emerging market for wireless portable devices is being driven by the cash-rich telecommunications vendors who see a future as rosy for wireless commerce as the recent past (and present) has been for desktop-based e-commerce. Leading telecom trailblazers Nokia of Finland, Ericsson of Sweden, and Motorola of the U.S. are ramping up for the anticipated wireless Internet explosion and are now making handsets with WAP capabilities generally available.

By 2004, it is estimated that there will be more than one billion cellular phones in circulation and around 700 million wireless commerce users. By this time, the number of wireless data users worldwide will have grown rapidly from the 31.7 million estimated in 1999 to around 750 million. In developed countries, the percentage of wireless subscribers using data will be above 70 percent, with the highest (79 percent) in Japan. Some analysts predict that within three years, more people will be accessing the Internet from mobile phones than from PCs. One of the main reasons for this is that, unlike with computers, people keep mobiles with them at home, in the office, and on the move.

The first devices now entering the marketplace are slow and restricted both in format and content, but they point the way to the future. WAP personal digital assistants and cellular phones are now able to browse the Internet and access sites and services specially designed for them using WML.

WAP will provide business with a new channel for existing and future services that can be reached by their customers day or night wherever they go. The uses of

WAP-enabled portable devices are not restricted to only content push services such as accessing the latest sports results, news, and weather. Users will be able to access sites allowing them, for example, to reserve seats at restaurants, theaters, and hotels, and to conduct transactions such as purchasing financial services and buying concert tickets.

By late 1998, WAP 1.0 had been superficially tested but had generated enough results to determine that it had a few flaws. Forum members declared an interest in developing enhancements to the standards, to extend the penetration of WAP. The enhancements were of such great consequence to the future of WAP's success that the Forum decided to discard WAP 1.0, and eliminate backwards compatibility in the attempt to create a workable and successful solution. The next release was to be an important baseline.

WAP 1.1 was announced in May of 1999; and soon after, WAP-enabled terminals started to enter the market. The WAP standard's goal is to enable all wireless devices equipped with a WAP microbrowser to access live information resources and applications. Content and application developers support palmtops, laptops, and standard and smart mobile phones. They also support a range of input and output devices including touch screens and bitmapped displays. Since the publication of WAP 1.1, the gap between current wireless data and the third generation networks expected to roll out in 2003/2004 has started to be bridged.

WAP 1.2 was announced in December of 1999, with a maintenance release 1.2.1 (formally known as WAP June 2000) increasing interoperability. WML is the markup language of WAP. Because WAP 1.1 is an important baseline, and because of the prevalence of WML 1.1 (as specified in WAP 1.1) devices in the marketplace, it is this version we will use throughout this book. We will also make you aware of changes introduced in WML 1.2 (in WAP 1.2) and WML 1.3 (in WAP June 2000) by highlighting the relevant version differences.

What's in This Book

This book will provide you with all you need to create a WAP application using WML. It starts by introducing you to the WAP technology and its concepts, and showing you how to download, install, and test your own WAP development environment.

Once you have your WAP development environment installed, you'll start to develop an example application. The aim of this approach is to demonstrate how you can use all the various WML and WMLScript features in a real environment, instead of using abstract examples. We'll build the site as we go through the book. Each time a concept or feature is explained, it will be integrated into the example application.

The site will go through three phases. In the first phase, we're going to develop some static cards using WML. This will get you into the swing of things and show you how to develop WML code to present information on wireless Internet devices, such as PDAs, palmtops, and cellular phones. In the second phase, we're going to use WMLScript to add some process logic to our example site, such as checking that values are entered correctly and performing mathematical calculations. In the third phase, we're going to turn the site into a fully functional WAP site that generates WML cards dynamically.

Once we have created our site and taken a complete tour of the WAP site creation process, we'll look at how we can internationalize our site to make it accessible by people using WAP-enabled devices all over the world! Now all that's left for you to do is create your own WAP site!

Chapter 1

Introducing WAP and WML

This chapter introduces you to the Wireless Application Protocol (WAP) and the key markup language you'll need to grasp to develop content for WAP-enabled wireless devices. This language, called Wireless Markup Language (WML), is supplemented by its own scripting language, called WMLScript, which will be introduced before a discussion on WAP architecture, standards, devices, and what the future holds in this fast-moving technological environment.

What Is WAP?

Wireless Application Protocol (WAP) is a set of standards designed to extend Internet services to mobile phones, pagers, and personal digital assistants (PDAs). The development of WAP is coordinated by an industry-wide group of companies under the banner of the WAP Forum. The WAP Forum was created to apply the best principles of Internet application development to the wireless environment. See the sidebar later in this chapter for more on the WAP Forum.

WAP has become the de facto worldwide standard for the presentation and delivery of wireless information and telephony services on mobile phones and other wireless devices. It is an open protocol that provides the same development standards to all vendors irrespective of the underlying network system. It is designed to work under the low bandwidth constraints of wireless networks. These constraints are currently around 10Kbps compared with the standard 56Kbps on home computers using domestic telephone lines with standard dial-up modems. As most wireless computing devices have limited processing power and memory, and are designed with screen displays and small multifunction keypads, WAP was developed with these limitations in mind. WAP was created to address three main issues related to data communications across wireless networks: low bandwidth, high latency, and connection availability.

Because WAP is an open protocol, a number of manufacturers are producing a wide range of WAP-enabled devices. These manufacturers in turn are able to source from a large range of WAP-specified components because the server technology is also open. This general openness and adoption of common standards means that developers, manufacturers, and content providers are able to adopt WAP with confidence and benefit from the economies of scale.

WAP uses a client/server architecture that employs an unsophisticated wireless-based microbrowser and requires only limited resources and a WAP gateway to deliver content from the server where it is stored. It is a standard independent of the air interface, the user interface, and the underlying data bearer. Therefore, it is entirely interoperable. Because WAP is based on existing Internet technologies, it leverages the massive investment in similar conventional Web tools, applications, servers, and their developers while considering the restricted bandwidth, processing power, and memory currently available on wireless portable devices.

Web content is available over existing wireless communication networks through a WAP gateway. Figure 1.1 illustrates how an established WWW infrastructure, based on the Hypertext Transfer Protocol (HTTP), uses a WAP gateway to interface with the wireless network by translating HTTP requests into wireless device requests.

FIGURE 1.1:

The WAP gateway

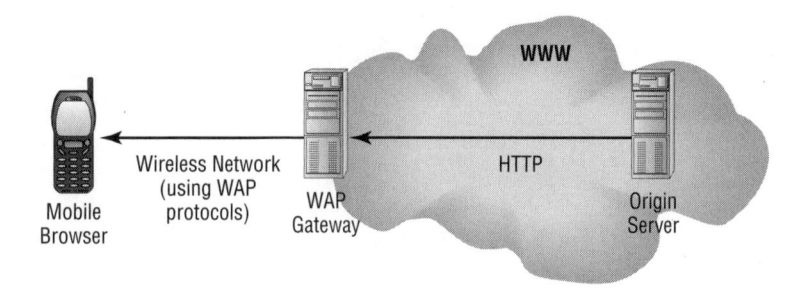

The 1997 WAP Forum specification is unique in that it is truly global and spans the numerous airlink standards. WAP specifies guidelines for the implementation of microbrowsers and the network-resident servers that connect portable wireless devices to the network infrastructure and the Web. For the carriers, the creation of WAP means minimum risk and investment, new sources of revenue, and a more attractive, comprehensive suite of value-added services. For users, it provides easy access via WAP-enabled handheld devices to the Web and secure access to corporate intranets. Manufacturers also benefit from the provision of a global, open, de facto standard. They're provided with a complete new range of marketing opportunities and revenue streams, while the content providers and developers are confronted with the huge untapped market of wireless customers and the prospect of 100 million WAP-enabled devices by mid-2001.

What Is WML?

Wireless Markup Language (WML) is to WAP and its handheld devices what Hypertext Markup Language (HTML) is to the Web and browsers such as Netscape and Internet Explorer. It describes how content is presented to the wireless device, allowing you to display information, present input options, and tell user agents (programs that interpret WML, WMLScript, and other forms of code—typically a microbrowser in a mobile phone) how to respond once an option has been selected using the keypad.

WML is a subset or an application of the eXtensible Markup Language (XML), and because WAP uses a similar model as the Internet, it allows content developers to quickly become proficient with this relatively simple tag-based language while allowing a clear development path. WML is based on the World Wide Web Consortium (W3C) guidelines for wireless access and works similarly to HTML to deliver Web text using simple markup tags.

WML's user interface is a WAP microbrowser optimized to map onto mobile wireless devices. A WML document is called a *deck*, which is comparable to an HTML page. Unlike the flat structure of HTML content, WML documents—or decks—are divided into separate units of user interaction. Each unit is called a *card*, and WAP services are created by letting the user navigate between the cards of one or more decks in much the same way hyperlinks are used within and between HTML documents.

WAP gateways provide the interface between the network and Internet or intranet services. From this gateway, WML content is accessed over the Internet using the standard HTTP mechanism.

WAP developers and content providers can get up to speed quickly with WML, as it follows the same programming model as the Web development model. It is a tag-based language specified as an XML document type, so all existing XML tools and some HTML development environments can be used to develop WAP applications. As standard HTTP is used for communication between gateway and servers, developers can use off-the-shelf Web servers to deploy their applications. Standard tools such as ColdFusion and CGI scripting languages such as Perl, PHP, and ASP generate content for dynamic WML applications.

The WML specification was developed by the WAP Forum and defines the syntax, variables, and elements to be used in a valid WML file. The WML 1.1 Document Type Definition (DTD) is available from www.wapforum.org/DTD/wml_1.1.xml, and all WML applications must correspond to it. The microbrowser that all WAP-compliant wireless devices are loaded with is able to handle all entities in the WML 1.1 DTD.

The WAP gateway translates wireless device requests into HTTP requests and then redirects the Web server's HTTP responses to the device. WML files being sent to WAP-enabled handheld devices are compressed into a binary format by the WAP gateway. It is possible to translate HTML into WML using a number of available filter tools, but in practice, the differing user interfaces employed between the desktop and wireless environments make specific WML-tailored solutions the norm.

A WAP emulator is a program that implements a WAP microbrowser, but is designed to run on a non-WAP device, such as a Windows PC. Emulators are often used by developers to speed up the development process, as well as to reduce the costs of using WAP during testing each time a change is made. They are also useful to see how a real WAP device will look, because many of these emulators mimic the look and feel of real WAP devices. A list of available emulators is provided in later chapters. When a WAP emulator is used, a WAP gateway is not required because WML files are downloaded from a Web server or local file, and the emulator renders it in the Emulator window. Figure 1.2 shows this process.

FIGURE 1.2:

Displaying WAP content using a gateway and an emulator

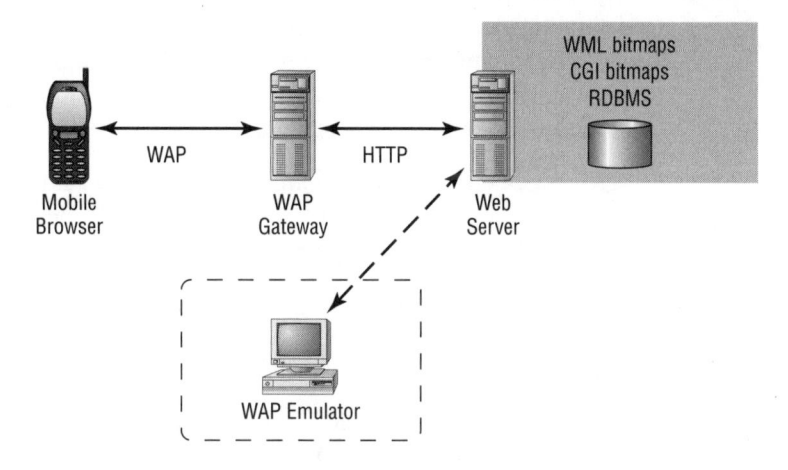

Applications and services written in WML become available to all network devices that are WAP compliant, delivering a *write once, use anywhere* tool. WML developers can map soft keys (appropriated to physical keys on the WAP-enabled device by the manufacturer) for easy user input and take advantage of features designed to maximize the effect of displaying text on a limited screen. Low-resolution graphics known as WBMPs can be used, and as bandwidth increases, so too will the resolution of the graphics supported by the WAP specification. As long as a recipient device is WAP compliant, the size of the device's display is automatically accounted for by the microbrowser and the use of standard HTTP header mechanisms to learn about a device's capabilities. These header mechanisms allow the developer to customize applications to take advantage of different device characteristics. This technique is known as *device sensing* and is the same in principle as the HTML of many Web sites that detect which Web browser and version you are running to provide an optimal display and to allow support for browser-specific features.

While WML is good at things like event processing, input and output handling, and rendering, it has no practical processing abilities. It is, therefore, supplemented by the WMLScript scripting language.

What Is WMLScript?

In addition to WML, the WAP Forum provides a scripting language called *WMLScript*. WMLScript is used alongside WML (or independently of it) to provide intelligence in the form of procedural logic to client services. WMLScript is to WML what JavaScript is to HTML. In fact, WMLScript is based on ECMAScript, a derivative of JavaScript, and has been designed to support the relatively low bandwidth restrictions applicable to handheld wireless devices.

WMLScript enhances the capabilities of WML in a number of ways. With it, you can access user agent facilities, check user input, generate local messages and dialogs, and execute user agent software.

This functionality allows you to locally program things like error messages and alerts for faster viewing, add to your wireless address book, and interrogate SIM cards.

WMLScript defines functions containing flow control logic constructs such as `while`, `if`, and `for`, which can be called from the main body of the WML program.

Even so, WMLScript still lacks basic programming features such as arithmetic functions, string handling, and WML 1.1 program interfacing capabilities. It therefore has to rely on a set of standard libraries to access functions relating to dialog presentation, floating point numbers, string conversion, and integer handling.

WMLScript is compiled by a WAP gateway into binary form to reduce the code's size and therefore minimize transfer time. It defines a byte-code representation and a byte-code interpreter for optimal utilization of current low bandwidth channels and wireless device memory restrictions. In brief, WMLScript uses the following syntax rules:

- The smallest unit of execution in WMLScript is a statement, and each statement must end with a semicolon (;).
- WMLScript is case sensitive.
- Comments can either be single-line (beginning with //) or multi-line (bracketed by /* and */). This syntax is identical to that of both C++ and Java.
- A literal character string is defined as any sequence of zero or more characters enclosed within double (" ") or single (') quotes.
- Boolean literal values correspond to true and false.
- New variables are declared using the var keyword (i.e., var x;).
- WMLScript has no type checking done at compile-time or runtime, and no variable types are explicitly declared. Internally, the following data types are supported:
    - Boolean
    - Integer
    - Floating point
    - String
    - Invalid

You do not need to specify the type of any variable because WMLScript automatically attempts to convert between the different types as required. It is also worth noting that WMLScript is not object-oriented, so it is not possible to create your own user-defined data types programmatically.

WMLScript allows a variety of operators that support value assignment operations, arithmetic operations, logical operations, string operations, comparison operations, and array operations. WMLScript operators and expressions are nearly identical to those of the JavaScript programming language.

Although WMLScript does not support the creation of new objects via object-oriented programming, the six libraries that are provided help in the handling of many common tasks. The Lang library includes functions for data type manipulation, absolute value calculations, and random number generation. The optional Float library includes `sqrt()`, `round()`, and `pow()` functions but is supported only on those wireless devices with floating point capabilities. The String library contains a set of functions for performing string operations. Some of the functions included in this library are `length()`, `charAt()`, `find()`, `replace()`, and `trim()`. A URL library is provided for handling both absolute URLs and relative URLs. Extraction functions let you retrieve individual components from absolute and relative URLs, and include `getPath()`, `getReferer()`, and `getHost()`. A WMLBrowser provides `go()`, `prev()`, `next()`, `getCurrentCard()`, and `refresh()`, where WMLScript can access the associated WML context. Finally, a Dialogs library provides a set of typical user-interface functions including `prompt()`, `confirm()`, and `alert()`.

The WAP Forum

The Wireless Application Protocol Forum was created in 1997 to provide a worldwide open standard for the delivery of Internet-based services to wireless handheld devices. It was formed by an alliance of partners made up of telephone manufacturers, Motorola, Ericsson, Nokia, and Unwired Planet, a US software company that changed its name to Phone.com (which recently merged with Software.com to become Openwave).

Before the formation of this group, the concerned players were all working independently to address the issue of developing a schema to increase the capabilities of wireless telephony platforms. Ericsson had begun work with a protocol called ITTP (Intelligent Terminal Transfer Protocol) with the aim of making it easy to add services to wireless platforms. Nokia was working on their Smart Messaging concept, and Unwired Planet on their Handheld Device Markup Language (HDML), a language similar to HTML but focused on small-screen devices such as PDAs and mobile phones. The phone companies were also working, in conjunction with the World Wide Web Consortium (W3C), on specifications to provide wireless transmission of Internet data.

Continued on next page

All this proprietary-based work came to a head in 1997 when a US network operator called Omnipoint received several different responses from the different phone companies to a tender request they had issued for the supply of wireless information services. Omnipoint recommended that the various vendors get together and define a common standard. Thus the WAP Forum was born with a mission to create a global wireless specification to work across the different wireless technologies.

WML was formed by utilizing many of the concepts in Phone.com's HDML within the industry-standard framework of XML, practically guaranteeing its long-term success and ability to evolve without limitation.

The WAP Forum published the WAP 1.0 specification for product interoperability and content/application development in 1998, having based their work on Internet standards and technology. After WAP 1.0 was released, the WAP Forum was then opened up for membership by all organizations interested in the area.

As of early 2001, there were well over 600 members from the leading wireless device manufacturers, wireless operators, and software development companies. By 2003, it is predicted that over 90 percent of all mobile phones dispatched will be equipped with a WAP browser.

The goals of the WAP Forum are to bring Internet content and advanced data services to wireless portable devices; create a global open protocol that works across all wireless technologies; allow the creation of applications and content that can be scaled across a wide range of devices and wireless bearer networks; and use existing standards and technology wherever appropriate.

The WAP Architecture

WAP's architecture applies Internet standards to microbrowser technology with the wireless device controlling how server WAP content is displayed. The protocol model is based directly on the familiar World Wide Web model, but has been optimized to provide functionality across wireless networks between wireless terminals.

The architecture is designed so that only the minimum of memory and processing resources are used by the wireless device, allowing the greatest range of low intelligence handsets to be equipped with the microbrowser. However, the architecture also allows more sophisticated devices to take advantage of higher-quality content delivery through the inclusion of animation, graphics, and scripting.

The WAP programming model is based upon the very flexible and powerful World Wide Web programming model. In this model, applications and content are presented in standard data formats and are read by Web browsers. The Web browser sends requests for data objects to a Web server, and the Web server responds with the data encoded using the standard formats. Figure 1.3 illustrates this process.

FIGURE 1.3:

World Wide Web programming model

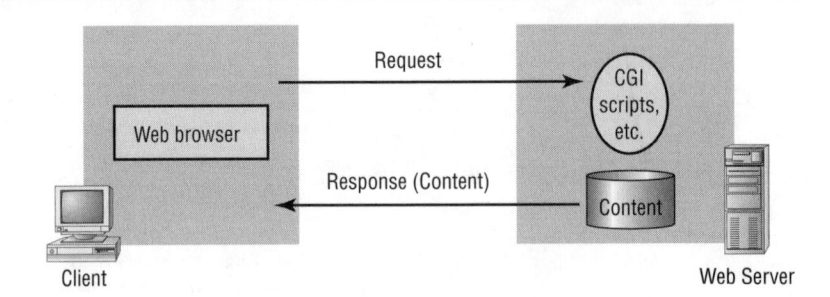

The World Wide Web standards specify a standard naming model. Under this model, all servers and content are named with an Internet-standard Uniform Resource Locator (URL). It enables Web browsers to correctly process content based on a specific content type. Also defined are standard content formats such as Hypertext Markup Language (HTML) and standard protocols such as the Hypertext Transport Protocol (HTTP), which allows any Web browser to communicate with any Web server.

The World Wide Web standards also define three types of servers: an *origin server* on which given WAP content sits or is to be dynamically created; a *proxy server*, which acts both as a server and a client for the purpose of making requests on behalf of other clients; and a *gateway server*, which acts as an intermediary for some other server.

The proxy server normally resides between clients and servers that have no means of direct communication. Requests are serviced by the proxy program or passed on, with possible translation, to other servers. The proxy server implements the client and server requirements of the World Wide Web specifications. Unlike a proxy, a gateway receives requests as if it were the origin server for the requested resource. The requesting client may not be aware that it is communicating with a gateway.

The WAP programming model is simply standard Web programming with a WAP gateway in the middle of the request/response cycle. A cell phone or other wireless terminal requests, in byte code, a given URL; the WAP gateway server decodes and decompresses this, then sends it on to the appropriate origin server as an ordinary HTTP request. The process is then repeated, in reverse, on the response side of the cycle.

This programming model has ensured that application developers have a smaller learning curve with a proven architecture and the ability to leverage existing tools. The WAP programming model has had to take into account the more restricted limitations of the wireless environments, but, wherever possible, existing standards have been used or have been adopted as the starting point for the WAP technology.

Figure 1.4 illustrates this WAP programming model. A user presses a key on their WAP phone. The key has a URL request assigned to it, which the client (user agent) passes to the WAP gateway using the WAP protocol. The WAP gateway then creates a normal HTTP request for the specified URL and passes it on to the origin server for processing. The URL may refer to a static file or some form of script application. If a static file has been referenced, the origin server adds an HTTP header to the file. If a script application has been specified, then the origin server runs the application. The origin server then returns the WML document (deck) incorporating the HTTP header or any output resulting from a script application. The WAP gateway then verifies the HTTP header and the WML content, encodes them into binary format, and creates a WAP response containing the WML that it sends to the client. Upon receipt of this response, the client processes it and displays the first card of the WML deck to the user.

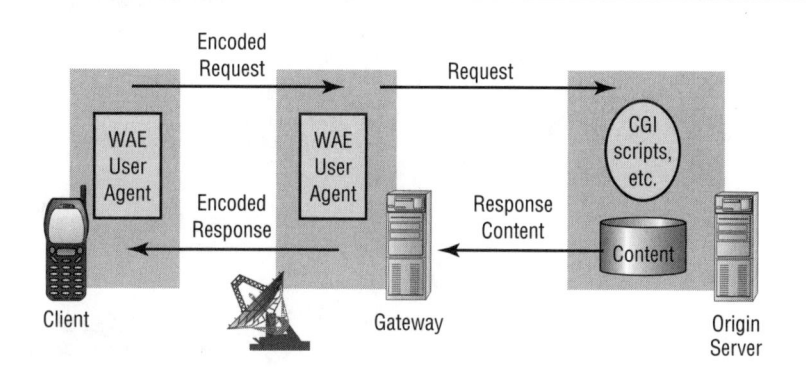

FIGURE 1.4:
The WAP programming model

So, WAP applications and content use formats based upon World Wide Web formats, and a set of standard communication protocols is used to transport content. The WAP microbrowser acts in the same way as a Web browser, coordinating the user interface.

WAP uses standard World Wide Web URLs to identify WAP content on origin servers and identify local resources in a device. It uses content typing consistent with World Wide Web typing, allowing user agents to process the content based on its type, and standard World Wide Web–based content formats for display, calendar, electronic business-card objects, images, and a scripting language. It also uses standard communication protocols, allowing the communication of browser requests from the wireless terminal to the network Web server.

The WAP Protocol

WAP is a layered communications protocol, an implementation of which is embedded in all WAP-enabled user agents. Its structure is very similar to the well-established International Standards Organization (ISO) network model with a transport protocol similar to the generally fixed-line HTTP. However, in this case, it is focused on broadcast requirements, which use less bandwidth. The WAP protocol architecture is shown in Figure 1.5 alongside a typical Internet Protocol stack. It consists of layers, which describe and specify the application/browser (WAE), sessions (WSP), transactions (WTP), security (WTLS), transports (WDP), and bearers (SMS, USSD, CSD, IS-136, CDMA, etc.).

FIGURE 1.5:

WAP and Internet Protocol stacks

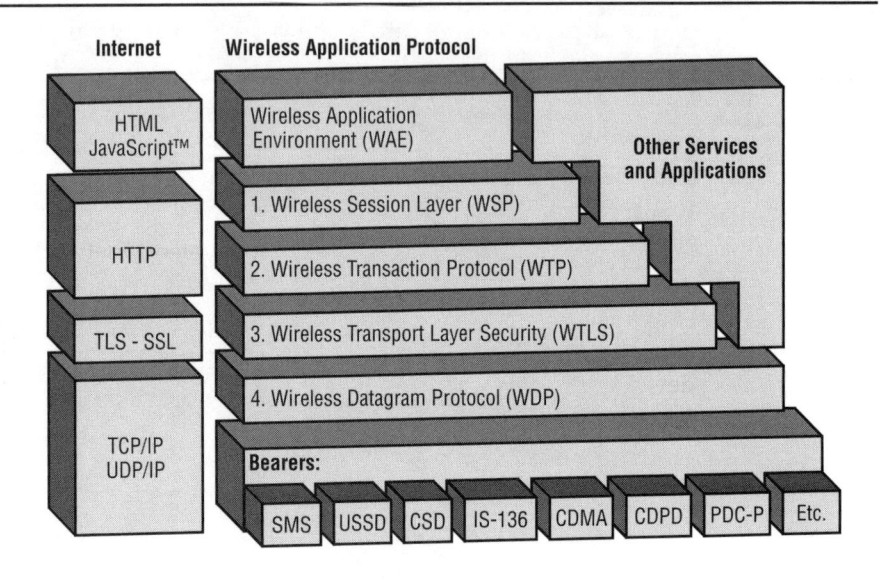

Following are brief descriptions of the main features of the Wireless Application Protocol layers.

Wireless Application Environment (WAE)

The *WAE* is the top layer of the WAP stack and is of most interest to content developers because it contains, among other things, device specifications and the content development programming languages, WML and WMLScript. It is an application environment that is based on a combination of mobile telephony technologies and the World Wide Web. The purpose of the WAE is to establish an environment to build applications and services. The WAE includes a microbrowser environment that defines how the wireless device interprets and presents WML and WMLScript. It also contains components that specify the following:

- WML for creating WAP applications
- WMLScript to enhance the logic capabilities of WML
- Wireless Telephony Application Interface (WTAI), which provides telephony services for WML decks running on phone-based devices
- Content formats that define a set of data formats, including images, phone book records, and calendar information

WAE depends upon a WAP-compatible proxy server to translate between WAP and HTTP transactions and WAP and Internet Protocols.

Wireless Session Protocol (WSP)

The *WSP* is a sandwich layer that links the WAE to two session services: one connection-oriented service that operates above the Wireless Transaction Protocol and one connectionless service operating above the Wireless Datagram Protocol. It is basically a binary-formatted tokenized version of HTTP, designed to provide low bandwidth browser handling on long latency networks. Unlike HTTP, WSP has been designed by the WAP Forum to provide fast connection suspension and reconnection. It has also been designed to provide content push capabilities that allow unsolicited transmission of data to user agents, which in turn allows WAP device users to be alerted, for example, to incoming e-mails, telephone calls, and faxes.

Wireless Transaction Protocol (WTP)

The *WTP* runs on top of a datagram service such as User Datagram Protocol (UDP) and is part of the standard suite of TCP/IP protocols used to provide a simplified protocol suitable for low bandwidth wireless stations. It offers three classes of transaction service: unreliable one-way request, reliable one-way request, and reliable two-way request response. WTP supports protocol data unit concatenation and delayed acknowledgment to help reduce the number of messages sent, and to attempt to optimize the user experience by providing the information that is needed when it is needed.

Wireless Transport Layer Security (WTLS)

WTLS incorporates security features that are based upon the established Transport Layer Security (TLS) protocol standard. It includes data integrity checks, privacy, service denial, and authentication services. Developers can access WTLS by using HTTPS instead of HTTP in the URL.

Wireless Datagram Protocol (WDP)

The *WDP* allows WAP to be bearer-independent by adapting the transport layer of the underlying bearer. The WDP presents a consistent data format to the higher layers of the WAP protocol stack, thereby offering the advantage of bearer independence to application developers.

Bearers

Below the WDP sit all of the *bearer* networks. These include Short Message Service (SMS), a facility for sending short messages; Unstructured Supplementary Service Data (USSD); Code Division Multiple Access (CDMA), for the reuse of scarce radio resources in adjacent areas; and Cellular Digital Packet Data (CDPD).

Through the Internet Protocol stack, the WAP client communicates with the WAP gateway, which sits between the wireless carrier's network on one side and the public Internet or corporate intranet on the other. Gateways can be located within carrier or corporate firewalls or both. In addition to taking care of various housekeeping tasks such as keeping track of the WAP client's bookmarks and managing its cache, the WAP server handles the interface between the two sets of network protocols, wireless (WAP) and wired (TCP/IP).

WAP Standards

As much as possible, WAP uses existing Internet standards for the basis of its own architecture and is designed to allow standard Internet servers to provide services to wireless devices. However, Internet standards such as HTML, HTTP, TLS, and TCP, which require large amounts of mainly text-based data to be sent, are inefficient over wireless networks. Traditional HTML content cannot be displayed well on the small-sized displays of mobile phones and pagers, and navigation around and between screens is not easy in one-handed mode. So Internet standards such as HTML, HTTP, TCP, and TLS are not appropriate for the restrictions associated with wireless networks.

WAP does, however, use many other Internet standards such as eXtensible Markup Language (XML), User Datagram Protocol (UDP), and Internet Protocol (IP) to communicate with wireless devices. So WAP is based on familiar standards such as HTTP and TLS, but has been optimized for the constraints of the wireless environment. For example, a WAP gateway is required to communicate with other Internet nodes using HTTP, and the WAP specification requires devices to use standard URL addressing to request services.

So WAP has been optimized with the restrictions of the wireless environment in mind. It is designed for low bandwidth and long latency, and uses binary transmission for greater compression of data. WAP sessions deal with intermittent coverage and operate using IP over a large variety of wireless transports whenever possible.

It is important that WAP standards complement existing standards. For example, instead of the WAP specification designating how data is transmitted over the air interface, it is designed to sit on top of existing standards so that the bearer's standard is used with the WAP protocol.

The WAP Forum works closely with the World Wide Web Consortium and other bodies such as the European Telecommunications Standards Institute (ETSI), the Cellular Telecommunications Industry Association (CTIA), and the Internet Engineering Task Force (IETF) to ensure that the future versions of HTML, HTTP, and TCP take the special needs of wireless devices into account and can be supported in the WAP framework. The WAP Forum also works closely with these bodies and others as they become members of the Forum to address the enhanced capabilities of third generation (3G) wireless networks expected to emerge around 2003 and 2004. Some countries, such as Japan and Finland, plan to have 3G services in use as early as 2001.

When the WAP Forum identifies a new area of technology with no existing standards specification, it works to submit its specification to related standards groups, believing that active participation leads to the best standards. With this approach, the WAP Forum hopes to produce open, not proprietary, standards through industry consensus and with no one vendor receiving favorable treatment. To date, the WAP Forum's membership role of contributing companies stands at over 100 who subscribe to the notion of the development of open standards as the best way to produce solutions for wireless Internet access.

WAP Devices

As well as being air-interface independent, the WAP specification is also device independent, specifying the minimum functionality a device must have, but designed to accommodate any functionality above that minimum.

A *WAP device* is a combination of hardware and software capable of running a WAP-compliant microbrowser such as a WAP-enabled mobile phone or a PDA. The use of proxy technology and compression in the network interface reduces the processing load so that inexpensive CPUs can be used in the handset, further reducing power consumption and extending battery life.

A PC can also be used as a WAP device if you download a WAP phone emulator from one of the developer sites. The emulator allows you to use a *virtual phone* on your desktop. Some major suppliers, such as Ericsson, Nokia, and Openwave, have developer sites where you can download software development kits (SDKs) containing WAP emulators.

A WAP phone can run any WAP application in the same way that a Web browser can run any HTML application. Once you have a WAP phone, you can access the Internet simply by entering URLs (or clicking bookmarked ones) and following the links that appear.

Using these devices, easy and secure access to Internet content and services such as banking, leisure, and unified messaging is made available. Furthermore, access is not restricted to the Internet; WAP devices will be able to deal with intranet information in the same way as Internet content because both are based upon HTML. This gives corporations the means of offering their employees information related to their work at any time, while on the move. This may also be extended to the corporation's customers and suppliers by making restricted access to company extranets available, thereby opening up the supply chain to interrogation and analysis. Of course, such corporate information will need to be reconfigured into a format suitable for small-screen viewing by reprogramming in WML or passing the pages through special HTML-to-WML filters.

With the wide range of WAP-enabled wireless devices now hitting the market, users will have significant options available to them when purchasing terminals and the applications they support. Following is a selection of WAP phones that have been announced recently:

Nokia 7110 and Nokia 7610 These two mobile phones are physically identical. The Nokia 7110 is targeted at the 900/1800MHz GSM market (Europe, Africa, Asia Pacific), whereas the Nokia 7610 is targeted at the 900/1800MHz TDMA market (USA). The user agent in both models is Nokia's WAP1.1 microbrowser. Both phones support WTLS.

Motorola Timeport P7389 The Timeport is a tri-band 900/1800/1900MHz GSM mobile phone that can be used in much of the world. It uses the UP.Browser 4.*x*, supporting not only WML and WMLScript 1.1, but also HDML 3. The Timeport supports WTLS.

Mitsubishi Trium Geo The Trium Geo was the first pre-pay WAP phone available. It's marketed by the UK carrier BT Cellnet and is notable for allowing the user to optionally disable WMLScript processing. Like most of the initial WAP phones, it does not support WTLS.

Sony CMD-Z5 Sony's Z5 is a dual-band 900/1800MHz GSM mobile phone containing Microsoft's Mobile Explorer, which is both a WML microbrowser and an HTML browser. It, too, does not support WTLS.

Device manufacturers can guarantee that their applications were developed to run on equipment that has the minimum functionality specified by the WAP specification while adding features that go beyond this minimum.

Because the WAP specification is so open, the services available to these devices will be wide-ranging in their nature. Information will be available via both push and pull technologies, and users will be able to interact with services by both voice and data. However, as the screen sizes and current speed and processing limitations make the types of services offered restrictive, it's unlikely that we'll see current Web-browsing patterns replicated via WAP-enabled devices until bandwidth capabilities significantly increase. Short of an increase in bandwidth, the user-interface consideration is unlikely to change in the short term as manufacturers strive to design devices that are light and fit comfortably in the palm of the hand. Therefore, the type of information service that content providers will offer in the short term will be real-time, specific services such as news, weather, stock prices, and ticketing.

The Future

In the next few years, mobile phones will start to benefit from very high bandwidth capabilities. Two-and-a-half and third generation communications systems (2.5G/3G) will allow enhanced services such as full-motion video images, multimedia, high fidelity sound, and fast access to the Internet. The 2.5G/3G systems will allow much higher capacity and data rates than can be offered by the restricted bandwidth currently available.

These wireless devices will be supported by a number of emerging technologies, including the following:

GPRS (General Packet Radio System)   A packet-switched wireless protocol with transmission rates from 115Kbps to 171Kbps. It will be the first service available to offer full instant wireless access to the Web. It will require new handsets to support the higher data rates. A main benefit is that users are always connected and online, and will be charged only for the amount of data that is transported. A user can make and receive voice calls while at the same time downloading data. For GSM providers, this new technology will increase data rates of both circuit switching (High Speed Circuit Switched Data [HSCSD]) and packet switching (GPRS) by a factor of 10 to 15 times.

EDGE (Enhanced Data Rate for GSM Evolution)   A higher bandwidth version of GPRS with speeds of up to 384Kbps, or twice that available from GPRS alone. It evolved from GSM, which is the prevailing standard throughout Europe and the Asia Pacific region—some 50 percent of the world's population. For GSM providers, this new technology will increase data rates of both circuit switching (HSCSD) and packet switching (GPRS) by a factor of 20 to 30 times.

HSCSD (High Speed Circuit Switched Data)   A new high-speed implementation of GSM data techniques. It uses four radio channels simultaneously and will enable users to access the Internet via the GSM network at very much higher data rates than at present. Data rates can be transmitted at 38.4Kbps or even faster over GSM networks.

UMTS (Universal Mobile Telecommunications System)   UMTS will allow a future mass market for high-quality wireless multimedia communications that will approach two billion users worldwide by the year 2010. Scheduled to launch commercially in 2002, it is set to be the technology that will allow the emergence of a new wireless Information Society. It will deliver low-cost, high-capacity wireless communications, offering data rates of 1Mbps to 2Mbps with global roaming and other advanced UMTS services.

Bluetooth   A specification for short-range radio links between wireless devices (a low-power radio technology being developed to replace cables and infrared links with wireless transceivers fitting onto a single chip). Devices such as printers, desktops, mobile phones, and PDAs will use the technology, and it has the potential to be used for wireless LANs. It is a de facto standard with a throughput of around 1Mbps, and delivers opportunities for rapid ad hoc connections and the possibility of automatic connections between devices. For example, a user could walk into their office and have their mobile phone's address book automatically synchronize with their PC's address book. Bluetooth is considered complementary to WAP technology, and when used together, they open up an unlimited variety of applications, such as long-distance (WAP) remote control of home and office devices.

Note that all of these emerging technologies center around significant increases in the bandwidth available to wireless devices.

So what is the future for WAP? It has been designed to be independent of the underlying network technology. The original constraints WAP was designed for—intermittent coverage, small screens, low power consumption, wide scalability over bearers and devices, and one-handed operation—are still valid in 2.5G and 3G networks.

The rapid growth of the use of the Internet and the huge growth of the use of wireless technologies are creating a demand for wireless access to the Internet, intranets, and other data networks. People want at least the same speed and power as they can currently achieve when using the Web via a desktop (and more) as they are offered connection technologies such as ISDN, with bandwidths of around 64/128Kbps, and the potential high-speed connections that will be available with the introduction of much faster services such as GPRS, EDGE, and eventually 3G systems.

What attracts the network operators is that WAP is a low-cost network upgrade that can be integrated seamlessly with no downtime on the network infrastructure. And *bridging* 2.5G technologies such as GPRS can be upgraded to 3G standards, ensuring that an operator's investment is protected. In the meantime, we must live with the restrictions, and it is reasonable to expect WAP to develop into optimized support for multimedia applications and continue to be relevant over the short and medium term.

In this chapter, you've been introduced to some key features such as WAP, WML, WMLScript, and the WAP architecture. WAP standards and devices have also been discussed together with a look at what the future holds in this quickly moving market. The next chapter, "Getting Started," will focus on WML and get you going with your first WML applications, showing you the tools you'll need to develop, implement, view, and test WML applications.

Chapter 2

Getting Started

The aim of this book is to guide you through the process of understanding how to use the Wireless Markup Language (WML) to create services that can be accessed on any WAP-enabled wireless device when supported by the scripting language WMLScript. This chapter gets you started on this by introducing you to the WML structure and the tools you'll need to start developing and viewing your first WML programs. You'll write and test your first simple program, and you'll be introduced to the example application you'll be developing throughout the rest of the book.

WML Structure

This section introduces you to the main elements you need to understand before you can get started with WML. It discusses key concepts such as how WML is structured into decks made up of one or more cards and how each card is composed of components such as tags, elements, and variables.

Cards and Decks

WML applications use a card and deck metaphor. A user interaction is represented by a *card*, while a complete task is represented by a *deck*. Applications can be thought of as a series of tasks or a collection of one or more decks.

A deck is the smallest unit of WML that a Web server can send to a microbrowser, and it consists of one or more cards with which a user is likely to interact. (A WML deck is really just a single file with the WML extension. That's why it's the smallest unit the server can send!) Figure 2.1 illustrates the card and deck structure. When a user agent receives a deck, it usually activates the first card in the deck, although you can direct it to any card in the deck. Depending on the card definition, the user can respond by entering text or choosing an option. WAP-compliant wireless devices with larger displays typically present each card as a single screen. Some smaller devices present each card as a collection of screens.

FIGURE 2.1:

The card and deck structure

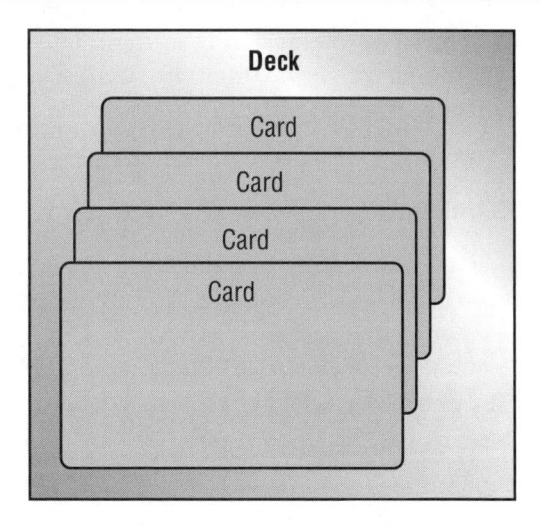

As a deck consists of one or more cards, and a single interaction between a user agent and a user is a card, multiple screens can be downloaded from the server to the client in a single transaction. Using WMLScript, user selections or entries can be routed to and handled by already loaded cards, thereby eliminating excessive communication with remote servers and improving performance.

The task performed by a deck might be, for example, the input of a set of specific requirements for booking a theater ticket. The deck might contain one card prompting the user to enter their choice of show, one prompting them to enter the date of the show, another prompting them to enter the time of the show, and so on. When the collection of card activities making up the deck is completed, the data would be sent to the server, and the next stage of the process would be activated. Another deck containing the next set of user interactions would be sent back from the server to the user's device.

Let's take a look at a sequence of events that might occur in a simple application used for accessing a user's bank details.

The user of the application enters the service's URL, probably through a bookmark, and the bank application's server transmits a deck to the user's wireless device. The deck might contain a Greeting card and two additional cards requesting a username and a password.

The user responds by entering their username and password, and the device's microbrowser reconnects to the server and passes the input to a program known as a Common Gateway Interface (CGI). This software verifies the user, gathers their specific account details, and formats a new deck.

The new deck is then sent back to the user's device with an Account Information card linked to a Search card and an End Session card. The user can then either end the session by selecting the End Session card or request a search of their account data by selecting the Search card. If the user selects the Search card, they need to enter search criteria and make a request. The server is accessed, the required data is gathered, and a new deck is formatted. A new deck containing a Search Result card, and additional Search and End Session cards, is transmitted back to the user's device. The process proceeds until the user ends the session by selecting the End Session card.

WML defines elements and attributes that let you specify the user-interface components, or the cards. Elements and attributes will be discussed further in following sections. Wireless device microbrowsers can navigate from one card to another.

A card can specify multiple user actions by including one or more of the following:

- Formatted text, including text, images, and links
- Input elements, which let the user enter a string of text, including numbers
- Fieldset elements, which act as organizational containers for other elements
- Select elements, which let the user choose from a list of options

Elements

WML is defined by a set of *elements* that specify all markup and structural information for a WML deck. Elements are identified by *tags,* which are each enclosed in a pair of angle brackets. Unlike HTML, WML strictly adheres to the XML hierarchical structure, and thus, elements must contain a start tag; any content such as text and/or other elements; and an end tag. Elements have one of the following two structures:

```
<tag> content </tag>
```

This form is identical to HTML.

`<tag/>`

When an element cannot contain visible content or is empty, such as a line break, this form can be used.

Table 2.1 lists the majority of valid elements. For details on all elements, refer to Appendix A, "WML Reference."

TABLE 2.1: Valid WML Elements

Category	WML Elements	Purpose
Decks and cards	card	Defines a card
	template	Defines a template
	head	Defines head information
	access	Defines access control information
	meta	Defines meta information
Events	do	Defines a do event handler
	ontimer	Defines an ontimer event handler
	onenterforward	Defines an onenterforward handler
	onenterbackward	Defines an onenterbackward handler
	onpick	Defines an onpick event handler
	onevent	Defines an onevent event handler
	postfield	Defines a postfield event handler
User input	input	Defines an input field
	select	Defines a select group
	option	Defines an option
	optgroup	Defines an option group
	fieldset	Defines a set of input fields
Text formatting	br	Defines a line break

Continued on next page

TABLE 2.1 CONTINUED: Valid WML Elements

Category	WML Elements	Purpose
	p	Defines a paragraph
	table	Defines a table
	tr	Defines a table row
	td	Defines a table cell (table data)
Tasks	go	Defines a go task
	prev	Defines a prev task
	refresh	Defines a refresh task
	noop	Defines a noop task
Variables	setvar	Defines and sets a variable
	timer	Defines a timer
Anchors	a	Defines an anchor
	anchor	Defines an anchor
Images	img	Defines an image

Attributes

Attributes describe various aspects of the element. Some attributes are mandatory, while others are optional and may have default values. You can include attributes in many WML elements. You always specify attributes in the start tag of an element, using the following syntax:

```
<tag attribute1="value1" attribute2="value2" attribute3="value3"...>
```

You separate each attribute value pair with white space, which may be a tab, new line, carriage return, or space character, and you must enclose the value in double quotation marks (" "). Attribute names must be lowercased.

Comments

As with most programming languages, WML provides a means of placing comment text within the code. *Comments* are used by developers as a means of documenting programming decisions within the code to allow for easier code maintenance. WML comments use the same format as HTML comments and use the following syntax:

```
<!-- a comment -->
```

The WML author can use comments anywhere, and they are not displayed to the user by the user agent.

Some emulators may complain if comments are placed before the XML prologue. The *prologue* is the first few lines that define the document type and version. (See "The Deck Structure" later in this chapter for more on the prologue.) Note that comments are not compiled or sent to the user agent, and thus have no effect on the size of the compiled deck.

Variables

Because multiple cards can be contained within one deck, some mechanism needs to be in place to hold data as the user traverses from card to card. This mechanism is provided via WML variables. *Variables* can be created and set using several different methods. Following are two examples:

The *<setvar>* element   The <setvar> element is used as a result of the user executing some task. The <setvar> element can be used to set a variable's state within the following elements: <go>, <prev>, and <refresh>. The following element would create a variable named a with a value of 321:

```
<setvar name="a" value="321"/>
```

The input elements   Variables are also set through any input element (input, select, option, etc.). A variable is automatically created that corresponds with the named attribute of an input element. For instance, the following element would create a variable named b:

```
<select name="b" title="B Value:">
```

Using Variables

Variable expansion occurs at runtime, in the microbrowser or emulator. This means it can be concatenated with or embedded in other text. Variables are referenced with a preceding dollar sign, and any single dollar sign in your WML deck is interpreted as a variable reference.

```
<p> total price is $$ $(total) </p>
```

> **NOTE** WML is case sensitive. No case folding (the forcing of text to uppercase or lowercase) is performed when parsing a WML deck. All enumerated attribute values are case sensitive. For example, the following attribute values are all different: `id="Card1"`, `id="card1"`, and `id="CARD1"`.

The Deck Structure

A deck structure starts with a prologue that is followed by an optional header and then a sequence of cards. The WAP server uses the prologue to manage the compilation of WAP programs. As all WML programs are based on XML, they must always begin with a valid XML prologue, which for WML 1.1 is as follows:

```
<?xml version="1.0"?>
<!DOCTYPE wml PUBLIC "-//WAPFORUM//DTD WML 1.1//EN"
  "http://www.wapforum.org/DTD/wml_1.1.xml" >
```

The prologue is followed by the body of the deck, starting with the <wml> element. WML consists of a set of elements that may contain attributes. Attributes may, themselves, contain further elements. All elements have a unique code tag. For example, the <card> element has the following syntax:

```
<card
  id="ID"
  newcontext = "true | false"
  onenterbackward = "URL"
  onenterforward = "URL"
  ontimer = "URL"
  ordered = "true | false"
  title = "string"
>
```

You write content here.....

</card>

In this case, all attributes are optional and are used to describe things such as a unique identifier for the card. A card element can contain a mix of processing instructions, formatting information, and displayable content.

When a WAP user agent receives a deck, it searches the deck-level elements, looking for the first card in the deck. It then examines the attributes and displays its content.

The program proceeds in response to user input or other events, and a deck is often linked to other decks. Control of the application is allowed by the definition of different types of tasks that affect the execution order of the decks. Tables and binary bitmapped images can also be displayed.

WML handles input and output, content rendering, and event processing but has no serious processing functionality. Therefore, WMLScript code may be referenced to enhance the functionality of the application. A WAP browser must therefore contain a WMLScript Virtual Machine (VM) to run the compiled script. WMLScript lets you define function operations such as flow control statements (e.g., if, while, for), and it lets you call assignment statements and comparison operations.

Installing an SDK

To test and develop your WML code, you will need to install a software development kit (SDK) or microbrowser emulator. You shouldn't expect to write WML code without testing it on some kind of microbrowser, and the SDKs are very useful for testing your WML pages even if you have your own WAP-enabled phone or other device. The SDK you choose will depend upon a variety of factors, such as the wireless devices you want to support, the features you need, and your personal preferences. Before embarking on a major project, it's a good idea to consult the product suppliers and other developers before making your choice. However, to ensure your code will work correctly in as many microbrowsers and WAP-enabled devices as possible, it may be best to install several of the main SDKs available.

> **NOTE**
>
> It's important to understand that the results displayed by the examples given in the book may not look exactly the same as the figures and graphics shown. This if often true even between different versions of the same emulators. What's important is that the general functionality is the same, meaning that although it may look and feel a little different when used, it still performs the same. Incidentally, this problem also exists when using WAP-enabled devices, which is why extensive testing on all supported devices is so important.

WAP SDKs

There are a number of SDKs available to assist you in the speedy development of WAP-based services. These SDKs usually contain a microbrowser emulator, although a range of self-standing emulators are being developed by various WAP-related organizations. AnywhereYouGo.com is creating a comprehensive list of WAP development tools, and the main ones listed to date are shown in Table 2.2.

TABLE 2.2: WAP Development Tools

Supplier	Description
Ericsson `http://www.ericsson.com/`	The Ericsson WapIDE SDK 2 is an Integrated Development Environment (IDE) for developing WAP services. It consists of three main components: a WAP browser, an Application Designer, and a Server Toolset. Use the following link to access this kit: `http://www.ericsson.com/developerszone/`.
Motorola `http://www.motorola.com/`	The Mobile Application Development Kit (Mobile ADK) allows developers to create their own add-on voice and data solutions. It consists of tools for both WAP and VoxML applications. Use the following link to access this kit: `http://www.motorola.com/developers/wireless/`. This ADK has some limiting factors. One is the huge download; another is that it needs a recent (mid-2000) version of Internet Explorer.

Continued on next page

TABLE 2.2 CONTINUED: WAP Development Tools

Supplier	Description
Nokia `http://forum.nokia.com/`	The Nokia WAP Toolkit is a generic software tool that enables developers to create and test application software that will run on a Nokia WAP server. The Toolkit can also be used to demonstrate WAP applications. It provides an easy environment in which developers can write, test, and debug applications on a PC-based emulator. Use the following link to access this Toolkit: `http://www.nokia.com/corporate/wap/sdk.html`. Note that the Nokia Toolkit, because it's written in Java, runs not only on the Windows platform, but also on Linux, Solaris, etc.
Openwave `http://www.openwave.com/`	Now called Openwave after their merger with Software.com, Phone.com's UP.SDK is a free SDK that allows Web developers to quickly and easily create HDML and WML information services and applications. The SDK includes an emulator that accurately simulates the behavior of an UP.Browser-enabled device. Phone.com also provides a publicly available UP.Link. Use the following link to access this kit: `http://developer.openwave.com/`.
Dynamic Systems Research Ltd. (Wapnet) `http://www.wap.net/`	Wapnet provides an SDK with a set of comprehensive tools for developing WAP applications. Included are the WAR (Wireless Application Reader) browser together with a set of WML and WMLScript source code examples. Use the following link to access this SDK: `http://www.wap.net/`.
Inetis `http://www.inetis.com/`	The Inetis DotWAP SDK allows fast and simple WAP site construction without any WAP or WML knowledge. It runs on Win32 platforms and is freeware. Use the following link to access this SDK: `http://www.inetis.com/`.

NOTE The files in Table 2.2 are sometimes very slow to download because they can be very large—as much as tens of megabytes! Be careful in selecting your SDK, because not all versions are free, and some require extra software.

The Nokia WAP Toolkit requires the latest release of Java. Check the Nokia site for more details and be prepared to register with Nokia as a WAP developer (for free) before entering the Nokia Forum, where you will find the links to the software.

The Ericsson SDK is also a large download because it includes a copy of the Xitami intranet Web server, although you do not have to install it if you already have it or a similar Web server installed. A local host server such as Xitami will help with the creation of your WML pages, should make loading pages quicker, and will allow the testing of dynamic content.

The Openwave UP.SDK is faster than either the Nokia or the Ericsson SDKs, although it may not be as suitable for developing and testing dynamic WML pages. There is also a microbrowser available from Openwave, but again, it is quite a large download. Their microbrowser uses a local server with a full-screen-height browser display.

WAP Emulators

Instead of installing an entire WAP SDK, you can install a WML emulator. An *emulator* simply lets you view the contents of your WML files as they would be seen on the screen of a WAP-enabled device. In many cases, a WAP SDK will provide little more than a WML emulator together with some example code. By using just an emulator, you will, therefore, still be able to see the output of your WML code, and the download time will be much less.

Again, while the emulators do a great job, they are not perfect. Try a few different ones, and you will quickly decide which you like the most. When the time comes to develop a real (commercial) WAP site, you will need to do a lot more testing, first with other SDKs/emulators and then with all the WAP-enabled devices you plan to support.

The following lists some of the WAP emulators that are available at the time of writing this book:

Klondike WAP Browser   Produced by Apache Software (www.apachesoftware.com). Klondike looks a lot like a Web browser and is therefore very easy to use for beginners. You can access local WML files easily. It also supports drag-and-drop, making local file use very easy.

M3Gate   Produced by Numeric Algorithm Laboratories (www.numeric.ru). M3Gate is a fast, stand-alone program that uses the Web browser as its gateway. It has full support for WML, WMLScript, WBMP images, Unicode, bookmarks, Multiple Character sets, and a choice of *skins* (additional handsets). It also supports drag-and-drop, making local file use very easy.

Yospace   Produced by Yospace (www.yospace.com). WAP developers can use the desktop edition of the emulator to preview WAP applications from their desktop, safe with the knowledge that the emulator provides a reasonably faithful reproduction of the actual handset products. You can plug in support for additional handsets as they become available (skins). Yospace is bundled with a collection of simple command-line tools (e.g., WML encoder, WMLScript compiler) for easy integration into your existing development environment.

EzWAP   Produced by EZOS (www.ezos.com). EZOS provides EzWAP, the first platform-independent WAP browser, which enables all kinds of computing systems to access the wireless Internet: wireless devices (e.g., PDA, Pocket PC, PC Companions), wireless computing and embedded systems, and PCs running Microsoft Windows NT, 2000, or CE.

WAPalizer   Produced by Gelon (www.gelon.net). The script fetches WML pages from WAP sites and converts them to HTML on the fly. In reality, it is not technically an emulator, because it does not interpret WML code, but HTML. This means that you will be able to view most WAP pages, but some pages, especially those with a lot of input forms, are very difficult to convert to HTML. Gelon also has a range of other pseudo-emulators that look like real WAP phones.

Ericsson R380 Emulator   Produced by Ericsson (www.ericsson.com/developerszone). The R380 WAP emulator is intended to be used to test WML applications developed for the WAP browser in the Ericsson R380. The emulator contains the WAP browser and WAP settings functionality that can be found in the R380.

WinWAP   Produced by Slob-Trot Software Oy Ab (www.winwap.org). WinWAP is a WML browser that works on any computer with 32-bit Windows installed (Windows 95, Windows 98, and Windows NT). You can browse WML files locally from your hard drive or the Internet with HTTP (as with your normal Web browser). It also looks and feels a lot like a normal Web browser.

WAPman for Windows 95/98/NT   Produced by wap.com.sg (www.wap.com.sg/downloads). The WAPman is a portable browsing device, combining access to the Internet with the properties of a mobile phone. With its unique WAP gateway structure, the WAPman has fast downloading capability and is highly compact and portable, functioning as a wireless commerce and lifestyle portal.

WAPsilon   Produced by Wappy (wappy.to). WAPsilon converts WAP sites to HTML that can be viewed on their site or on their device. WAPsilon can be integrated into your Web site or plugged into your browser. Like WAPalizer, it technically is not an emulator, because it does not interpret WML code, but HTML.

Opera   Produced by Opera (www.opera.no). Opera is actually an excellent HTML Web browser that now also supports WML. An interesting idea, because it's very convenient to browse both HTML and WML with the same product. This is one to watch.

WAPEmulator   Produced by Wapmore (www.wapmore.com). Their emulator is available on the Wapmore site. There is a new Netscape version that is not as functional as the Internet Explorer version.

Wireless Companion   Produced by YOURWAP.com (www.yourwap.com). With the Wireless Companion, you may access any WAP and Web content over the Internet including the free personal wireless services at YOURWAP.com.

Some Design Considerations

Wireless devices are limited by the size of their displays and keypads. It's therefore very important to take this into account when designing a service. Typically, today's WAP-enabled wireless devices have displays that range from sub-VGA graphics to screens that can display no more than four lines of 32 characters. So as a WAP device application or service designer, you must take this into account.

As this book goes to press, there are announcements of all types of amazing new WAP-enabled devices that offer far better features, but as is usual practice with software development, it's wise to support the minimum platform for the widest market appeal. It is, however, also possible to detect the device type and offer the extra features where available.

Typical WAP services might include buying tickets, viewing train time tables, checking into flights, and looking up things like sports results, stock values, and phone numbers. People accessing such services are not going to use their devices to surf the Internet in the traditional sense, as the restricted interface will not accommodate this way of working. So you must ensure that you keep things simple and easy to use. You should always keep in mind that there are no standard microbrowser behaviors and that the data link may be relatively slow, at around 10Kbps. However, with GPRS, EDGE, and UMTS, this may not be the case for long, depending on where you are located.

Continued on next page

> The following are general design tips that you should keep in mind when designing a service:
>
> - Keep the WML decks and images to less than 1.5KB.
> - Keep text brief and meaningful, and as far as possible try to precode options to minimize the rather painful experience of user data entry.
> - Keep URLs brief and easy to recall.
> - Minimize menu levels to prevent users from getting lost and the system from slowing down.
> - Use standard layout tags such as <big> and <b>, and logically structure your information.
> - Don't go overboard with the use of graphics, as many target devices may not support them.

A Simple WML Program

By now, we are assuming that you have downloaded and installed either a WML SDK or an emulator. If you haven't done so, we suggest you do this now, so that you can write your first WML deck. It contains just one card and will display the message "This is my first WML Card" in your WML emulator (see Figure 2.2).

FIGURE 2.2:

A one-card WML program

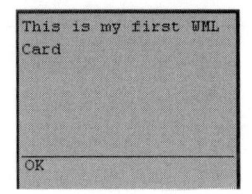

```
This is my first WML
Card



OK
```

This test will enable you to see how your emulator accesses local files and check that it is working as it should. When working with local WML files, it's best to select an emulator that makes it easy to do so. Some emulators assume you only want to enter a remote URL. The best ones for local file use will either remember the last open file folder or accept dragged-and-dropped files. Both Klondike and M3Gate accept drag-and-drop files at this time.

Before going any further, decide which text editor you want to use to create your WML files. We use Wordpad—it comes free with Windows 95, 98, and NT, and includes most of the editing functions you could ever need for editing WML files. Once you have decided which editor you are going to use, use it to create an empty file named `myfirst.wml`.

> **NOTE**
>
> If you are using Wordpad or Notepad, the DOC or TXT extensions, respectively, will be appended to your file unless you specify another extension when saving the file. So, make sure to add the WML extension when saving. If you forget and the file is saved with the DOC or TXT extension, just manually change the extension to WML.

Now that you have created your file, type the following text into it:

```
<?xml version="1.0"?>
<!DOCTYPE wml PUBLIC "-//WAPFORUM//DTD WML 1.1//EN"
  "http://www.wapforum.org/DTD/wml_1.1.xml" >
<wml>
  <card id="First">
    <p>
      This is my first WML Card
    </p>
  </card>
</wml>
```

> **TIP**
>
> If you don't want to type this text, the file, `myfirst.wml`, is provided on the CD that comes with this book—you can simply copy this file onto your hard drive.

Now, read the instructions provided with your emulator to find out how to open a WML file on your hard disk and display its contents on your emulator. We recommend that you don't skip this test and that you spend time getting to know how your emulator accesses local files—you will find this essential for the early stages of creating and testing WML code as you'll use this mechanism to test and view the results of your WML programs without having to download it from a Web server.

Testing Your Program

By creating and displaying the `myfirst.wml` file, you performed the simplest type of test—creating a WML file locally on your hard disk, then viewing it using an emulator.

This is by far the most efficient way of developing and testing WML files. Since your aim is, however, to develop a service that is going to be available to WAP phone users, you should upload your WML files onto a server once you have developed them locally and test them over a real Internet connection. As you start developing more complex WAP services, this is how you will identify and rectify performance problems, which could, if left alone, lose your site visitors.

In uploading the file `myfirst.wml` to a server, you will be testing your WML emulator to see how it looks and behaves, and checking your Web server to see that it is set up correctly. Now start your emulator and use it to access the URL of `myfirst.wml`. For example, the URL might look something like this:

```
http://ourwebsite.com/wapstuff/myfirst.wml
```

Configuring Web Servers to Deliver WAP Content

If you are using a commercial or free host/server, ask their technical support staff if they support WAP (most already do). If not, you can ask them if they could do so. It's a very simple change.

If you need a server to host your WAP site, here are a few top-rated hosts that support WAP:

www.TierraNet.com

www.Verio.com

www.NetNation.com

www.Web2010.com

www.HiWay.com

If you have your own server, then you simply need to add support for the MIME types and extensions listed in Table 2.3. Instructions follow on how to configure the two leading Web servers.

TABLE 2.3: MIME Types for WML Files

MIME Type	File Extension
text/vnd.wap.wml	WML
text/vnd.wap.wmlscript	WMLS
application/vnd.wap.wmlc	WMLC
application/vnd.wap.wmlscriptc	WMLSC
image/vnd.wap.wbmp	WBMP

Apache This popular Web server runs predominantly on Unix or Linux systems, so we're providing instructions for configuring such a server. Locate the file srm.conf, which is usually in /etc/httpd/conf, and add the following lines to the file:

```
AddType text/vnd.wap.wml .wml
AddType text/vnd.wap.wmlscript .wmls
AddType application/vnd.wap.wmlc .wmlc
AddType application/vnd.wap.wmlscriptc .wmlsc
AddType image/vnd.wap.wbmp .wbmp
```

Save the file and restart Apache, for example, by issuing the command **/etc/httpd/bin/apachectl restart**. Be aware that the ResourceConfig variable in the httpd.conf file can override the srm.conf file, meaning you'll have to modify whatever file that variable indicates instead of srm.conf.

If you do not have your own Apache server, but you know that the server you use—for example, your ISP's Web server—is Apache, then all may not be lost. If your Web server administrator hasn't disabled this feature for security reasons, you can achieve the same results by writing a file called .htaccess containing the lines above to each directory that contains your WML files. In fact, the .htaccess file is hierarchically cumulative—place it in your root directory for it to apply to all subdirectories.

Microsoft IIS To configure a Microsoft IIS server to deliver WAP content, you need to perform the following:

1. Open the Internet Service Manager console and expand the tree to view your Web site entry. You can add the WAP MIME types to a whole server or individual directories.

2. Open the Properties dialog box by right-clicking the appropriate server or directory, then choose Properties from the menu.

3. From the Properties dialog, choose the HTTP Headers tab, then select the File Types button at the bottom right.

4. For each MIME type listed earlier in Table 2.3, supply the extension with or without the dot (it will be automatically added for you), then click OK in the Properties dialog box to accept your changes.

The Example Application

Through the course of this book, we're going to develop an example application. The aim of this approach is to demonstrate how you can use all of the various WML and WMLScript features in a real environment instead of using just abstract examples. We'll build the site as we go through the book. Each time a concept or feature is explained, it will be integrated into the example application.

In the example application, you are going to create a WAP service for a cinema that will let users review the movies currently being shown and book tickets for them via their WAP-enabled mobile phones. The idea is that once the users have booked the tickets, they can just arrive on the night of the movie and pick their tickets up without worrying about ticket availability and the inconvenience of waiting to purchase them.

The First Steps

The following sections walk you through the site you're going to create. When you first log on, you are presented with a series of choices, as shown in Figure 2.3.

FIGURE 2.3:

The Choice card

```
FirstUnwired.com
1▶View Movies
2 Ticket Prices
3 View Account

Help
```

Figure 2.3 demonstrates how you can present a list of options to users and let them choose one, so that the appropriate card is displayed. In Figure 2.3, the View Movies option lists the movies that are currently available. In our example, there are only two. See Figure 2.4.

FIGURE 2.4:

A card listing movies

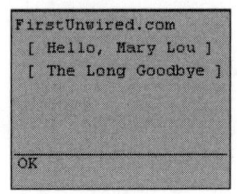

```
FirstUnwired.com
[ Hello, Mary Lou ]
[ The Long Goodbye ]


OK
```

In Figure 2.5, you see that the card for each movie provides a short critique of the movie with an option to book tickets for that particular movie.

FIGURE 2.5:

Movie Critique card

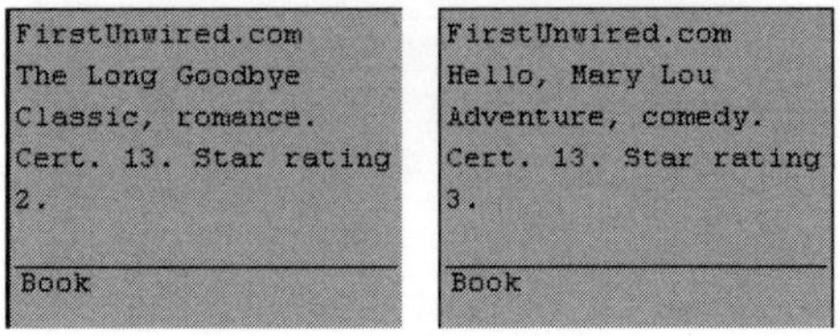

```
FirstUnwired.com
The Long Goodbye
Classic, romance.
Cert. 13. Star rating
2.

Book
```

```
FirstUnwired.com
Hello, Mary Lou
Adventure, comedy.
Cert. 13. Star rating
3.

Book
```

Performing Some Validations with WMLScript

Until now, the whole example application has been created using WML. Now, WMLScript comes into play. If a user chooses to book a ticket in either of the cards shown in Figure 2.5, a WMLScript function is called that performs the following processing:

- If the user has logged on to the system in the current session, a card appears that lets them choose how many tickets they want to book for each row (the tickets in each row are priced differently).

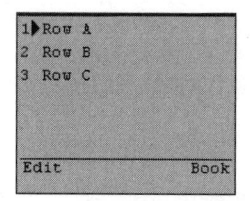

```
1▶Row A
2  Row B
3  Row C



Edit              Book
```

- If the user has not yet logged on to the system in the current session, they are presented with a logon screen that prompts them to enter their mobile phone number, followed by a screen that asks for their password. By requiring such information at logon, the logon screen provides security, which is important since the user is about to perform a financial transaction (book a ticket).

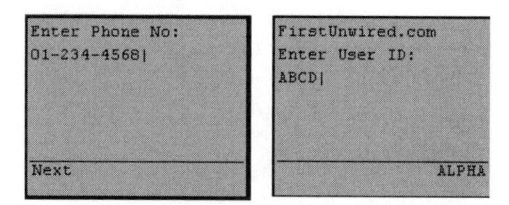

```
Enter Phone No:         FirstUnwired.com
01-234-4568|            Enter User ID:
                        ABCD|



Next                                ALPHA
```

- When the user enters their phone number and password, these details are sent to the server.

The Server Side Programming

In the next process, the WML code runs a servlet, written in Java, on the server. The servlet checks whether the entered values exist on the server. If they do, they are stored in a file on the server. If they do not, the user is prompted to register for the service, and the server then records the values the user enters.

Once the user has registered or logged on, they are presented with the card requesting them to enter the number of tickets they want to book in each of the rows A, B, and C, as shown earlier. Once they have entered this information, the server is polled by calling a Java servlet to check that the number of tickets they booked is still available. If they are not available, a response is returned to the mobile phone telling them how many tickets are left in the row or rows that the user specified and prompting them to reenter a number of tickets.

Once they have entered a valid number of tickets, a WMLScript function is called to perform the following functions:

- Calculating the total number of tickets booked
- Calculating the total price of the booked tickets

Finally, the WMLScript function performs the following validations:

- If the total price is less than the cost of one of the cheapest tickets (indicating no tickets were booked), the following alert is displayed:

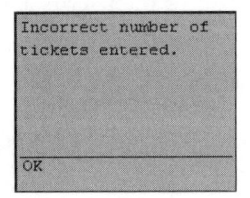

```
Incorrect number of
tickets entered.




OK
```

Once the validations have all been completed, the total price of the tickets booked is displayed on the mobile phone, as shown in Figure 2.6.

FIGURE 2.6:

Tickets Reserved screen

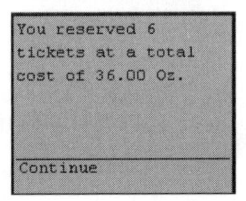

```
You reserved 6
tickets at a total
cost of 36.00 Oz.




Continue
```

If the user chooses to book the tickets, a Java servlet is called on the server to check that the user has enough money in their account to pay for the tickets. If they do, the total cost of the tickets booked is deducted from their account.

As the Choice card shows back in Figure 2.3, the user has three choices when they first access the FirstUnwired.com service:

- View Movies
- Ticket Prices
- View Account

We've just looked at what happens when they choose the first option. The second option calls a Java servlet on the server that retrieves the ticket prices from the server and generates the WML code required to display these prices. Because the Java servlet generates the WML on the fly, this is known as a *dynamic* WML page, as opposed to a fixed or *static* page that has been coded by hand. Dynamic WML can be produced by a wide variety of server side technologies, such as Perl, PHP, ASP, and others.

The third option calls a WMLScript function that tests to see whether the user has already logged on to the service in the current session. If they have, a Java servlet is called that retrieves their account information from the server, then generates the WML code required to display their account details. If they have not, they are prompted to log on to the service before their account details are displayed.

The example application performs a typical range of functions that a WAP service may perform. Note that it is by no means complete—error trapping is minimal, and the security is not what you would want to use in the real world. Furthermore, to keep the server side simple, all the data is stored by the servlet using plain text files. In a real-world application, it's more likely that you would be using a database for this type of work, such as MySQL, SQL Server, Oracle, and others. What this application will do is get you started using WML and WMLScript. You will use all the typical interactions between WML and WMLScript on the client side and some typical server side interactions, too.

Once you have completed this book, you will be ready to develop real WAP services—that is, a complete WAP site that anyone in the world with a WAP-enabled device can access! You will be comfortable in the knowledge that you have already mastered many of the features that you'll want to use in your WAP application and have all the information you need to take the next step: getting your service online. In the next chapter, you will take your first step in that direction by creating your first WML pages.

Chapter 3

Your First WML Pages

We've already had a brief look at WML and WMLScript. Now let's start looking at how we can use WML to create a WAP site! In this chapter, we're going to examine some of the basic elements of WML 1.1, including the following:

- How to define cards
- How to include and format text
- How to include and format images
- How to navigate with user agent buttons
- How to use lists to navigate within a deck

While reviewing these basic elements, we'll also create a simple WAP site with a splash screen, welcoming users to the WAP site. You no doubt have come across many Web sites that employ splash screens. These are often full of gadgets and all sorts of files that take forever to download. Naturally, with a WAP site, you should keep your splash page simple; otherwise, your visitors may well run out of patience waiting for it to download and go elsewhere instead. We're going to create a simple splash screen that will include our site name, FirstUnwired.com, and a company logo.

Getting Started

So let's go! First, we'll need to create the file in which we'll add the WML. Open whichever tool or editor you're going to use to develop your WAP site and create a new file named `cinema.wml`. Note the WML extension, indicating this is a WML file.

Now that you have created the file, add the following lines (called the XML prologue) to the top of it:

```
<?xml version="1.0"?>
<!DOCTYPE wml PUBLIC "-//WAPFORUM//DTD WML 1.1//EN"
  "http://www.wapforum.org/DTD/wml_1.1.xml" >
```

If you don't want to type this in, you can copy and paste it from the `prologue.wml` file on the CD under the directory /Examples.

TIP

Alternatively, if the editor you are using supports macros or templates, you could define one and have the editor create the XML prologue for you each time you start a new deck.

The WAP server uses the XML prologue to manage the compilation of WAP programs. As all WML programs are based on XML, they must always begin with a valid XML prologue, which for WML 1.1 is as that given above.

Now that you have entered the prologue, you can start using WML. The first thing you'll want to do is define the beginning and the end of the WML deck, using the <wml> element.

TIP

Remember that a deck is simply a WML file that contains one or more cards that will be downloaded to the user agent.

As with all elements, the <wml> element has a start and an end tag. It is structured as follows:

```
<wml>

    WML deck contents

</wml>
```

NOTE

When developing WML files, we find it useful to always put in both the start and the end tags for each element at the same time. This prevents you from forgetting to put the end tag of an element in and, subsequently, spending a lot of time trying to work out why your WML won't work!

So let's put the <wml> element into cinema.wml. It should now look like this:

```
<?xml version="1.0"?>
<!DOCTYPE wml PUBLIC "-//WAPFORUM//DTD WML 1.1//EN"
  "http://www.wapforum.org/DTD/wml_1.1.xml" >

<wml>

</wml>
```

Now that you have defined the beginning and end of the deck, you can put the first card into it. A card is defined by the <card> element, including the start and end tags. Before going any further, we have to give the card a name. To specify a card's name, you use the id attribute. In this case, the card will be named Splash, so enter **<card id="Splash">** in the start tag.

> **TIP** There is no convention in WML for specifying which card is displayed first in the user agent—the first card in the deck is always displayed first.

Your text should now look like this:

```
<?xml version="1.0"?>
<!DOCTYPE wml PUBLIC "-//WAPFORUM//DTD WML 1.1//EN"
   "http://www.wapforum.org/DTD/wml_1.1.xml" >

<wml>

   <card id="Splash">

   </card>

</wml>
```

Formatting Text

We can now start entering the card contents. We are going to display the text "FirstUnwired.com" together with a company logo.

Let's first look at how to enter the text "FirstUnwired.com." Any text in a card has to be within a <p> element. Go ahead and add the <p> element containing "FirstUnwired.com."

Your text should now look like this:

```
<?xml version="1.0"?>
<!DOCTYPE wml PUBLIC "-//WAPFORUM//DTD WML 1.1//EN"
   "http://www.wapforum.org/DTD/wml_1.1.xml" >

<wml>

   <card id="Splash">
```

```
    <p>
      FirstUnwired.com
    </p>
  </card>

</wml>
```

Let's now look at this in your SDK. Start your SDK and open the file `cinema.wml`. It should look something like Figure 3.1.

FIGURE 3.1:

The splash screen

As far as splash pages go, even if we are limited by bandwidth, ours could use a bit of spicing up! Let's add some formatting. The `<p>` element includes two attributes: `align` and `mode`. They have the following syntax:

```
<p align="alignment" mode="wrapmode">
  content
</p>
```

In this syntax, `align` is the alignment of the paragraph. This can be `left`, `center`, or `right`. And `mode` is the wrap mode. By default, word wrapping is used. You can prevent word wrapping by defining `mode` as `nowrap`.

Let's use the `align` attribute in the `<p>` element to define the alignment of the text as `center` and also display "FirstUnwired.com" in bolded big typeface. To display text in bold, you use the `<b>` element. To display text in a big font, you use the `<big>` element. You can nest elements within other elements, so there is no problem in having the same text within several elements.

NOTE Not all user agents support the `<big>` element.

Now try adding the `align="center"` attribute to the `<p>` element and the `<b>` and `<big>` elements to `cinema.wml`. You should end up with something like this:

```
<?xml version="1.0"?>
<!DOCTYPE wml PUBLIC "-//WAPFORUM//DTD WML 1.1//EN"
  "http://www.wapforum.org/DTD/wml_1.1.xml" >

<wml>

  <card id="Splash">
    <p align="center">
      <b><big>FirstUnwired.com</big></b>
    </p>
  </card>

</wml>
```

The code should look like Figure 3.2 when displayed in your user agent.

FIGURE 3.2:

Splash screen using formatted text

Adding Images to WML Cards

Let's finish the splash page with an image. The WML language allows you to include images in formatted text.

> **NOTE** Not all user agents currently display images. You can, however, write decks containing images and send those decks to such devices.

You use the `<img>` element to include images in your WML cards. The image appears wherever you put the `<img>` statement within the text.

The `<img>` element has the following syntax:

```
<img alt="text" src="url" localsrc="imgfile"/>
```

The `alt` attribute specifies the text to display if the user agent does not support images or cannot find the specified image—rather than displaying an error message.

The `src` attribute specifies the URL of the image to display. The `localsrc` attribute specifies an image that is stored in the user agent ROM (read-only memory) or the Web server. If you specify a valid image in the `localsrc` attribute, the user agent ignores the `src` attribute.

WAP has its own graphic format, WBMP (Wireless BitMap). Some user agents may accept the other Internet graphics formats, such as JPEG and GIF, but as WBMP is the de facto WAP image format and is likely to be supported by the widest range of user agents, we recommend that you use this.

We have included a file named `funwired.wbmp` on the CD under the directory /Examples. Now add the `<img>` element to your WML file to include an image above the text "FirstUnwired.com." You should end up with something like this:

```
<?xml version="1.0"?>
<!DOCTYPE wml PUBLIC "-//WAPFORUM//DTD WML 1.1//EN"
   "http://www.wapforum.org/DTD/wml_1.1.xml" >

<wml>

  <card id="Splash">
    <p align="center">
      <b><big>FirstUnwired.com</big></b>
      <img src="cinema.wbmp" alt="FirstUnwired.com"/>
    </p>
  </card>

</wml>
```

Moving Around

So far, we have only one card in our example. We now want to be able to go from the Splash card to an Index card, letting users choose what they want to do. There are two basic ways in which you can let users move from one card to another: by pressing a button on their mobile phone or by choosing an option from a list.

In our example application, we are going to define a button on the user agent to display the next card when it is pressed.

Navigating with User Agent Buttons

WML 1.1 defines a number of "buttons" that all WAP-compatible devices must support. We put *buttons* in quotation marks because they do not necessarily have to be buttons per se—they are actually commands that can be executed by any type of user interaction, such as pressing actual buttons or an area on a touch-sensitive screen, or even using a voice command.

In our example, we are using buttons on a mobile phone. The button on the top-left side of the keypad will be used as the Accept button, which is what we will use to let the user make an affirmative choice. We'll leave the top-right button alone for now—this could be useful later for performing actions based on the relevant context.

To define the action that is executed when a button is pressed, use the <do> element. The <do> element looks something like this:

```
<do type="accept" label="Next">
  <go href="#NextCard"/>
</do>
```

This <do> element defines the Accept button so that it is labelled "Next" on-screen, and when it is pressed, the card NextCard is displayed using the <go> element with the href attribute. Instead of displaying the NextCard card (which, in this case, is in the same deck), we could display a card in another deck, execute a WMLScript, or execute a program such as a Java servlet or Perl script.

Defining Buttons

Let's now create a new card in cinema.wml and define the Accept button in the Splash card so that it displays the new card. We'll name the new card Index.

Remember, to define a new card, we use the <card> element. In the meantime, we'll leave the card empty. By adding the new card, the deck cinema.wml will look like this:

```
<?xml version="1.0"?>
<!DOCTYPE wml PUBLIC "-//WAPFORUM//DTD WML 1.1//EN"
  "http://www.wapforum.org/DTD/wml_1.1.xml" >

<wml>

  <card id="Splash">
    <p align="center">
      <b><big>FirstUnwired.com</big></b>
    </p>
  </card>

  <card id="Index">
  </card>

</wml>
```

Now, let's use a <do> element to display the new card, Index, when the Accept button is pressed and give it the label "Enter." cinema.wml will now look like this:

```
<?xml version="1.0"?>
<!DOCTYPE wml PUBLIC "-//WAPFORUM//DTD WML 1.1//EN"
  "http://www.wapforum.org/DTD/wml_1.1.xml" >

<wml>

  <card id="Splash">
    <do type="accept" label="Enter">
      <go href="#Index"/>
    </do>
    <p align="center">
      <b><big>FirstUnwired.com</big></b>
    </p>
  </card>

  <card id="Index">
  </card>

</wml>
```

Now, open `cinema.wml`. The first screen that is displayed should now look something like Figure 3.3.

FIGURE 3.3:

Splash screen with redefined buttons

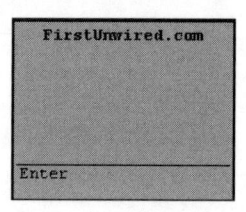

Navigating with Lists

Buttons aren't the only tool available to let users navigate between cards. You can also let users choose options from a list on-screen, then display a card depending on the chosen option.

In WML, you have the choice of two types of lists: one that uses the `<option>` element nested within the `<select>` element and another that uses the `<go>` element nested within the `<anchor>` element. The difference between the two is in the presentation on-screen and the mechanism for selecting an option.

The WML code for the first type of list, using the `<option>` element from within the `<select>` element, looks like this:

```
<select name="choice">
  <option onpick="#Movies"> View Movies </option>
  <option onpick="#Prices"> Ticket Prices </option>
  <option onpick="#Directions"> Directions </option>
</select>
```

Be sure to place the `<select>` element inside a `<p>` tag pair for it to work. The minimal code to display the `<select>` list would look something like this:

```
<?xml version="1.0"?>
<!DOCTYPE wml PUBLIC "-//WAPFORUM//DTD WML 1.1//EN"
    "http://www.wapforum.org/DTD/wml_1.1.xml" >

<wml>

  <card>
    <p>
```

```
            <select name="choice">
              <option onpick="#Movies"> View Movies </option>
              <option onpick="#Prices"> Ticket Prices </option>
              <option onpick="#Directions"> Directions </option>
            </select>
          </p>
        </card>

</wml>
```

The list will look something like Figure 3.4 when displayed on-screen.

FIGURE 3.4:

List using the `<option>` element

> 1 ▶ View Movies
> 2 Ticket Prices
> 3 Directions
>
> OK

The WML code for the second type of list, using the `<go>` element nested within the `<anchor>` element, looks like this:

```
<anchor title="Movies">
  <go href="#Movies"/>View Movies
</anchor>
<br/>
<anchor title="Prices">
  <go href="#Prices"/>Ticket Prices
</anchor>
<br/>
<anchor title="Directions">
  <go href="#Directions"/>Directions
</anchor>
```

So, the minimum code required to implement this example of the `<anchor>` element would be as follows:

```
<?xml version="1.0"?>
<!DOCTYPE wml PUBLIC "-//WAPFORUM//DTD WML 1.1//EN"
  "http://www.wapforum.org/DTD/wml_1.1.xml" >

<wml>
```

```
      <card>
        <p>
          <anchor title="Movies">
            <go href="#Movies"/>View Movies
          </anchor>
          <br/>
          <anchor title="Prices">
            <go href="#Prices"/>Ticket Prices
           </anchor>
          <br/>
          <anchor title="Directions">
            <go href="#Directions"/>Directions
          </anchor>
          <br/>
        </p>
      </card>

    </wml>
```

The list will look something like Figure 3.5 when displayed on-screen.

FIGURE 3.5:

List using the `<anchor>` element

```
[ View Movies ]
▶[ Ticket Prices ]
[ Directions ]


Prices
```

The only real difference between the two types of lists is their presentation. Right now, let's look more closely at the first type of list—using the `<select>` element.

Navigating with Selection Lists

What we want to do here is let users choose what they want to do next: choose a movie they want to read more about and perhaps book tickets for it, or just view ticket prices.

First, we'll create two new cards, which we'll leave empty for the moment. They'll serve as cards to which we can create links. We'll give them the card IDs Movies and Prices.

Go ahead, create the two new cards. Once you have created them, the file `cinema.wml` should look like this:

```
<?xml version="1.0"?>
<!DOCTYPE wml PUBLIC "-//WAPFORUM//DTD WML 1.1//EN"
  "http://www.wapforum.org/DTD/wml_1.1.xml" >

<wml>

  <card id="Splash">
    <do type="accept" label="Enter">
      <go href="#Index"/>
    </do>
    <p align="center">
      <b><big>FirstUnwired.com</big></b>
    </p>
  </card>

  <card id="Index">
  </card>

  <card id="Movies">
  </card>

  <card id="Prices">
  </card>

</wml>
```

Now, we want to create a selection list using the `<option>` element within a `<select>` element in the Index card. This will enable users to choose whether they want to view the list of movies currently being screened or view the ticket prices, sending them to the appropriate card when they make their choice. The `<option>` element has the following syntax:

```
<option title="label" value="value" onpick="url">

    content

</option>
```

In this syntax, `title` defines the label that is displayed for the Accept key, `value` defines the unique value that will be assigned to the surrounding `<select>` name when the user chooses the option, and `onpick` specifies the URL to open when the user chooses the option.

Let's now add two `<option>` elements nested within a `<select>` element in the Index card. The first `<option>` element will have the title Movies, the card ID Movies for the `onpick` attribute, and the text "View Movies."

> **NOTE** WAP supports relative URLs. This means that since we are jumping to a card from within the same deck, we have to enter only the card ID and not the URL in the `onpick` attribute.

The second `<option>` element will have the title Prices, the card ID Prices for the `onpick` attribute, and the text "Ticket Prices."

> **TIP** Before editing the `cinema.wml` file, note that the `<select>` element within which the `<onpick>` element is nested must itself be nested within a `<p>` element.

Now you have all the information you need to create the selection list in the Index card, so give it a go!

Once you have added the list to the Index card, the `cinema.wml` file should look something like this:

```
<?xml version="1.0"?>
<!DOCTYPE wml PUBLIC "-//WAPFORUM//DTD WML 1.1//EN"
   "http://www.wapforum.org/DTD/wml_1.1.xml" >

<wml>

   <card id="Splash">
     <do type="accept" label="Enter">
       <go href="#Index"/>
     </do>
     <p align="center">
       <b><big>FirstUnwired.com</big></b>
     </p>
   </card>

   <card id="Index">
     <p>
```

```
        <select>
          <option title="Movies" onpick="#Movies">
            View Movies</option>
          <option title="Prices" onpick="#Prices">
            Ticket Prices</option>
        </select>
      </p>
    </card>

    <card id="Movies">
    </card>

    <card id="Prices">
    </card>

</wml>
```

Now try viewing cinema.wml in your user agent. Navigate to the Index card, which should now look something like Figure 3.6.

FIGURE 3.6:

The Index card

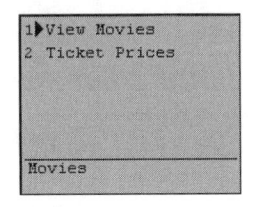

Now that you know how to use selection lists, using the <onpick> element nested within the <select> element, let's try using an anchored list to navigate.

Navigating with Anchored Lists

What we're going to do is create a list of two movies. (We never claimed that the example was going to be totally realistic—you'll have to wait until you get to Chapter 7, "Making Your Service Dynamic," for that!) In the meantime, we'll create a list of two movies using WML. These movies are: *Hello, Mary Lou* and *The Long Goodbye*. Before creating the list, we'll create the two cards that will display information about the two movies. This time, we won't leave the cards empty; we'll include a short description of the film (remember to keep this very short, as it is targeting users who'll be using mobile phones), the certification, and our own star rating. We'll let you decide what description, certification, and star rating you give the movies! We'll give the new cards the IDs Movie1 and Movie2.

Once you have added the two new cards, your `cinema.wml` file should look something like this:

```
<?xml version="1.0"?>
<!DOCTYPE wml PUBLIC "-//WAPFORUM//DTD WML 1.1//EN"
  "http://www.wapforum.org/DTD/wml_1.1.xml" >

<wml>

  <card id="Splash">
    <do type="accept" label="Enter">
      <go href="#Index"/>
    </do>
    <p align="center">
      <b><big>FirstUnwired.com</big></b>
    </p>
  </card>

  <card id="Index">
    <p>
      <select>
        <option  title="Movies" onpick="#Movies">
          View Movies</option>
        <option title="Prices" onpick="#Prices">
          Ticket Prices</option>
      </select>
    </p>
  </card>

  <card id="Movies">
  </card>

  <card id="Movie1">
    <p>
      Hello, Mary Lou
      Adventure, comedy.  Cert. 13.  Star rating 3.
    </p>
  </card>
```

```
<card id="Movie2">
  <p>
    The Long Goodbye
    Classic, romance.  Cert. 13.  Star rating 2.
  </p>
</card>

<card id="Prices">
</card>

</wml>
```

Now that we've created the two new cards, we can create the anchored list that will enable users to navigate to them. To create an anchored list, include a `<go>` element that is nested within an `<anchor>` element. The `<anchor>` element has the following syntax:

```
<anchor title="label"> text </anchor>
```

In this syntax, `title` defines the label that is displayed for the Accept key, and `text` is the text displayed on-screen that represents the task that is performed by choosing the anchor.

Nested within the anchor must be one of three elements: `<go>`, `<prev>`, or `<refresh>`. In our example, we're going to use the `<go>` element, which will specify the card to jump to when the anchor is selected. This has the following syntax:

```
<go href="url" sendreferer="boolean" method="method"
  accept-charset="charset" />
```

In this syntax, `href` is the URL that is opened when the `<go>` element is called. This can be relative. `sendreferer`, if set to `true`, causes the device to set the HTTP_REFERER header to the relative URL of the calling deck; `method` is the HTTP method that is called with the request, and this can be `get` or `post`; and `accept-charset` is the character set to be used by the application.

In our example, we'll be using only the `href` attribute for now. Now, let's add the anchored list to the Movies card. The first `<anchor>` element includes the text "Hello, Mary Lou," and the second will include the text "The Long Goodbye." They will both have the title Info, and they will both have nested within them a `<go>` element, including the `href` attribute that links to the card that includes the movie's description.

`cinema.wml` should now look something like this:

```wml
<?xml version="1.0"?>
<!DOCTYPE wml PUBLIC "-//WAPFORUM//DTD WML 1.1//EN"
  "http://www.wapforum.org/DTD/wml_1.1.xml" >

<wml>
  <card id="Splash">
    <do type="accept" label="Enter">
      <go href="#Index"/>
    </do>
    <p align="center">
      <b><big>FirstUnwired.com</big></b>
    </p>
  </card>

  <card id="Index">
    <p>
      <select>
        <option title="Movies" onpick="#Movies">
          View Movies</option>
        <option title="Prices" onpick="#Prices">
          Ticket Prices</option>
      </select>
    </p>
  </card>

  <card id="Movies">
    <p>
      <anchor title="Info">
        <go href="#Movie1"/>Hello, Mary Lou
      </anchor>
      <br/>
      <anchor title="Info">
        <go href="#Movie2"/>The Long Goodbye
      </anchor>
    </p>
  </card>

  <card id="Movie1">
    <p>
      Hello, Mary Lou
```

```
            Adventure, comedy.  Cert. 13.  Star rating 3.
        </p>
    </card>

    <card id="Movie2">
        <p>
            The Long Goodbye
            Classic, romance.  Cert. 13.  Star rating 2.
        </p>
    </card>

    <card id="Prices">
    </card>

</wml>
```

Now try viewing `cinema.wml` in your user agent. Navigate to the Movies card, which should now look something like Figure 3.7.

FIGURE 3.7:

The Movies card

```
[ Hello, Mary Lou ]
[ The Long Goodbye ]




Info
```

In this chapter, we covered some of the basics of WML—creating lists, formatting text, creating cards, and including the WML 1.1 prologue. In the next chapter, we're going to go on to use some of the more advanced features of WML 1.1.

Chapter 4

Spicing It Up

In this chapter, we're going to look at some of the advanced features of WML and build some of them into our example application. We'll be looking at the following features:

- Letting users input data
- Using variables
- Using WML events

Once you have finished this chapter, you'll have a good idea of what advanced WML features are available and how to use them in your own WML applications.

Letting Users Input Data

WML enables users to input information in two ways: by entering text and by selecting items from a list. Since most users will be using their mobile phones to enter information, you should try to limit the amount of text that users enter and let them choose items from lists wherever possible.

If you've ever tried entering text on a mobile phone keypad, you'll know why we say this—it's a long and often frustrating process. There are, of course, other ways of letting users input text, such as voice recognition and handwriting recognition, but neither of these are yet at a stage where they can be used as a reliable means of data input.

In the following sections, we'll look at how you can let users enter text and the ways in which you can let users choose options from lists.

Letting Users Enter Text

WML includes the `<input>` element for letting users enter text. This element lets you capture the text they input into a variable and gives you some control over the format of the text.

The `<input>` element has the following syntax:

```
text

<input
  name="variable"
```

```
    size="input area"
    title="label"
    format="mask"
    maxlength="number"
    emptyok="true|false"
 />
```

- `text` is the prompt the user is given to enter some text.
- `size` is the size of the input area (field). For example, if you want a user to enter a password of five letters, you type **size="5"**.
- `title` is the label you want to give the text. This label may be used by the user agent to prompt the user to enter the text.
- `format` is a mask that defines the format of the text to be entered (see Table 4.1).

TABLE 4.1: Input Formatting Codes

Tag	Description
A	Any symbolic or uppercase alphabetic character (no numbers)
a	Any symbolic or lowercase alphabetic character (no numbers)
N	Any numeric character (no symbols or alphabetic characters)
X	Any symbolic, numeric, or uppercase alphabetic character (not changeable to lowercase)
x	Any symbolic, numeric, or lowercase alphabetic character (not changeable to uppercase)
M	Any symbolic, numeric, or uppercase alphabetic character (changeable to lowercase); defaults to uppercase first character
m	Any symbolic, numeric, or lowercase alphabetic character (changeable to uppercase); defaults to lowercase first character

- `maxlength` is the maximum length of the text to be input.
- `emptyok` specifies whether the field can be left empty. `true` lets the user leave the field empty; `false` will let them continue only once they have entered something. The default is `false`.

Now that we've explored how to let users enter text using a keypad, let's look at how to let users enter text by selecting an option from a list.

Letting Users Enter Options from a List

In the previous section, we looked at letting users input information by entering text manually. A more useful method of letting users enter information is by having them choose the information they want to enter from a list, where possible. You can do this when what they need to enter is one of a fixed number of options that can be presented in a list.

We've already looked at using the `<select>` element earlier in this book, when we talked about navigating with lists. You can also use the `<select>` element to assign a value to a variable depending on the option that was chosen from the list. To do this, add the `<option>` element's `value` attribute to the `<select>` element, which has the following syntax:

```
text

<select
  title="label"
  name="variable"
  value="default">

    <option value="value">content</option>
    <option value="value">content</option>

</select>
```

- *text* is the prompt that is displayed to the user.
- *title* is a title for the select statement.
- *name* is the variable to which the selected value is stored.
- *value* is the initial value of the variable. Set the `value` attribute of the `<select>` element to be the same as the `value` attribute of the `<option>` element that you want initially selected.
- *option* is a list item, within which is the value stored in the `name` variable when an item is chosen, and *content* is the list text.

Now let's see how we can use these two ways of letting users input data in our example application.

So far, when users have accessed our site, we have not asked them to log on. So, let's use the <input> element to ask them to log on to the site by entering a password and their phone number. To do this, we'll create a new WML file that will deal with all aspects of the users' accounts. We'll call it account.wml. We'll start by simply asking users to log on. We'll ask them to enter a five-letter user ID and a phone number in the format (NNN) NNN-NNNN.

Note that we are going to include two parentheses and one hyphen in the number format. This is done by simply adding the characters to the number formatting. For example, in this case, in the format attribute of the <input> element, we're going to add the parentheses and hyphen to the format mask:

```
<input name="TELNO" format="(NNN) NNN-NNNN"/>
```

You can add any characters to input text in this way.

So, let's now create the first part of account.wml. We'll call the card in which we ask for the username and password Login; define the Accept button to display "Continue"; and display a card named Details once the button is pressed. We'll leave Details empty for the moment, and we'll leave the checking of the password and telephone number to later in this book!

Once you have created account.wml, it should look something like this:

```
<?xml version="1.0"?>
<!DOCTYPE wml PUBLIC "-//WAPFORUM//DTD WML 1.1//EN"
   "http://www.wapforum.org/DTD/wml_1.1.xml" >

<wml>

  <card id="Login">
    <do type="accept" label="Continue">
      <go href="#Details"/>
    </do>
    <p>
      Enter User ID:
      <input name="UID" format="AAAAA"/>
      Enter Phone No:
      <input name="TELNO" format="(NNN) NNN-NNNN"/>
    </p>
  </card>

  <card id="Details">
  </card>

</wml>
```

Try opening the `account.wml` deck on your emulator. It should look something like Figure 4.1.

FIGURE 4.1:

The Password screen

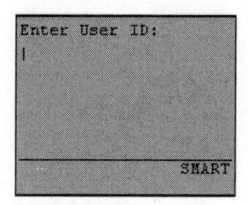

[screen: Enter User ID: | SMART]

Try entering five uppercase letters. You'll notice that once you type the fifth letter, "OK" appears, letting you know that you have entered the required amount of letters. You can go to the next screen by clicking OK (the Accept button).

> **NOTE** Although you defined the user ID and telephone number on the same card, they may not be both displayed at the same time on some emulators or WAP devices. This is to maximize the usability of WML programs on small mobile phone screens by simplifying data input.

If your WML emulator has displayed only the first input field, you must click Accept to go to the next input field. Now enter a number. You may notice as you enter numbers that hyphens are automatically inserted as defined in the `format` attribute of the `<input>` element for the number. This will look something like Figure 4.2 on your emulator.

FIGURE 4.2:

The Phone Number screen

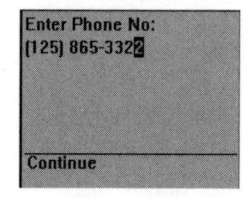

[screen: Enter Phone No: (125) 865-332_ | Continue]

Notice that once you have entered the required number of numbers (10), the caption "Continue" appears at the bottom of the screen, indicating that you can click the Accept button to continue.

Not all WML emulators will implement these features consistently, such as automatically displaying the hyphens or showing the Continue buttons when a field is full. However, most user agents (microbrowsers) in WAP devices function more reliably than most emulators.

We've now examined two ways in which you can allow users to enter data: by typing text on the keypad or by selecting items from a list. We used text typing with the <input> element in our example application. We'll also enable users to select items from lists in our example application, but before doing that, let's take a look at variables and how we can use them in WML.

Using Variables

We've already discussed variables in the preceding sections: In the <input> element, we stored the entered data in variables named UID and TELNO in our example application. We also looked at variables in the <option> element when using lists, where a value is stored in a variable when an option is chosen.

We'll now discuss some ways in which we can use variables. In this section, we're going to look at how to display variable values in WML, how to explicitly set variable values, and how to send variable values to other applications.

Before we go any further in discussing variables, though, we'd like to highlight the following two points:

- WML variables do not have to be declared before use.
- WML variables are case sensitive.

Displaying Variable Values

You can use variables in your WML code in formatted text, URLs, selection items, or default values. To display a variable value, reference the variable using the syntax $variable. For example, to display the value of a variable named var, you use the following WML text:

```
<p>
    $var
</p>
```

Setting Variable Values

You can explicitly set a variable value to anything in WML, using the `<setvar>` element. This element lets you set a variable value when you execute a `<go>`, `<prev>`, or `<refresh>` element. These elements are discussed later, in "Using WML Events." You must specify one `<setvar>` element for each variable you want to set. The `<setvar>` element has the following form:

```
<setvar name="name" value="value"/>
```

For example, to set the variable `username` to `Paul`, you type the following line:

```
<setvar name="username" value="Paul"/>
```

Passing Variable Values to Other Applications

You'll be doing a lot of this in the next two chapters. WML has no processing logic, and you'll want to do something with the data input by users. Therefore, you'll be passing variables to WMLScript for client side processing or to server side applications written using technologies such as Java servlets or Perl.

You can pass variables to other applications in either of two ways:

- By using the post method and the `postfield` attribute within a `<go>` element
- By using the variables to set arguments in a URL string within a `<go>` element

We recommend that you use the post method with the `postfield` attribute to pass variable values to other applications, because it enables the WAP gateway to translate the variable data to the character set used by your application. The syntax of the post method and the `postfield` attribute within a `<go>` element is as follows:

```
<go href="URL" method="post">

    <postfield name="app_variable" value="$(variable)"/>

</go>
```

- *URL* is the URL to be called.
- *app_variable* is the application variable name.
- *variable* is the WML variable name.

For example, to call the URL http://*yourserver*/tickets.cgi with the variable price taken from the WML variable price, use the following command:

```
<go href="http://yourserver/tickets.cgi
➥?price=$(price)&number=$(number)"/>
  <postfield name="price" value="$(price)"/>
  <postfield name="number" value="$(number)"/>
</go>
```

To pass the variable as an argument within a <go> element, using the same URL and variables as given above, use the following command:

```
<go href="http://www.mobileminx.com/tickets.cgi?price=$
  (price)&number=$(number)"

</go>
```

Referencing Variables in the Example Application

Now let's go back to our example. In the last part of the example, we asked users to enter a user ID and telephone number to access a card named Details, which for the moment is blank. Let's display the text "User ID" followed by "Account Details" in this card, displaying the value entered for the user ID in the UID field. When the user enters their user ID, we write this to the variable UID. Therefore, to display the value of UID, we refer to $UID in the WML code. Once we have done this, account.wml will look something like the following:

```
<?xml version="1.0"?>
<!DOCTYPE wml PUBLIC "-//WAPFORUM//DTD WML 1.1//EN"
  "http://www.wapforum.org/DTD/wml_1.1.xml" >

<wml>

  <card id="Login">
    <do type="accept" label="Continue">
      <go href="#Details"/>
    </do>
    <p>
      Enter User ID:
      <input name="UID" format="AAAAA"/>
      Enter Phone No:
      <input name="TELNO" format="(NNN) NNN-NNNN"/>
    </p>
```

```
    </card>

    <card id="Details">
      <p>
        $UID Account Details
      </p>
    </card>

</wml>
```

Figure 4.3 shows what the Details card should look like when it is displayed on your emulator.

FIGURE 4.3:

The Account Details screen

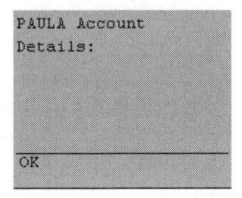

Acting on Variables Set by the User

Now that we know how to reference variables, let's look at how we can let users input data by selecting an option from a list, then display that data on-screen. Do you remember that in the previous chapter, we had an option to view ticket prices, which called a card named Prices that we left blank? Let's now let users choose one of three rows—rows A, B, and C—from a list, and then display a new card—RowPrice—that displays the ticket price for seats in that row. We'll say that tickets in row A cost $4.25, tickets in row B cost $5.00, and tickets in row C cost $5.25. We'll use the <select> element with the <option> element's value attribute to do this.

Let's now use the <select> element to let users choose a row in the Prices card, then display the cost of tickets in the chosen row in the RowPrice card. The file cinema.wml will look like the following:

```
<?xml version="1.0"?>
<!DOCTYPE wml PUBLIC "-//WAPFORUM//DTD WML 1.1//EN"
  "http://www.wapforum.org/DTD/wml_1.1.xml" >

<wml>
```

```
<card id="Splash">
  <do type="accept" label="Enter">
    <go href="#Index"/>
  </do>
  <p align="center">
    <b><big>FirstUnwired.com</big></b>
  </p>
</card>

<card id="Index">
  <p>
    <select>
      <option title="Movies" onpick="#Movies">
        View Movies</option>
      <option title="Prices" onpick="#Prices">
       Ticket Prices</option>
    </select>
  </p>
</card>

<card id="Movies">
  <p>
    <anchor title="Info">
      <go href="#Movie1"/>Hello, Mary Lou
    </anchor>
    <anchor title="Info">
      <go href="#Movie2"/>The Long Goodbye
    </anchor>
  </p>
</card>

<card id="Movie1">
  <p>
    Hello, Mary Lou <br/>
    Adventure, comedy.  Cert. 13.  Star rating 3.
  </p>
</card>

<card id="Movie2">
  <p>
    The Long Goodbye <br/>
    Classic, romance.  Cert. 13.  Star rating 2.
```

```
      </p>
    </card>

    <card id="Prices">
      <do type="accept" label="View Prc">
        <go href="#RowPrice"/>
      </do>
      <p>
        Select a row to view its price.
        <select title="tktprices" name="tPrice">
          <option value="4.25">Row A</option>
          <option value="5.00">Row B</option>
          <option value="5.75">Row C</option>
        </select>
      </p>
    </card>

    <card id="RowPrice">
      <do type="accept" label="Return">
        <go href="#Prices"/>
      </do>
      <p>
        Ticket price = $(tPrice)
      </p>
    </card>

</wml>
```

Now try viewing cinema.wml on your emulator. When you get to the Prices card, it should look something like Figure 4.4. When you select a row, then click the Accept button, the RowPrice card will look something like Figure 4.5.

FIGURE 4.4:

The Prices screen

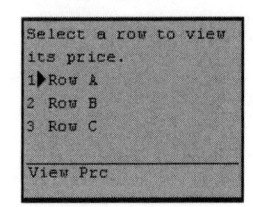

FIGURE 4.5:

The Ticket Price screen

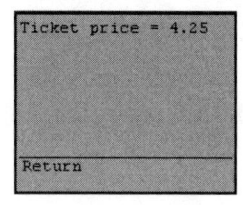

[Screen display showing "Ticket price = 4.25" with a "Return" option]

Variable Escaping

Variable escaping is the method of replacing characters in a variable with an *escape sequence*. The method is defined in URI Generic Syntax RFC 2396 and describes replacing certain characters that might be construed as something else with a percent sign (%) followed by character codes. Letters, digits, and some punctuation marks are considered safe characters and do not need to be escaped. The following example shows a string before and after variable escaping:

- Before escaping: "@ $4.25 * 2 = $8.50"
- After escaping: "%40+%244.25+*+2+%3D+%248.50"

Microbrowsers must implement automatic escaping for those tasks where escaping is required—for example, href, src, onenterforward, onenterbackward, ontimer, and onpick. As you can expect, you can force or prevent escaping at any time by utilizing a *conversion mode*. See Table 4.2 for the conversion modes.

TABLE 4.2: Variable Conversion Modes

Mode	Usage	Description
escape	$(var:escape)	Forces escaping of the variable's value
unesc	$(var:unesc)	Reverses the action of escaping the variable's value
noesc	$(var:noesc)	Prevents escaping of the variable's value

In this section, we've shown you how to use variables in WML—inputting values to variables, referencing variable values, passing variables to other applications, and explicitly setting variable values. In the next section, we're going to look at WML events and discuss how you can use WML events in your application.

Using WML Events

WML links tasks to events. There are two types of events: *intrinsic events* and *user events*. Intrinsic events are triggered by the user agent itself, whereas user events are triggered by a user action. Let's look at these two types of events in more detail and at what specific events are available to WML programmers.

Intrinsic Events

All intrinsic events are bound to tasks using the `<onevent>` element. The `<onevent>` element has the following syntax:

 `<onevent type="type">task</onevent>`

- *task* defines the task to perform when the intrinsic event is triggered.
- *type* defines the intrinsic event type. You can define both card-level and deck-level events.
  - A card-level event is defined within a `<card>` element and applies only to the card in which it is defined.
  - A deck-level event has to be defined within a `<template>` element and applies to the whole deck. For full details of the `<template>` element, refer to Appendix A, "WML Reference."

If a deck includes both a deck-level event and a card-level event, the card-level event overrides the deck-level event. Table 4.3 lists the intrinsic event attributes and describes when they are triggered.

TABLE 4.3: Intrinsic Event Attributes

Attribute	Description
onpick	Triggers when a user selects an item from an `<option>` list
onenterforward	Triggers when a user enters a card through a `<go>` element or through any other mechanism
onenterbackward	Triggers when a user enters a card through the `<prev>` element or through pressing the Back key
ontimer	Triggers when a `<timer>` element expires

Table 4.4 lists the elements that can be performed as a result of an intrinsic event.

TABLE 4.4: Intrinsic Event Tasks

Event	Action
`<go>`	Opens the specified URL
`<prev>`	Pops the current URL off the history stack and opens the previous URL in the stack
`<noop>`	Does nothing; useful for overriding deck-level `<do>` elements
`<refresh>`	Refreshes the specified variables within the current card (If any variables are currently on display, the new refreshed variable value is displayed.)

Let's now add an intrinsic event to our example application. We could use the timer event to add a small animation to our splash screen by displaying a series of cards, each after a timer has expired. Before doing so, though, we'll take a quick look at the `<timer>` element.

The `<timer>` element has the following syntax:

```
<timer name="variable" value="value"/>
```

- *variable* is the variable in which the timer is stored.
- *value* is the timer value. This is in 10ths of a second, so the value 10 equals 1 second.

We're going to create an exploding star. We'll do this by creating two new cards, named Splash1 and Splash2. First, in the card Splash, we'll delete the following lines:

```
<do type="accept" label="Enter">
  <go href="#Index"/>
</do>
```

In their place, we'll include the following lines:

```
<onevent type="ontimer">
  <go href="#Splash1"/>
</onevent>
<timer value="10"/>
```

We'll also add an asterisk to the center of the card, so it will now look like the following:

```
<card id="Splash">
  <onevent type="ontimer">
    <go href="#Splash1"/>
  </onevent>
  <timer value="10"/>
  <p align="center">
    <b><big>FirstUnwired.com</big></b>
    <br/>
    <br/>
    <br/>
    *
  </p>
</card>
```

In card Splash1, we'll include the same timer, as well as the next part of the animation. Splash1 will look like the following:

```
<card id="Splash1">
  <onevent type="ontimer">
    <go href="#Splash2"/>
  </onevent>
  <timer value="10"/>
  <p align="center">
    <b><big>FirstUnwired.com</big></b>
    <br/>
    <br/>
    \ | /
    <br/>
    -- --
    <br/>
    / | \
  </p>
</card>
```

Finally, in card Splash2, we'll include the final part of the animation, before moving on to the card Index. Splash2 will look like the following:

```
<card id="Splash2">
  <onevent type="ontimer">
    <go href="#Index"/>
  </onevent>
  <timer value="10"/>
```

```
            <p align="center">
              <b><big>FirstUnwired.com</big></b>
              <br/>
              \   |   /
              <br/>
              <br/>
              --       --
              <br/>
              <br/>
              /   |   \
            </p>
          </card>
```

So go ahead, have some fun by adding these cards to the file cinema.wml, and have a look at it on your emulator. The cards will look like Figures 4.6, 4.7, and 4.8.

FIGURE 4.6:

The Splash card

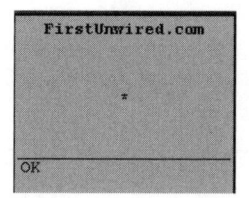

FIGURE 4.7:

The Splash1 card

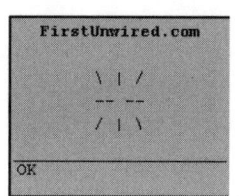

FIGURE 4.8:

The Splash2 card

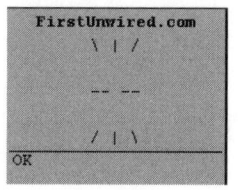

Now that we've looked at intrinsic events, let's move on to user events.

User Events

User events are triggered by an action taken by a user. That action may be pressing a button, touching an icon on a touch-sensitive screen, or executing a voice-activated command. The <do> element enables you to bind a user event to a task. The <do> element has the following syntax:

```
<do
  type="event"
  label="label"
  name="name"
  optional="true|false">

  task

</do>
```

> **NOTE** The button, icon, or voice command to which these events are tied depends on the user agent. What the events actually do, however, is up to you, the WML programmer.

- *event* specifies the event to which the task is bound. Table 4.5 lists the user events that you can use.

TABLE 4.5: User Events

Event	Description
accept	Acceptance of the proposal displayed to the user; synonymous with OK
delete	Delete the selected item
help	Ask for help
prev	Display the last URL in the history stack
options	Display the options available to the user
reset	Reset the current context
unknown	Any <do> element

- *label* is a label that is displayed to indicate to the user the meaning of the event, whether it be pressing a button, touching an icon, etc.
- *name* identifies the binding between the task and the event. If you do not include a name, this value defaults to the value in the type attribute.
  - If you give a card-level task and event binding the same name as the deck-level task and event binding, the element bound at the card level overrides that bound at the deck level.
- The optional attribute, if set to true, instructs the user agent to ignore the element.
- *task* defines the task to perform when the user event is triggered; these are the same as the intrinsic event tasks listed in Table 4.4 earlier: <go>, <prev>, <noop>, and <refresh>.

We've already used user events in our example application. For example, the lines

```
<do type="accept" label="Continue">

    <go href="#Details"/>

</do>
```

bind a <go> task to the pressing of the Accept button.

Let's now add a new user event to our example application. In your emulator, open the file account.wml. Log in with a user ID and phone number, then go to the Account Details screen and press the Back button. Notice that when you go back to the initial screen where you entered your user ID and password, the values you entered are still there. It would make more sense to let users clear them so they can reenter them if they made a mistake. We can do this by binding the Options button to the <refresh> task.

Before doing so, though, we'll take a quick look at the <refresh> task. The <refresh> task has the following syntax:

```
<refresh>

    <setvar name="variable" value="newval"/>

</refresh>
```

You can include as many `<setvar>` elements as you like within the `<refresh>` element.

Now we're going to bind the Options button to the `<refresh>` task to refresh the variables UID and TELNO to null values. This will leave the card Login looking something like the following:

```
<card id="Login">
  <do type="accept" label="Continue">
    <go href="#Details"/>
  </do>
  <do type="clear" label="Clear">
    <refresh>
      <setvar name="UID" value=""/>
      <setvar name="TELNO" value=""/>
    </refresh>
  </do>
  <p>
    Enter User ID:
    <input name="UID" format="AAAAA"/>
    Enter Phone No:
    <input name="TELNO" format="(NNN) NNN-NNNN"/>
  </p>
</card>
```

Once we've completed the Login card, the file account.wml should look like this:

```
<?xml version="1.0"?>
<!DOCTYPE wml PUBLIC "-//WAPFORUM//DTD WML 1.1//EN"
  "http://www.wapforum.org/DTD/wml_1.1.xml" >

<wml>

  <card id="Login">
    <do type="accept" label="Continue">
      <go href="#Details"/>
    </do>
    <do type="clear" label="Clear">
      <refresh>
        <setvar name="UID" value=""/>
        <setvar name="TELNO" value=""/>
      </refresh>
```

```
    </do>
    <p>
      Enter User ID:
      <input name="UID" format="AAAAA"/>
      Enter Phone No:
      <input name="TELNO" format="(NNN) NNN-NNNN"/>
    </p>
  </card>

  <card id="Details">
    <p>
      $UID Account Details
    </p>
  </card>

</wml>
```

We've finished looking at some of the more advanced features of WML. These have included the following:

- Letting users input data
- Using variables
- Using WML events

In the next chapter, we're going to look at WMLScript, which will enable us to add some client side processing logic to our example application.

Chapter 5

Adding Intelligence with WMLScript

WML is fine for creating static pages that display information that doesn't change. But WML, like all languages, does have limitations—it can't perform calculations, verify user input beyond making sure that entered data is formatted correctly, or carry out any logic processing. Enter WMLScript. WMLScript is a scripting language that is derived from ECMAScript, which in turn was derived from JavaScript. It was defined to enable client side procedural logic and to reduce the amount of bandwidth required to execute services on user agents. As a result, WMLScript performs client side processing. This means that when a WMLScript program is called by a user agent, it is downloaded from the server to the user agent, then executed by the user agent. Needless to say, WMLScript has to be lightweight to be downloaded over the limited bandwidth. Some typical uses of WMLScript are checking user input, performing calculations, validating data, and displaying dialogs, alerts, and confirmations, all done on the WAP device—without the need to communicate with the server, which is very efficient in terms of speed.

In this chapter, you'll learn how to create WAP services with WMLScript functions that will perform the following roles:

- Define the process logic for the service
- Perform mathematical functions
- Perform data validation
- Display alerts

The beginning of this chapter covers the background information you'll need to be able to program with WMLScript. The rest of this chapter covers how the WMLScript functions that perform the actions just listed are built.

WMLScript Characteristics

WMLScript is function oriented. This means that it doesn't have a main program from which all functions are called. Instead, a series of functions are stored in a file, on a server. Each file containing WMLScript functions is called a compilation unit or program. Just as the Web server stores WML files with the extension WML, WMLScript files are similar text files but with the extension WMLS. When a user agent calls a WMLScript function, the WAP gateway delivers the whole WMLScript file to the WAP device for execution of individual functions.

Both WML and WMLScript can call WMLScript functions. WML uses the following syntax to call a WMLScript function:

```
<go href="filename.wmls#function_name(arguments)"/>
```

which is the same syntax used to call another card. WMLScript uses a syntax you would expect from an ECMAScript language, notably

```
function_name(arguments);
```

which calls a function within the same WMLScript program. But to call a function in a different WMLScript program, the following syntax is used:

```
use url OtherWMLScript "other_filename.wmls";
OtherWMLScript#function_name(arguments);
```

In this section, we'll be looking at some considerations you should bear in mind when developing programs in WMLScript.

WMLScript Interpreter Architecture

When a WMLScript function is called by a user agent, it is retrieved from the server where it is stored by the WAP gateway and compiled into a binary format. It is then interpreted by the WMLScript byte-code interpreter on the user agent. When a user agent calls a WMLScript function, it specifies the parameters it wants to pass to the function and the compilation unit holding the function. The function can contain any amount of instructions, calls to other functions, and calls to the standard WMLScript library functions. The WMLScript library functions add a lot of functionality to WMLScript, without which WMLScript would be limited in use.

While the function is being executed, the WMLScript interpreter records the following state information:

- The Instruction Pointer, which records the instruction that is currently being executed
- The current values of the variables being used by the function
- The operand stack, which records expression values and the arguments that are passed between calling and called functions
- The function call stack, which records the standard library, and the WMLScript function details and their return addresses

The WMLScript byte-code interpreter executes the functions in the order in which they are called.

Error Handling

WMLScript provides no inherent error-handling capability. Therefore, when you design services using WMLScript, you must try to prevent errors from happening and provide verification wherever possible. One way in which you can prevent errors from occurring is by making sure that users enter data in the user agent in the correct format. This is called *input validation*. Preventing errors in the first place is better than writing lots of code to handle the errors. For example, if you ask a user to enter a number value of two digits, you can make sure they enter two digits using the `format` attribute of the `<input>` element. In the WML code, this would look as follows: `<input format="NN">`. Refer to Table 4.1 (in the previous chapter) for information on specifying data entry formats.

Debugging WMLScript

WMLScript offers very few debugging tools at this time. This means that you should develop your WMLScripts as small blocks of code, making sure that each one works correctly before moving on to the next. We've found that one of the most difficult types of problem to solve is when your WMLScript just won't compile. When this happens, the best solution, given the lack of more powerful debugging facilities, is to try to identify the problematic section of code by commenting out other sections of the code, then call the script again until it compiles.

> **WARNING** Be very careful when using this technique, however, as you may comment out a statement that is required by an uncommented area of code, thereby causing additional problems!

Once you have your code compiling, debugging entails verifying that your WMLScript will produce the expected result. We find it very useful to send variable values to the WML browser where you can view them. Most WML SDK providers also provide their own debugging aids, such as the ability to see the current variable values stored in the WML browser context.

Consult your SDK documentation for more information on debugging facilities.

WMLScript Overview

Before we start developing programs using WMLScript, it is essential that we take a quick look at some of the more important things to bear in mind when developing WMLScript. We promise to make this as painless as possible—just bear with us, and we'll be onto the more exciting stuff shortly.

Lexical Structure

The *lexical structure* defines the overall syntax of WMLScript, including case sensitivity and comments. When you develop WMLScripts, bear in mind the following rules about the WMLScript lexical structure:

- WMLScript is case sensitive. This means that *myvar* is not the same as *myVar*.
- WMLScript ignores spaces, tabs, line breaks, and all other editing characters that are entered between tokens, except for those defined from within strings.
- Statements are separated by a semicolon (;).
- Blocks of statements are enclosed in braces ({}).

Comments

You can include single lines as *comments* by preceding them with two forward slashes (//), as in other languages such as C++ or Delphi.

You can include multiple lines as comments by preceding the lines with a forward slash followed by an asterisk (/*) and ending them with an asterisk followed by a forward slash (*/).

Following is an example with both single- and multiple-lined comments:

```
//This is a comment that will be ignored by the compiler.

/*All these lines are
comments that will be
ignored by the compiler.*/
```

Literals

WMLScript lets you use five types of literals. These are as follows:

- Integer
- Floating point
- String
- Boolean
- Invalid

The following sections describe each of these literals.

Integer Literals

Integer literals can be expressed in decimal, hexadecimal, or octal form and must comply with the following rules:

- *Decimal integers* can include any combination of numbers from 0 to 9. For example, 36.
- *Hexadecimal integers* can include the characters 1 to 9, a to f, and A to F. They must begin with 0x or 0X. For example, 0x5E.
- *Octal integers* can be any combination of numbers from 0 to 7, but they must begin with a 0. For example, 045.

Floating Point Literals

Floating point literals can contain a decimal point as well as an exponent. An exponent is indicated by an e or E followed by an integer, which may be positive or negative. The exponent indicates the number's base 10 logarithmic value. For example, the number 42.67 can be expressed as any of the following:

- 42.67
- 42.67e0
- 0.4267e2
- 4267e-2

String Literals

String literals can contain any characters apart from those that are listed in the following section, "Escaping," which require escape sequences. String literals must be surrounded by single or double quotes (' ' or " ").

Here are some examples of valid string literals:

```
"The heroes welcome"
"Massive 50% reductions"
'November 5, 1999'
```

Escaping Certain characters have to be *escaped* (preceded with a certain character) if you want to include them in character strings. Table 5.1 lists those characters and provides the escape sequence for each one.

TABLE 5.1: Character Escape Sequences

Description	Sequence
Apostrophe or single quote	\'
Double quote	\"
Backslash	\\
Forward slash	\/
Backspace	\b
Form feed	\f
New line	\n
Carriage return	\r
Horizontal tab	\t
A character with the encoding specified by the two hexadecimal digits hh (Latin-1 ISO8859-1)	\xhh
A character with the encoding specified by the three octal digits ooo (Latin-1 ISO8859-1)	\ooo
A Unicode character with the encoding specified by the four hexadecimal digits hhhh	\uhhhh

Boolean Literals

Boolean literals can have one of two values: `true` or `false`. This is also sometimes known as the *truth* value.

Invalid Literals

WMLScript supports a special *invalid literal* to denote invalid values. The return value from any invalid literal is `invalid`, as shown in the following example:

```
a = 1/0;
if (a == invalid) {
    // Division by zero error
}
```

WMLScript Variables

WMLScript variables have to be declared within the function that they are used in or passed as function parameters, and they must also be declared before they can be used. Moreover, all variable names must be unique within the function they are declared in.

Declare variables using the var keyword. Note that you can declare multiple variables on the same line by separating each variable with a comma. Indicate the end of your variable declarations using a semicolon. You can, optionally, initialize variables when you declare them. If you don't initialize your variables, they will be automatically initialized with an empty string value `""`. Because of this, you must initialize a variable with a value if you want to perform arithmetic functions on the variable. This effectively gives the variable a data type without having to explicitly declare its type.

Here are some example variable declarations:

```
var myString = "Hello, world";
var myNum = 0;
var myName;
var myList1, myList2, myList3;
```

In the declarations above, `myString` is automatically given the data type String, and `myNum` Integer. The other variables will be assigned a type when they are first assigned a value. It is not good programming practice to leave the data type assignment to be set automatically, and we recommend you always assign a value to every new variable declaration.

Data Types

WMLScript supports five *data types*: Boolean, integer, floating point, string, and invalid. WMLScript is a weakly typed language, meaning that you do not have to define variable types in their declarations. Instead, WMLScript automatically converts from one data type to another as needed. This flexibility is also the cause of many programming errors, so care must be taken when using variables.

One widely used technique for keeping track of a variable's data type is to prefix the variable with a unique identifier, denoting its type.

For example, all integer variables would start with i or int, and all strings with s or str. While standards do exist for other languages, many developers use their own variations, which is fine as long as they are used consistently.

Numeric Values

You can use integers and floating point numbers in your WMLScripts. The size of an integer is 32 bits; therefore, integer values can range from –2147483648 to 2147483647.

You can get the maximum number of integer values during runtime using the maxInt and minInt functions from the Lang library as follows:

```
var maxVal = Lang.maxInt();   //maxVal = 2147483647
var minVal = Lang.minInt();   //minVal = -2147483648
```

The size of floating point numbers is also 32 bits; thus, floating point values can range from 0.40282347E+38 to 1.17549435E–38.

You can get the maximum number of floating point values during runtime using the maxFloat and minFloat functions from the Lang library as follows:

```
var maxVal = Lang.maxFloat();   //maxVal = 0.40282347E+38
var minVal = Lang.minFloat();   //minVal = 1.17549435E-38
```

WMLScript handles floating point numbers using the following rules:

- If an operation results in a floating point number that is not part of the set of finite real numbers (it is not a number supported by the floating point format), the result is invalid.
- If an operation results in a floating point underflow, the result is zero (0.0).
- *Negative zero* and *positive zero* are equal.

String Values

String values can contain any characters. WMLScript includes a String library that lets you manipulate strings.

Boolean Values

You can use *Boolean values* to determine truth or not truth. You can initialize or assign a value to a Boolean variable explicitly, or assign a value as the result of a logical expression evaluation.

WMLScript Operators

The following sections provide a brief explanation of the *WMLScript operators*. WMLScript supports the following types of operators:

- Assignment operators, which assign values to operands
- Arithmetic operators, which perform arithmetic functions
- String operators, which enable you to manipulate strings
- Logical operators, which enable you to evaluate operands
- Relational operators, which compare operands
- Array operators, which enable you to manipulate strings as arrays
- Comma operators, which let you combine multiple evaluations in one expression
- Conditional operators, which assign a value to an expression based on the Boolean result of an initial statement
- typeof operators, which describe the type of the given expression
- isvalid operators, which check whether or not a variable or expression is valid

Assignment Operators

Assignment operators assign values to operands. WMLScript supports all the usual assignment operators, including =, +, +=, *=, /=, etc. Assignment is made by value only, so assignment of one variable to another does not bind the two variables—only the value is copied.

```
var a = 1; // Assign 1 to variable a.
var b = a; // Copy contents of a to variable b.
a = 2;     // a now contains 2, but b still contains 1.
```

When a variable is assigned a value that includes the same variable, the abbreviated assignment can be used. The following two lines produce the same result.

```
a = a + b;
a += b;
```

See Appendix B, "WMLScript Reference," for a complete list of the WML assignment operators. In the meantime, here are some further examples:

```
var myNum = 0;
var TotVal = myNum;
totPrice = quantity * unitPrice;
```

Arithmetic Operators

WMLScript supports all of the basic, complex binary, and unary operators.

- The basic operators perform all of the basic operations that you'd expect: *, /, +, -.

- The complex binary operators perform the regular complex binary tasks, which include remainder (%), bitwise left shift (<<), bitwise right shift (>>), bitwise right shift with zero fill (>>>), bitwise AND (&), bitwise OR (|), and bitwise XOR (^).

- The unary operators perform the basic unary operations: +, -, decrement (--), increment (++), and bitwise NOT (~).

For a full list of arithmetic operators, see Appendix B, "WMLScript Reference."

String Operators

You can use *string operators* to concatenate strings. WMLScript also includes the String library, which lets you manipulate strings. For full information on the String library, refer to Appendix B, "WMLScript Reference." Here's an example of string *concatenation* (concatenation is when strings are added together):

```
var surfsUp = "Big " + "waves";  //surfsUp = "Big waves"
surfsUp += " today";             //surfsUp = "Big waves today"
```

Logical Operators

The logical AND operator && evaluates the first operand and tests the result. If the result is `false` or `invalid`, the operation returns the first operand result and the second operand is not evaluated. If the first operand is `true`, the operation returns the result of the second operand.

Here is an example of logical operators:

```
surferOK = (sunShines && beachIsClose) ||
(!noWaves && !sharks);
```

The logical OR operator || evaluates the first operand and tests the result. If the result is `true` or `invalid`, the operation returns the result of the first operand and the second operand is not evaluated. If the first operand is `false`, the operation returns the result of the second operand.

> **NOTE** WMLScript converts variables to Boolean when they hold the result of a logical operator.

Relational Operators

WMLScript supports the standard set of *relational operators*: < (less than), > (greater than), <= (less than or equal to), >= (greater than or equal to), == (equal to), and != (not equal to). Note the use of a double equals sign in *equal to*. When these relational operators are used on nonnumeric values, variables, and expressions—for example, Boolean, string and `invalid`—some special rules apply.

Boolean For Boolean, `true` is larger than `false`.

String Comparison is performed character by character based on the order of the character codes in the string values. Character codes are defined by the character set supported by the WMLScript Interpreter.

Invalid If at least one of the operands is `invalid`, the result of the comparison is `invalid`.

Note the following results of comparisons:

```
result = (1 < 2);          // result is true.
result = (1 == 2.0);       // result is false.
result = (true > false);   // result is true.
result = ("a" < "b");      // result is true.
```

```
result = ("a" < "aa");        // result is true.
result = ("a" < "invalid");   // result is true.
result = ("a" < invalid);     // result is invalid.
result = (true == invalid);   // result is invalid.
```

Array Operators

WMLScript does not support arrays as such. However, you can use the String library to manipulate strings as if they were arrays by using a specified operator to separate elements. Element indexes start at 0.

Here is an example of how you can use a string as an array:

```
var array = "ABC,DEF,GHI,JKL";
var myElement = String.elementAt(array,2,","); // myElement = GHI
```

> **NOTE** Because indexes start at 0, you need to use an index of 2 to obtain the third element of the array. This is a common cause of difficult-to-find errors.

Comma Operators

Comma operators let you combine multiple evaluations in one expression.

> **NOTE** Commas that are used to separate multiple parameters in a function call or to separate multiple variables in a variable definition are not comma operators.

Here is an example of how comma operators are used:

```
for (minutes=1, cost=50; minutes < 20; minutes++,cost++) {
   totCost += (minutes*cost);
}
```

Conditional Operators

You can use *conditional operators* to assign a value to an expression based on the Boolean result of the initial statement. Conditional operators take three operands. The Boolean value of the first operand decides whether the result of the operation is the evaluation of the second or third operand, according to the following rules:

- If the value of the first operand is `true`, the result of the operation is the evaluation of the third operand.

- If the value of the first operand is `false`, the result of the operation is the evaluation of the second operand.

Here is an example of a conditional operator:

```
var goodDay = (surfsUp && haveBoard) ? "Yes" : "No";
```

which is equivalent to the following `if` statement:

```
var goodDay;
if (surfsUp && haveBoard) {
    goodDay = "Yes";
} else {
    goodDay = "No";
}
```

typeof Operators

The *typeof operator* returns a value that describes the type of the given expression, according to Table 5.2.

TABLE 5.2: *typeof* Return Values

Operator Type	Return Value
Integer	0
Floating point	1
String	2
Boolean	3
Invalid	4

Here are examples of the typeof operator:

```
a = 1234;      t = typeof a;   // t is 0.
a = 12.34;     t = typeof a;   // t is 1.
a = "12.34";   t = typeof a;   // t is 2.
a = true;      t = typeof a;   // t is 3.
a /= 0;        t = typeof a;   // t is 4.
```

isvalid Operators

The *isvalid operator* checks whether or not a variable or expression is valid. The isvalid operator returns a Boolean true or false depending on the validity of the variable or expression.

- If the result of an expression is invalid or a variable is not a valid type, the value false is returned.
- If the result of an expression is not invalid or a variable is a valid type, the value true is returned.

Here are examples of the isvalid operator:

```
var a = 12.34;
var b = "any string";
var v = isvalid a;     // v is true.
var w = isvalid a/0;   // w is false.
var x = isvalid b;     // x is true.
```

WMLScript Type Conversions

WMLScript performs *type conversions* wherever possible. If the conversion is logical, then it's likely that it will be performed. The following cases are of importance:

- Boolean true is converted to the string "true".
- Boolean false is converted to the string "false".
- The empty string "" is converted to Boolean "false".
- All other strings are converted to Boolean "true".
- The empty string "" cannot be converted to a number.
- Nonzero numbers are converted to Boolean "true".
- Zero numbers are converted to Boolean "false".
- A failed type conversion returns invalid.

WMLScript Statements

Statements are a combination of expressions and keywords. A single statement can span multiple lines, and multiple statements can be included in one line.

The following sections describe the WMLScript statements.

Empty Statements

Use *empty statements* when a statement is required syntactically, but there is no operation to be performed.

Here is an example of an empty statement:

```
while (calcVal() <= maxVal) ;
```

which is far from clear to a maintainer of your code, or even yourself if you revisit it after some time. When combining the empty statement with a loop statement, it is more understandable when written in the following way:

```
while (calcVal() <= maxVal) {
   ;  // Perform calcVal until it returns a value greater than maxVal
}
```

Expression Statements

Expression statements perform all WMLScript operations, such as calculations, assigning values to variables, and making function calls.

Here are some example expressions:

```
var isGood = "Beach" + "Sun";   // isGood is "BeachSun".
var price = qty * unitPrice;    // price is qty times unitPrice.
row++;                          // row is incremented.
```

Block Statements

A *block statement* is a set of statements enclosed by braces ({}). Because the set of statements is enclosed by braces, they are processed as one statement.

Here is an example of a block statement:

```
{
   totalUnits += individualUnits;
   totalPrice += individualUnits * individualPrice;
}
```

if Statements

The *if statement* lets you conditionally perform one of two operations, depending on the Boolean value of the condition.

If the condition is `true`, the first operation is performed. If it is `false` or `invalid`, the second operation is performed. `if` statements can be nested.

Here is an example of an `if` statement:

```
if (weather == "sun") {
    temperature = "high";
} else {
    temperature = "low";
}
```

Variable Statements

Variable statements declare variables. Variable statements also let you initialize variables, but if you choose not to initialize a variable, it will be initialized with an empty string by default.

Variables must be declared before they are used. Declarations may be placed within a block statement, but unlike many other programming languages, the block does not affect their scope—the variables are still available outside the block in which they are declared. If the declaration includes an initialization, the variable is reinitialized on every execution of the block.

Here is an example of the use of variable statements:

```
var resting = true;
if (daylight) {
    var action;
    if (resting) {
        var treesPlanted = 0;
    } else {
        treesPlanted++;
        action += "tree planting ";
    }
}
```

All variables are available everywhere. The variable `action` is initialized as the empty string `""`. Whenever `resting` is `true`, `treesPlanted` is set to 0, and should `resting` be `false`, `treesPlanted` is incremented and `"tree planting "` is added to the `action` string.

while Statements

A *while statement* performs the defined statement for as long as the specified expression is true.

Here's an example of a while statement:

```
var announcement = "";
var countdown = 10;
while (countdown > 0) {
    announcement += countdown + ",";
    countdown--;
}
announcement += "lift off!";
// announcement = "10,9,8,7,6,5,4,3,2,1,lift off!";
```

for Statements

The *for statement* performs a loop. It can have up to three optional statements, which are enclosed in braces and divided by semicolons. In most applications we can think of, all three would be used. The first statement initializes a counter. For as long as the second statement is true, the following statement in braces is executed. The third statement increments the counter.

Here is an example of a for statement:

```
for ( var counter = 0; counter < 10; counter ++) {
    var price += counter;
}
```

break Statements

break statements terminate the current while or for loop and execute the statements following the terminated loop. You cannot use break statements outside of a while or for loop.

Here is an example of a break statement:

```
for (var each = 0; each < max; each++) {
    if (each == last) {
        break;
    }
    total += each;
}
```

continue Statements

continue statements terminate the execution of a block of statements in a `while` or `for` loop and continue execution of the next loop. If you use a `continue` statement in a `for` loop, the counter is incremented and the loop continues processing. If you use a `continue` statement in a `while` loop, it jumps to the condition.

You cannot use a `continue` statement outside of a `while` or `for` loop.

Here is an example of a `continue` statement:

```
for (var each = 0; each < max; each++) {
    if (each == last) {
        break;
    }
    if (each == omit) {
        continue;
    }
    total += each;
}
```

return Statements

The *return statement* exits a function, specifying the value to be returned. A function may have more than one `return` statement, though if you omit a `return` statement from a function, the function returns an empty string `""`.

Here is an example of a `return` statement:

```
function CalculatePrice ( unitPrice, numOrdered ) {
    return unitPrice * numOrdered;
}
```

Reserved Words

Reserved words are used by WMLScript programs and can't be used as identifiers. In WMLScript 1.1, the reserved words are as follows:

- WMLScript keywords: `access, agent, break, continue, div, div=, domain, else, equiv, extern, for, function, header, http, if, isvalid, meta, name, path, return, typeof, url, use, user, var, while`

- Non-WMLScript keywords: `delete, in, lib, new, null, this, void, with`

- Future reserved keywords: `case, catch, class, const, debugger, default, do, enum, export, extends, finally, import, private, public, sizeof, struct, super, switch, throw, try`
- WMLScript literals: `true, false, invalid`

Pragmas

A *pragma* is a directive that directs the compiler to perform a specific task during compilation. WMLScript supports the following three types of pragmas:

- `url` pragmas, which enable WMLScript files to access external functions in other WMLScript files
- `access` pragmas, which enable you to restrict access to WMLScript files to caller files of a specified domain and path
- `meta` pragmas, which let you include information in WMLScript files that is used only by its origin server, specify properties that are interpreted as HTTP headers, and specify user agent–specific information

WMLScript Libraries

WMLScript lacks many of the features you'd expect to find in a programming language; however, this downfall is redressed with the use of standard libraries. These libraries enable WMLScript to provide a good level of functionality, while keeping its core language lightweight. This is similar in design to the first versions of the C language.

Each library contains a number of functions. You call a standard WMLScript library function by typing the library name, followed by a dot (.), then the function name, plus any arguments you want to pass to the library.

WMLScript includes six libraries:

- The Lang library provides a number of WMLScript language–related core functions. These include arithmetic functions, random number functions, conversion functions, user agent functions, and flow control functions.

- The Float library provides a number of floating point number–related functions. These include arithmetic functions and user agent functions.
- The String library functions perform element manipulation functions, string manipulation functions, and string conversion functions.
- The URL library functions perform URL management, retrieval, and the resolving of functions.
- The WMLBrowser library enables WMLScript to exercise navigation control over the WML browser.
- The Dialogs library enables you to display messages in the WML browser, prompting the user for responses.

The WMLScript libraries are described in full detail in Appendix B, "WMLScript Reference."

Connecting WML and WMLScript

Most often, your WMLScript programs will be invoked from WML decks. To WML, the functions in your WMLScript programs are identified just like other external resources—by using a URL. To call your WMLScript functions from your WML code, you use the following syntax:

```
href="filename.wmls#function(arguments)"
```

This can be called from a link (for example, an `onpick` element), from an event (for example, `<do type="accept">`), or from anchors (for example, a `<go>` element).

You can invoke WMLScript functions from WML, but how can you invoke WML code from WMLScript? To return processing to the WML code, you use the WMLScript statement:

```
WMLBrowser.go("filename.wml#Card_id");
```

`WMLBrowser` is a call to the standard WMLScript library WMLBrowser. And `go` specifies that function of the WMLBrowser library to be executed. The `go` function calls a WML deck (and optionally a card), which is displayed in the browser. In this example, the card `Card_id` of deck `filename.wml` is displayed.

Calling a WMLScript Function

Let's now start adding some logic to our example application. When a user chooses View Account Details from the main index, `cinema.wml#Index`, the deck `account.wml` opens at the first card, which requires the user to enter their user ID and phone number. At the moment, every time a user chooses View Account Details, they have to enter their user ID and phone number, even if they have already done so in the same session. As you can imagine, this would start to be annoying after a while. Why not, once a user has entered these details in a session, skip this input screen and go straight into letting them view their account details or buy a ticket?

If a user has chosen to reserve tickets for a movie, the card that lets them reserve tickets is `account.wml#Choose`. However, in real life you'd want users to identify themselves before they reserve tickets by logging on. At the moment, they go straight to the ticket reservation card, whereas if they have not already logged on, they should have to do so before they're able to reserve any tickets.

Our first piece of WMLScript is going to eliminate the extra steps required for the users to identify themselves.

If someone goes to `cinema.wml` and picks the option View Account Details in the card Index, control is passed to the Details card in `account.wml` using the following line:

```
<option onpick="account.wml#Details">View Account</option>
```

And if the user chooses Reserve in the movie detail cards Movie1 and Movie2, again control is passed to the Choose card in `account.wml` using the following line:

```
<do type="accept" label="Buy">
    <go href="account.wml#Choose"/>
</do>
```

Now that we know the movie the user has chosen to reserve tickets for and that we want to send them to the buy card in `account.wml`, we have to set some variables. These variables can be set using the `<setvar>` element nested in a `<go>` element. We'll create a variable called MOVIE to record the movie that was chosen. This can also be used to identify that the user has chosen to reserve tickets and not to view their account details, so we want the user to go to the reserve ticket card (`account.wml#Choose`).

The first step is to add the appropriate statement to `cinema.wml#Moviex` to set these variable values. We will set variable MOVIE to 1 if they chose *Hello, Marie Lou* and 2 if they chose *The Long Goodbye*.

```
<setvar name="MOVIE" value="x"/>
```

As long as the variable MOVIE is correctly initialized, we can use it to decide what happens when `account.wml` is called:

- If the user hasn't logged in (that is, no user ID has been entered), go to the Login card.
- If MOVIE is either 1or 2, go to the buy tickets card.
- If MOVIE is an empty string " ", go to the view account details card.

This logic is going to be carried out by a WMLScript function, named ProcessDeck, in a WMLScript file, named `script.wmls`.

Let's now edit the statements. On the Index card, we'll change the `<option onpick>` element for the View Account Details option to invoke ProcessDeck to perform the logic that depends on the contents of the variable MOVIE:

```
<option onpick="script.wmls#ProcessDeck()"> View Account</option>
```

Now we'll edit the `<do type="accept">` element on the Movie1 card to set the variable MOVIE to 1:

```
<card id="Movie1">
  <do type="accept" label="Reserve">
    <go href="script.wmls#ProcessDeck()">
      <setvar name="MOVIE" value="1"/>
    </go>
  </do>
  <p>
     Hello, Mary Lou <br/>
     Adventure, comedy.  Cert. 13.  Star rating 3.
  </p>
</card>
```

Note the structure of the `<go>` element. To nest the `<setvar>` element in the `<go>` element, the single `<go>` element has been separated into a start and end tag. Now we perform similar edits on the Movie2 card, setting the variable MOVIE to 2.

```
<card id="Movie2">
  <do type="accept" label="Reserve">
    <go href="script.wmls#ProcessDeck()">
      <setvar name="MOVIE" value="2"/>
    </go>
  </do>
  <p>
     The Long Goodbye <br/>
     Classic, romance.  Cert. 13.  Star rating 2.
  </p>
</card>
```

Now that we've set the variable MOVIE, we can create the WMLScript script.wmls (at last!). The file will look like this:

```
extern function ProcessDeck() {

  var strMovie  = WMLBrowser.getVar( "MOVIE" );
  var strUserID = WMLBrowser.getVar( "UID" );

  if ( strUserID == "" ) {
    WMLBrowser.go( "account.wml#Login" );
  } else {
    if ( strMovie != "" ) {
      WMLBrowser.go( "account.wml#Choose" );
    } else {
      WMLBrowser.go( "account.wml#Details" );
    }
  }
}
```

Let's take a look at what happened there. The function is called ProcessDeck. It is defined as being extern, as it interfaces with the WML code. Functions that are called by the WML browser must be external (extern), because they are accessed by an external file.

Next there are some variable definitions using the var command. Note that the type of integer is not defined—as we said earlier, WMLScript is a weakly typed language, meaning that variables will automatically take the type definition according to the values that are loaded into them.

To pass variables from the browser to the script, we use the standard WML-Browser library with the getVar function. The WMLBrowser library interfaces with the current WML browser context. For full details on the WMLBrowser library function, refer to Appendix B, "WMLScript Reference."

In our example, the values loaded into the variables are as follows:

- Variable `strUserID` will have the value `UID` passed to it from the WML card.
- Variable `strMovie` will have the value `MOVIE` passed to it from the WML card.

The rest of the script consists of `if` and `else` statements. You should already be comfortable with these statements, which will do the following:

- First, if `strUserID` (`UID` in the WML browser context) holds an empty string value, the Login logon card will be displayed, as the user has not yet logged on:

    ```
    if ( strUserID == "" ) {
      WMLBrowser.go( "account.wml#Login" );
    }
    ```

- Next, if `strMovie` (`MOVIE` in the WML browser context) does not hold an empty string value, the Choose card will be displayed, so the user can choose which tickets they want to reserve:

    ```
    if ( strMovie != "" ) {
      WMLBrowser.go( "account.wml#Choose" );
    }
    ```

- Finally, if neither of the above cases are true, the account Details card will be displayed:

    ```
    else {
      WMLBrowser.go( "account.wml#Details" );
    }
    ```

Using Variables in WMLScript

We've already seen how to use `WMLBrowser.getVar` to get variables from the WML browser context and how to declare variables using the var command. Let's now look a bit more closely at the use of variables in WMLScript. You can initialize variables with a value, but if you don't specify a value, the variable is initialized as an empty string. Here are some examples of var statements:

```
var A;                 // A = "" and is of type string.
var B = 1;             // B = 1 and is of type integer.
var C = "My";          // C = "My" and is of type string.
var D = "My "+"house"; // D = "My house" and is of type string.
```

When you use variables in WMLScript and you want to perform mathematical operations on variable values, the variables must be numerical. Since nonexplicitly initialized WMLScript variables are created as empty strings, you cannot perform mathematical operations on the variable value. Therefore, you should always initialize the variable with a number to declare its intended type. It is not considered good programming practice to allow variables to change type except under special circumstances.

Converting Variable Types

Under certain circumstances, you will have to convert variables from character strings to numbers. This most commonly happens under the following circumstances:

- You use `WMLBrowser.getVar` to retrieve a variable from the WML browser context. When you use `WMLBrowser.getVar`, variables are returned as character strings.

- You use a character string as an array of numbers. WMLScript does not support numerical arrays as such, but you can convert values from character strings into numbers. We'll talk more about this next.

Converting Values with the Lang Library

Time to talk more about the Lang library. The Lang library deals mainly, but not exclusively, with variable types. The function you'll find yourself using in the next example is the `parseInt` function—this converts a character into a number. The following is an example of this:

```
var A = "1";
var B = "2";
var C = A + B;   // C = "12" and is of type string.
```

Although A and B contain numbers, because they are surrounded by quotes, they are treated as character strings. Therefore, C will hold the value "12". If we wanted to carry out the addition, we would have to convert A and B to numbers:

```
var A1 = Lang.parseInt(A);
var B1 = Lang.parseInt(B);
var C1 = A1 + B1;          // C1 = 3
```

In the above example, C1 will now hold the value 3. Note that you could also convert the above values to numbers with a floating decimal point, using the

Lang.parseFloat function. For full details of the Lang library, see Appendix B, "WMLScript Reference."

In our application, we are going to use two types of operators: arithmetic operators and string operators.

Arithmetic operators include +, -, /, *, and div. They also include binary operators—these are described fully in Appendix B, "WMLScript Reference."

Here are some examples of arithmetic operators:

```
var A = 2 * 2;     // A = 4
var B = 4 / 2;     // B = 2
var C = A + B;     // C = 6
var D = A - B;     // D = 2
```

Manipulating Strings as Arrays with the String Library

The String library enables you to manipulate character arrays. We've found this library to be a powerful component of WMLScript, and it will be used extensively in the next example, so now is a good time look at the String library in more detail.

You can use the String library to perform array-type functions on character strings. In the example below, we are going to use two of the String library functions: elementAt and replace. For a full description of all the String library functions, refer to Appendix B, "WMLScript Reference."

The function elementAt retrieves the element at a given index number. The elementAt function syntax is as follows:

```
String.elementAt (string, index, delimiter);
```

- *string* is a character string or a variable containing a character string.
- *index* is the number of delimiters specified in the delimiter from the start of the string.
- *delimiter* specifies the delimiter.

Here are some examples:

```
var A = "ABC;DEF;HIJ;KLM";
var B = String.elementAt( A, 0, ";" );   // B = "ABC"
var C = String.elementAt( A, 1, ";" );   // C = "DEF"
var D = String.elementAt( A, 5, ";" );   // D = ""
```

The `replace` function replaces a given string with the specified string. The `replace` function syntax is as follows:

```
String.replace (string, oldPortion, newPortion);
```

Here are some examples of the `replace` function:

```
var A = "Hello, Paul";
var B = String.replace( A, "Paul", "John" );  // B = "Hello John"
```

Calculator and Validator

Now, let's work on a complete function named `CalculatePrice`. It does a number of things. First, it initializes the variable `strTicketPrice` as an array of the ticket prices—,5,7,9,—using commas as delimiters. You can accomplish this using the following statement:

```
var strTicketPrice = ",5,7,9,";
```

It can also build up a character string from the number of tickets chosen for rows A, B, and C in the Choose card in `account.wml`, again using commas as delimiters:

```
var strBuyTickets = ","+R1+","+R2+","+R3+",";
```

Next, it can replace any null values passed over from Choose with 0s, which will enable arithmetic functions to be correctly carried out on them, using the statement:

```
var strTicketArray = String.replace(strBuyTickets, ",,", ",0,");
```

It then initializes two variables that will be used later. The first indicates the amount of tickets that have to be bought before bulk purchase discounts can be applied. This is done with the following statement:

```
var iBulkDiscount = 25;
```

The second extracts the smallest ticket value from the string `strTicketPrice`. This is done with the following statement:

```
var strMinPrice =
    String.elementAt( strTicketPrice, 1, "," );
```

The smallest value from the string `strTicketPrice` is then converted into an integer using the following statement:

```
var iMinPrice = Lang.parseInt( strMinPrice );
```

Though we could have merged the two lines using two variables into one line using one variable, as in the following statement, this style is at times difficult for the beginner to understand, so we will not continue to use it:

```
var iMinPrice =
  Lang.parseInt(
       String.elementAt( strTicketPrice, 1, "," )
   );
```

This integer will be checked against the total price of the reservation—if this price is less than the total cost of one ticket, there must have been an input error. The function CalculatePrice then uses a for loop to calculate the total cost of the reserved tickets, as well as the total number of tickets reserved. Finally, it performs the validations on the total price of the reserved tickets and the total amount of tickets bought to see whether bulk purchase discount applies. Let's look at the code:

```
extern function CalculatePrice() {

    // A function to perform input validation and price calculation

    var R1 = WMLBrowser.getVar( "ROWA" );
    var R2 = WMLBrowser.getVar( "ROWB" );
    var R3 = WMLBrowser.getVar( "ROWC" );

    // strTicketPrice is a string array of ticket prices.
    var strTicketPrice = ",5,7,9,";  // least expensive first

    // Build comma delimited string array of tickets chosen per row.
    var strBuyTickets = "," + R1 + "," + R2 + "," + R3 + ",";

    // Replace all null values with 0s, for later processing.
    var strTicketArray = String.replace( strBuyTickets, ",,", ",0," );

    // Declare and initialize variables.
    var iTotalPrice   = 0;
    var iTicketPrice  = 0;
    var iNumTickets   = 0;
    var iBulkDiscount = 25;

    //  The price of the least expensive ticket
    var strMinPrice = String.elementAt( strTicketPrice, 1, "," );
    var iMinPrice   = Lang.parseInt( strMinPrice );
```

```
/**********************************************************
 * Loop that takes each element from the string arrays
 * (ticket prices and number of tickets reserved),
 * converts them to integers, then adds up the total
 * number of tickets reserved and total price of tickets
 **********************************************************/

for ( var row = 1; row <= 3; row++ ) {

  var strRowTickets = String.elementAt( strTicketArray, row, "," );
  var strRowPrice = String.elementAt( strTicketPrice, row, "," );
  var iRowTickets = Lang.parseInt( strRowTickets );
  var iRowPrice = Lang.parseInt( strRowPrice );

  iNumTickets += iRowTickets;
  iTicketPrice = iRowTickets * iRowPrice;
  iTotalPrice += iTicketPrice;
}

/**********************************************************
 * Some data validation:
 * 1. If the total price is less than the cost of one of
 *    the cheapest tickets, display "Incorrect number of
 *    tickets entered."
 * 2. If the total amount of tickets bought is greater
 *    than bulkDisk (the amount of tickets that qualify
 *    for a bulk purchase discount), display "You can get
 *    a discount by calling 1-800 555 1234."
 **********************************************************/

if (iTotalPrice < iMinPrice) {

  Dialogs.alert( "Incorrect number of tickets entered." );
  WMLBrowser.go( "account.wml#Problem" );

} else {

  if (iNumTickets > iBulkDiscount) {

    Dialogs.alert( "You can get a discount by calling
        ➥ 1-800 555 1234.");
```

```
            WMLBrowser.go( "account.wml#Problem" );

      } else {

            WMLBrowser.setVar( "NUMTICKETS", iNumTickets );
            WMLBrowser.setVar( "TOTALPRICE", iTotalPrice );
            WMLBrowser.go( "account.wml#Purchased" );
      }
   }
}
```

Note that this is not the most efficient WMLScript you can use, but we wanted to use it to demonstrate some of the concepts we introduced you to earlier.

We've already looked at the initializations, so let's look at the loop. The following statement initializes the counter row to the value 1, then executes the loop for as long as row is less than or equal to 3, and increments the count:

```
for ( var row = 1; row <= 3; row++) {
```

The next statements extract the values from the variables strTicketArray (the amount of tickets reserved in rows A, B, and C, respectively) and strTicketPrice (the prices of tickets in rows A, B, and C, respectively), using the counter row to increment the elements extracted in each loop. They both specify the comma as the delimiter between each element.

```
var strRowTickets = String.elementAt( strTicketArray, row, "," );
var strRowPrice = String.elementAt( strTicketPrice, row, "," );
```

For example, if the number of tickets reserved in rows A, B, and C are 2, 3, and 4, the element 2 will be extracted on the first loop, 3 on the second loop, and 4 on the third.

The next two statements convert the extracted values into integers. They were stored in the arrays as strings, so you cannot perform arithmetic functions on them.

```
var iRowTickets = Lang.parseInt( strRowTickets );
var iRowPrice = Lang.parseInt( strRowPrice );
```

The next three statements perform the required arithmetic:

```
iNumTickets += iRowTickets;
iTicketPrice = iRowTickets * iRowPrice;
iTotalPrice += iTicketPrice;
```

- `iNumTickets` keeps a running total of `iRowTickets` (the number of tickets reserved in rows A, B, and C).

- `iTotalPrice` keeps a running total of the total price of the tickets reserved for each row (`iRowTickets * iRowPrice`), which is the number of tickets reserved in rows A, B, and C multiplied by the price of the tickets in rows A, B, and C.

Validating Data

Here's one of the main uses of WMLScript: *data validation*. WML can make sure data is entered in the correct format, but WMLScript can ensure that data entered falls within a required range.

The first validation checks whether the total price of tickets reserved is less than the value of the ticket that has the lowest price tag.

```
if (iTotalPrice < iMinPrice) {

    Dialogs.alert( "Incorrect number of tickets entered." );
    WMLBrowser.go( "account.wml#Problem" );
}
```

If it is, the `alert` function from the Dialogs library is called. We haven't looked at the Dialogs library yet. It displays messages on the WML browser. The `alert` is just that—a way of alerting users of something. It displays the specified message, which in this case is `"Incorrect number of tickets entered."` Note that the `alert` statement is followed by the following statement:

```
WMLBrowser.go( "account.wml#Problem" );
```

The card that appears simply prompts the user to click the Return key, which returns the user to the Choose card so they can reenter the amount of tickets they want to reserve. This may seem superfluous, but if you don't include it, control drops down to the last statement, which displays the Purchased card in `account.wml`, informing the user that they have successfully reserved the tickets.

The second validation checks whether the total amount of tickets reserved exceeds the amount of tickets that qualify for the bulk purchase discount (this is initialized to 25), using the following statement:

```
if (iNumTickets > iBulkDiscount) {
```

If the total amount of reserved tickets does exceed the amount of tickets that qualify for the bulk purchase discount, the message "You can get a discount by calling 1-800 555 1234." is displayed, followed by the Problem card in account.wml. This is accomplished with the following statements:

```
Dialogs.alert( "You can get a discount by calling
➡  1-800 555 1234.");
WMLBrowser.go( "account.wml#Problem" );
```

These validations are on the values held by variables. It is also worth looking at variable type validations, although none of these are included in the example. You can check whether a value is an integer. The function String.parseInt(A) will return an invalid if A is not an integer. Therefore, the following code:

```
var A = WMLBrowser.getVar( "iNumTickets" );
var B = Lang.parseInt( A );
if (B) {
  // Do action if number is integer.
} else {
  // Do action if number is not integer.
}
```

will enable you to develop actions based on the type of a variable.

WMLScript Functions

WMLScript includes three types of functions: external functions, library functions, and internal functions. We have already seen the first two in use on numerous occasions. Nonetheless, we'll review all three.

External Functions

In script.wmls, the function ProcessDeck is defined in the following manner:

```
extern function ProcessDeck() {

  // Function definition

}
```

The extern function statement declares that the function is *external*, which means that the function can be called by files other than the one in which it was defined. The entire function code is surrounded by curly braces ({}).

Here is an example of a call to an external function named `ProcessDeck` in the file `script.wmls` from WML:

```
<option onpick="script.wmls#ProcessDeck()">
  View Account
</option>
```

However, if you want to call an external function in one WMLScript file from another WMLScript file, you must use the use pragma. The use pragma declares the URL of the WMLScript file that contains the function you want to access and assigns a name to that URL. To call the function, enter the name you assigned to the URL followed by the name of the function itself.

Here is an example of a call to an external function named `CalculatePrice` in the file `script.wmls` from another WMLScript file:

```
use url PriceCalc
  "http://www.firstunwired.com/script.wmls";

var result = PriceCalc#CalculatePrice();
```

For full information on the use pragma, see Appendix B, "WMLScript Reference."

Library Functions

Library functions are standard functions that are included in WMLScript. You call a WMLScript library function by typing the library name, followed by a period (.), followed by the function name. Here is an example of a library function call:

```
var strMovie = WMLBrowser.getVar( "MOVIE" );
```

The WMLBrowser library's `getVar` function returns a value from a variable in the current browser context (MOVIE). In this case, this value is used to initialize the variable `strMovie`.

Internal Functions

Internal functions can be accessed only from within the file in which they are declared. You call internal functions by typing the function name and a comma-separated list of arguments. The number of arguments entered with the function call must match the number of parameters listed in the function declaration. Internal functions can be called before their declarations.

The following section, "The Full Compilation Unit," includes the following function call:

```
iTotalPrice += CalcPrices( strTicketPrice, iRowTickets, row );
```

In this case, the variable `iTotalPrice` is a running total of the cost of the tickets bought in rows A, B, and C. Each time this line is executed (it is in a loop that executes three times), it calls the internal function `CalcPrices`, passing with it the current values in the following variables:

- `strTicketPrice`, which is the price of tickets in each of the rows A, B, and C
- `iRowTickets`, which is the number of tickets reserved in each of the rows
- `row`, which is the counter with the value 1, 2, or 3 (1 equates to row A, 2 equates to row B, and 3 equates to row C)

Following is the declaration of the function `CalcPrices`:

```
function CalcPrices ( strTicketPrice, iRowTickets, row ) {

   var strRowPrice  = String.elementAt( strTicketPrice, row, "," );
   var fRowPrice    = Lang.parseFloat( strRowPrice );
   var fTicketPrice = iRowTickets * fRowPrice;
   return fTicketPrice;
}
```

The parameters `strTicketPrice`, `iRowTickets`, and `row` accept the value of these three variables. The function then extracts the price of the tickets for each row from the array `strTicketPrice`, converts it to a floating point number (`var fRowPrice = Lang.parseFloat(strRowPrice);`), multiplies the number of tickets reserved in each row by the price of tickets in each row (`var fTicketPrice = iRowTickets * fRowPrice;`), and returns the result to the calling function (`return fTicketPrice;`). The calling function then adds the returned value to the running total: `iTotalPrice += CalcPrices( strTicketPrice, iRowTickets, row );`.

The Full Compilation Unit

If we include the local function call described above, the final WMLScript file, `script.wmls`, will look as follows:

```
extern function ProcessDeck() {

  // A function to decide which card in account.wml to display
```

```
        var strMovie  = WMLBrowser.getVar( "MOVIE" );
        var strUserID = WMLBrowser.getVar( "UID" );

        if ( strUserID == "" ) {
          // User has not logged on, force user to login.
          WMLBrowser.go( "account.wml#Login" );

        } else {

          if ( strMovie != "" ) {

            // User has chosen a movie.
            WMLBrowser.go( "account.wml#Choose" );

          } else {

            // User has chosen to view account details.
            WMLBrowser.go( "account.wml#Details" );
          }
        }
      }

      extern function CalculatePrice() {

        // A function to perform input validation and price calculation

        var R1 = WMLBrowser.getVar( "ROWA" );
        var R2 = WMLBrowser.getVar( "ROWB" );
        var R3 = WMLBrowser.getVar( "ROWC" );

        // strTicketPrice is a string array of ticket prices.
        var strTicketPrice = ",5.25,6.00,6.75,"; // least expensive first

        // Build comma delimited string array of tickets chosen per row.
        var strBuyTickets = "," + R1 + "," + R2 + "," + R3 + ",";

        // Declare and initialize variables.
        var iTotalPrice   = 0.00;
        var iNumTickets   = 0;
        var iBulkDiscount = 25;

        // The price of the least expensive ticket
```

```
var strMinPrice = String.elementAt( strTicketPrice, 1, "," );
var iMinPrice   = Lang.parseFloat( strMinPrice );

/***********************************************************
 * Loop that takes each element from the string arrays
 * (ticket prices and number of tickets reserved),
 * converts them to integers, then adds up the total
 * number of tickets reserved and total price of tickets
 ***********************************************************/

for ( var row = 1; row <= 3; row++ ) {

  var strRowTickets = String.elementAt( strBuyTickets, row, "," );
  if (strRowTickets == "") {
    // if price of ticket is null, replace with 0
    strRowTickets = "0";
  }
  var iRowTickets = Lang.parseInt( strRowTickets );

  iNumTickets += iRowTickets;
  iTotalPrice += CalcPrices ( strTicketPrice, iRowTickets, row );
}

/***********************************************************
 * Some data validation:
 * 1. If the total price is less than the cost of one of
 *    the cheapest tickets, display "Incorrect number of
 *    tickets entered."
 * 2. If the total amount of tickets bought is greater
 *    than bulkDisk (the amount of tickets that qualify
 *    for a bulk purchase discount), display "You can get
 *    a discount by calling 1-800 555 1234."
 ***********************************************************/

if (iTotalPrice < iMinPrice) {

    Dialogs.alert( "Incorrect number of tickets entered." );
    WMLBrowser.go( "account.wml#Problem" );

} else {

  if (iNumTickets > iBulkDiscount) {
```

```
            Dialogs.alert( "You can get a discount by calling
              ➥1-800 555 1234.");
            WMLBrowser.go( "account.wml#Problem" );

        } else {

            var strTotalPrice = String.format( "%1.2f", iTotalPrice );
            WMLBrowser.setVar( "NUMTICKETS", iNumTickets );
            WMLBrowser.setVar( "TOTALPRICE", strTotalPrice );
            WMLBrowser.go( "account.wml#Purchased" );
        }
    }
}

function CalcPrices ( strTicketPrice, iRowTickets, row ) {

    // a function to calculate running total of ticket prices

    var strRowPrice  = String.elementAt( strTicketPrice, row, "," );
    var fRowPrice    = Lang.parseFloat( strRowPrice );
    var fTicketPrice = iRowTickets * fRowPrice;
    return fTicketPrice;
}
```

This script uses the go function of the WMLBrowser library to execute new cards in the account.wml deck. We've not yet seen these cards, so let's take a look at them now.

The existing Login card needs modifying to check the user input; to do this, it calls the ProcessDeck function:

```
<go href="script.wmls#ProcessDeck()"/>
```

resulting in the Login deck looking like the following:

```
<card id="Login">
  <do type="accept" label="Continue">
    <go href="script.wmls#ProcessDeck()"/>
  </do>
  <do type="clear" label="Clear">
    <refresh>
      <setvar name="UID" value=""/>
      <setvar name="TELNO" value=""/>
    </refresh>
```

```
    </do>
    <p>
      Enter User ID:
      <input name="UID" format="AAAAA"/>
      Enter Phone No:
      <input name="TELNO" format="(NNN) NNN-NNNN"/>
    </p>
  </card>
```

The existing account Details deck needs modifying to display the movie index by using a go element:

```
<do type="accept" label="Return">
  <go href="cinema.wml#Index"/>
</do>
```

resulting in the Details deck looking like the following:

```
<card id="Details">
  <do type="accept" label="Return">
    <go href="cinema.wml#Index"/>
  </do>
  <p>
    $UID Account Details
  </p>
</card>
```

The new Choose card displays the row options for the chosen movie, prompting the user to enter the number of required tickets per movie. The price is calculated by calling the CalculatePrice function, as in the following complete deck:

```
<card id="Choose" ordered="false">
  <onevent type="onenterforward">
    <refresh>
      <setvar name="ROWA" value=""/>
      <setvar name="ROWB" value=""/>
      <setvar name="ROWC" value=""/>
    </refresh>
  </onevent>
  <do type="accept" label="Book">
    <go href="script.wmls#CalculatePrice()"/>
  </do>
  <p>
    Choose Tickets:<br/>
```

```
        Row A:
        <input title="Row A" name="ROWA" format="*N"/>
        Row B:
        <input title="Row B" name="ROWB" format="*N"/>
        Row C:
        <input title="Row C" name="ROWC" format="*N"/>
    </p>
</card>
```

The Purchased card is displayed by the `CalculatePrice` function, which sets the WMLBrowser context variables NUMTICKETS and TOTALPRICE, which are displayed in the following deck:

```
<card id="Purchased">
    <do type="accept" label="Continue">
        <go href="cinema.wml#Index"/>
    </do>
    <p>
        You reserved $NUMTICKETS tickets
        at a total cost of $TOTALPRICE.
    </p>
</card>
```

The final new card is the Problem card, which prompts the user to return to the Choose card after the browser has displayed a Dialogs warning.

```
<card id="Problem">
    <do type="accept" label="Return">
        <go href="Choose"/>
    </do>
    <p>
        Press Return continue.
    </p>
</card>
```

You have now built a WML service that incorporates many of the functions that can be carried out by WMLScript, including the following functions:

- Logical processing
- Data validation
- Arithmetic calculations
- Alert dialog display

In the next chapter, you're going to find out how to interface between the WML browser, WMLScript, and a Web server, which will enable you to create your own complete, fully functioning WAP service.

Note that all the source files for this application are included on the CD provided with this book.

Chapter 6

Tuning Your Service

This chapter discusses how you can use a WAP device's cache to increase the efficiency of sending and retrieving messages. The cache is used to reduce the amount of data traffic between your WAP device and the WAP gateway, and it accomplishes this by keeping a local store of information in the WAP device instead of repeatedly requesting it from a WAP server.

Before the cache is explained, the chapter gives an overview of the Hypertext Transfer Protocol (HTTP). HTTP is a very long-winded protocol that can use many hundreds of characters for the simplest requests and responses. The WAP gateway, through which all WAP applications must pass, converts HTTP messages into Wireless Session Protocol (WSP) messages, which is compatible with HTTP. You need to understand something of HTTP and HTTP caching before you can appreciate how caching is used in WAP to minimize message traffic. Some simple examples are given on how to dynamically generate the HTTP headers using a server scripting language such as PHP, VB, or ASP.

The chapter concludes with a brief explanation of how dynamic WAP applications can be developed using Java Server Pages (JSP). If you are not familiar with these server technologies, then you can safely skip them, as they are not essential to developing WAP applications.

HTTP Overview

HTTP is the text-based protocol Web clients and Web servers use to communicate with each other, and it is essentially the backbone of the Web. All HTTP transactions follow the same general format. Each client request and server response has three parts:

- The request or response line
- The request or response header section
- The request or response entity body

A client begins a transaction by contacting the server at a designated port number (by default, 80). It then sends a document request by specifying an HTTP command called a *method*, followed by a document address and an HTTP version number.

The HTTP method command consists of a Uniform Resource Locator (URL) that identifies the resource (usually a file) the client is querying and the HTTP version number. URL is a general term for all valid formats for addressing schemes supported on the Internet and World Wide Web. For example, you access any Web site by its URL, such as http://www.sybex.com, or a specific file, such as http://www.sybex.com/index.htm. You can also reference an FTP site with a URL, such as ftp://ftp.mirror.org.

The following lines of a client request contain header information, which provides information about the client and the data entity it is sending the server. The second part of a client request is the entity body, which is the data being sent to the server.

```
GET /glossary.html HTTP/1.0
```

This example uses a technique called the GET method to request the document glossary.html in the root directory, which uses version 1.0 of HTTP.

The client then sends optional header information, describing for the server its configuration and the document formats it will accept. Header information containing a header name and value is given line by line. To end the header, the client sends a blank line.

After sending a request and header, the client can transmit additional data. On receiving a request from a client, the server replies with a status line containing the following fields:

- The HTTP version, the version of HTTP that the server is using to respond
- The status code, a three-digit number indicating the server's result of the client's request
- The descriptive text, text describing the status code

Here is an example of such a status line:

```
HTTP/1.0 200 OK
```

This status line indicates that the server uses version 1.0 of HTTP in its response. Status code 200 (and the textual description of the code, "OK") indicates that the client's request was successful and the requested data will be supplied after the headers.

After the status line, the server sends header information to the client about itself and the requested document. Following is an example. Note that a blank line ends the header.

```
Date: Thu, 02 Sep 2000 12:24:02 GMT
Server: NCSA/1.5.2
Last-modified: Mon, 10 Jan 1999 09:12:22 GMT
Content-type: text/html
Content-length: 3234
```

After a successful request, the requested data is sent. This data is simply a stream of data of the type text/html and may come from a file (a static HTML page) or may be a generated response from a program (a dynamic HTML page).

After the server has finished sending the requested data, it maintains the connection and allows the client to make additional requests. The transaction carries on in this way, cycling back to the beginning until either the client or the server explicitly closes the connection. As many documents embed other data objects such as files, images, frames, and code (such as JavaScript, VBScript, or Java applets), if the object is embedded rather than referenced, this saves the client from having to make another connection to the server just to display the HTML page. However, externally referenced objects, such as images or Java applets, will require a separate server connection to be made.

HTTP does not maintain any information from one transaction to the next (known as a *stateless* protocol), so the next transaction needs to start all over again.

HTTP Methods

There are three main methods defined for HTTP:

- GET
- HEAD
- POST

NOTE Methods are case sensitive, so GET is different than get.

WAP applications concern themselves with only GET and POST, but the following sections briefly describe all three methods for your benefit.

The *GET* Method

GET is a request for information located at a specified URL on the server. It is the most commonly used method by browsers to retrieve documents for viewing. The result of a GET request can be generated in many different ways. It could be a file accessible by the server, the output of a program or CGI script, or possibly the output from a hardware device.

After a client uses the GET method in its request, the server responds with a status line, headers, and the requested data. If, due to an error or lack of authorization, the server can't process the request, it sends an explanation in the data portion of the response.

If GET is used to request a file, which is usually identified by its full path name on the server, you would see the following client and server transmissions. If the client transmits the following:

```
GET /glossary.html HTTP/1.1
Connection: Keep-Alive
User-Agent: Mozilla/4.0 (compatible; MSIE 5.01; Windows NT 5.0)
Host:
   www.org.com
Accept: image/gif, image/x-xbitmap, image/jpeg, image/pjpeg, */*
```

the server could reply as follows:

```
HTTP/1.1 200 Document follows
Date: Mon, 02 Oct 2000 11:12:08 GMT
Server: NATT/1.3.1
Last-modified: Sun, 01 Oct 2000 10:21:12 GMT
Content-type: text/html
Content-length: 2443
```

This would be followed by the body of the response, which in this example would be the text of the HTML at www.org.com/glossary.html.

The *HEAD* Method

The HEAD method requests only the header information on a file or resource, and the server sends no information in the data portion of the reply. The header information from a HEAD request is the same as the header information from a GET request. HEAD is not used by the client to retrieve a document but to find out information about it. There are many uses for the HEAD method, such as to find out when a document was modified, what type the document is, what type of server it resides on, and the document's size.

> **NOTE** Most of the header information provided by a server is optional and might not be given by all servers.

Web clients are often designed to allow flexibility in the server response and to take certain preset actions when the requested header information is not given by the server. An example HEAD request follows:

```
HEAD /glossary.html HTTP/1.1
Connection: Keep-Alive
User-Agent: Mozilla/4.0 (compatible; MSIE 5.01; Windows NT 5.0)
Host: www.org.com
Accept: image/gif, image/x-xbitmap, image/jpeg, image/pjpeg, */*
```

The server could reply:

```
HTTP/1.0 200 Document follows
Date: Mon, 02 Oct 2000 11:12:08 GMT
Server: NCSA/1.5.2
Last-modified: Sun, 01 Oct 2000 10:21:12 GMT
Content-type: text/html
Content-length: 2452
```

> **NOTE** The document body is not sent in response to a HEAD request.

The *POST* Method

The POST method allows data to be sent to the server in a client request. The data is sent to a server with accessible data handling like a CGI script. The method can be used for a range of purposes, such as providing input to database operations, interface programs, newsgroup postings, etc.

Such input is contained within the entity-body section of the client's request. After the server processes the POST request and headers, it passes the entity body to the program specified by the URL. URL encoding is often used to allow form data to be translated into a list of variables and values for CGI processing. Following is an example:

```
POST /cgi-bin/greeting.pl HTTP/1.1
User-Agent: Mozilla/4.0 (compatible; MSIE 5.01; Windows NT 5.0)
Accept: image/gif, image/x-xbitmap, image/jpeg, image/pjpeg, */*
Host: www.org.com
Content-type: application/x-www-form-uriencoded
Content-length: 28

month=september&date=12
```

In this example, a client request is used to send a greeting message from a form.

Other Methods

The following methods are available but are used less frequently:

LINK   Requests that header information be associated with a document on the server.

UNLINK   Requests dissociation of header information from a document on the server.

PUT   Requests that the entity body of the request be stored at the specified URL.

DELETE   Requests the removal of data at a URL on the server.

OPTIONS   Requests information about communications options available on the server. The request URL can be substituted with an asterisk (*) to indicate the server as a whole.

TRACE   Requests that the requested entity body be returned intact. Used for debugging.

Caching in HTTP 1.1

Caching is used to significantly improve performance. A *cache* is a program's store of response messages and the subsystem that controls its message storage, retrieval, and deletion. HTTP 1.1 caching is defined in RFC 2616. It is used to reduce the need to send requests and full responses; it accomplishes this by cutting down both the number of network round-trips and the bandwidth requirements. This concept will become important when we go on in the next section to discuss WAP caching, as the minimization of traffic is of particular importance in the low bandwidth world of wireless communications.

A Web cache sits between the Web servers and one or more clients monitoring requests for objects like HTML pages, images, and files. There are two types of caches. The first type is the cache implemented by the browser client, which is the type we are referring to here. The other type is a high-speed cache server, or *proxy server* as it's better known, usually located on your local Internet service provider (ISP) server or as a company firewall.

Regardless of the type of cache, its purpose is to save copies of accessed resources as they are requested by clients. If another request for the same object is made, the cache uses the copy instead of requesting the object from the origin (remote) server again. In this way, a cache reduces latency and thereby increases efficiency and response time, as requests can be satisfied from the local cache (proxy server) instead of the origin (remote) server. A cache also reduces data traffic, as cached objects are retrieved from the server only once. This reduces the amount of bandwidth the client uses, thus saving bandwidth requirements.

NOTE A proxy cache uses the same technique as a Web cache but on a much larger scale, often serving thousands of users in the same way. Proxy servers are often set on the firewalls of large companies, as popular objects need to be requested only once, and there are many users to be served.

There are two concepts that should be mentioned here. The first is the concept of *freshness*. In caching, this means that a cached object is able to be sent to a client without checking with the origin server. The second concept is that of *validation*. This is a means of informing a cache whether the copy that it has is still good. Together, freshness and validation are the most important ways that a cache works with content. A fresh object will be instantly available from the cache, while a validated object will avoid sending the entire object over again if it hasn't changed.

All caches have a set of rules that they use to determine when to serve an object from the cache if it's available. Some of these rules are set in the HTTP protocols, while others are set by the administrator of the cache. Generally, the following are the most common rules that are followed for a particular request:

1. If the object's headers tell the cache not to keep the object, it won't. Also, if no validator is present, most caches will mark the object as uncacheable.
2. If the object is authenticated or secure, it won't be cached.
3. A cached object is considered fresh if:
    a. It has an expiry time or other age-controlling directive set and is still within the freshness period.
    b. A browser cache has already seen the object and has been set to check its freshness only once a session.
    c. A proxy cache has seen the object recently, and it was modified relatively long ago.

   Fresh documents are served directly from the cache without checking with the origin server.
4. If an object is stale, the origin server will be asked to *validate* the object or, in other words, tell the cache whether the copy it has is still good. It does this by checking the date and time of the object; if the origin server copy is newer than the cache copy, it will retrieve the object, thus refreshing its cache.

Some HTTP Caching Features

While cultivating a thorough understanding of HTTP caching is beyond the scope of this book, a summary of some of the more important cache features follows:

- Cache correctness
    - A correct cache must respond to a request with the most up-to-date response held by the cache that is appropriate for the request.
    - If the cache cannot communicate with the origin server, then a correct cache *should* respond if the response can be correctly served from the cache; if not, it must return an error or warning indicating that there was a communication failure.

- Warnings
    - Whenever a cache returns a response that is fresh enough, it must attach a warning to the effect, using a Warning general-header.
- Explicit user agent warnings
    - Many user agents make it possible for users to override the basic caching mechanisms. For example, the user agent might allow the user to specify that cached entities are never validated, or it might habitually add "Cache-control: max-stale=3600" to every request indicating a freshness life of one hour.
- Exceptions to warnings
    - In some cases, the operator of a cache might choose to configure it to return stale responses even when not requested by clients. This may be necessary for reasons of availability or performance, especially when the cache is poorly connected to the origin server.
- Client-controlled behavior
    - The origin server is the primary source of expiration information. However, in some cases the client might need to control a cache's decision about whether to return a cached response without validating it. Clients do this using several directives from a mechanism called the Cache-control header.
- Server-specified expiration
    - HTTP caching works best when caches can entirely avoid making requests to the origin server. The primary mechanism for avoiding requests is for an origin server to provide an explicit expiration time in the future, indicating that a response might be used to satisfy subsequent requests. In other words, a cache can return a fresh response without first contacting the server.
- Age calculations
    - To know if a cached entry is fresh, a cache needs to know if its age exceeds its freshness lifetime. The current age of a cache entry is calculated by adding the amount of time (in seconds) since the cache entry was last validated by the origin server to the initial age. When a response is generated from a cache entry, the cache includes a single Age header in the response with a value equal to the cache entry's current age.

Caching in WAP

Most WAP microbrowsers contain a memory cache. Memory caches are used to store the decks that the user has visited most recently, so the deck can be quickly redisplayed without the need to request it again from the server.

> **NOTE** Although WAP devices are not obliged to contain a cache, most have some degree of cache control and maximize its use.

When the cache exceeds the WAP device's memory capacity, the least recently visited decks are dropped. A prime goal when you write WAP applications is to minimize wireless traffic as much as you can. The WAP caching model assists you in doing this.

The WAP cache specifications, WAP-120 (WAP Caching Model Specification from http://www.wapforum.org/what/technical.htm) and WAP-175 (WAP Cache Operation Specification from http://www.wapforum.org/what/technical.htm), define the caching model for the WAP device. It is an implementation of the HTTP 1.1 caching model described above and allows for the adoption of the HTTP model while providing support for low-end WAP devices. The specification addresses WAP device caching of fetched documents, files, etc., including WML decks, WMLScript functions, and any other fetched resources named with a URL. It also addresses the role and responsibility of the WAP gateway in the implementation of reliable caching and the support infrastructure needed to implement HTTP 1.1 caching on a WAP user agent.

The WAP Caching Model

As mentioned earlier, the WAP caching model is based on HTTP 1.1 caching as defined in RFC 2616. To allow for the operation of HTTP 1.1 caching on WAP-based devices, with their limited bandwidth and functionality, a number of extensions and clarifications have been added to the model.

When a WAP device caches a response, it caches the response text, caching-related headers, and all response validation–oriented information. All cache items are identified by the usual URL components such as domain name, path, port number, etc.

The most important HTTP header is the `Cache-control` header. It is used to control WML decks and WMLScript functions. You use the `Cache-control` header to control all caching entities used during the request and response sequence. `Cache-control` headers usually override a device's cache characteristics and must be passed through all proxies and gateways without alteration. A description of how to use this header follows:

- `Cache-control: max-age=<seconds>` defines the longest period that a URL is allowed to remain in a user agent's cache. This is a very commonly used instance of the `Cache-control` header, as it enables a URL to be cached only for a specific period of time. For example, a WML service that is updated on a regular basis, such as an airline booking system, can use this mechanism to ensure that users fetch only updated information from the server at a pre-calculated interval. Under these circumstances, only the information cached since the user's last request is fetched if the `max-age` has not expired. The following example defines the maximum age to be 10 minutes:

    `Cache-control: max-age=600`

- `Cache-control: no-cache` stipulates that the URL should never be cached. This is used in instances when you wish to turn off caching completely. This is required when dealing with scenarios in which information is constantly changing, such as a real-time stock-quote scenario where stock prices change instantaneously in response to market conditions. The following is the only way to write this header:

    `Cache-control: no-cache`

- `Cache-control: must-revalidate` defines whether the URL is validated when browsing back through the history list. See the following section on history stacks for a description. The following is the only way to write this header:

    `Cache-control: must-revalidate`

An alternative way of setting the refresh frequency is by use of the `Expires` header. With this method, the date at which the information becomes out of date is defined. The WAP device can then use this information to determine when to remove the URL from its cache and refetch the information. `Expires` dates should not be more than one year in the future.

- You can use `Expires: <date>` to specify the date after which the URL is to be removed from the cache. The following example defines the expiration date as a specific time (which may be in the past to prevent caching or in the future to enable caching):

   ```
   Expires: Thu 07 Jun 2001 18:41:00 GMT
   ```

> **NOTE** All WAP devices that contain a cache must faithfully implement resource caching as described in the HTTP 1.1 Caching Specification, RFC 2616.

History Stacks

HTTP 1.1 defines the concept of validation, which is the process of deciding if a cache entry is still valid or has expired. WAP devices usually contain a history stack that allows 10 or more items to be stored in much the same way that a Web browser allows you to return to your most recently accessed pages. The interaction between a WAP device cache and the WML history is controlled by `Cache-control: must-revalidate`. When using the device's built-in history mechanism, such as the PREV button to go back through tasks or the NEXT button to move forward through tasks, the device must attempt to use the cached resource. It is important that you understand this mechanism to ensure your applications behave in the correct way.

> **NOTE** All forward references are validated, while all backward references are not.

If, after a NEXT request, the device finds no URL in the cache, it places a request for it, stores the response back in the cache, and places (pushes) its URL on the history stack. If the URL is already in the cache, the WAP device validates it before using it for its response. The browser must support the following interaction between cached resources and the WML history:

- If `must-revalidate` is set and the cached resource is stale, then the WAP device must revalidate the resource when going back through the history. A refetch must use exactly the same method as the original request, including the same request entity (such as `POST`) without any user interaction.

- If a stale cached resource doesn't have the `must-revalidate` cache control attribute, the WAP device must not revalidate the entity when going back through the history.

So, the history normally shows the way things were at the time the user retrieved the resource. But if the `must-revalidate` attribute is set on a resource, the history will show the up-to-date version of the resource.

Navigating between Resources

Unless a cached resource's content type specifies some other cache validation, it does not require revalidation. For example, function calls within single WMLScript programs may occur without revalidation, with only the initial fetch needing to be checked for validity. Intra-deck navigation can occur without revalidation. In this case, only the initial fetch of the deck requires a check for resource validity.

NOTE As stated in HTTP specification RFC 2616, the WAP gateway must accurately implement the role of an HTTP 1.1 proxy with respect to caching and cache header transmission.

Preventing the Cache from Reading the WML Deck

As we have seen, after a WML deck has been downloaded to the WAP device, it lives in the WAP device's memory for a certain period of time. Until this period has expired, the deck will not be downloaded from the server but instead from the WAP device memory. This caching technique obviously speeds things up considerably.

There are times, however, when you might not want the deck to be read from the cache but from the server instead. An example of this might be where you have a deck containing cards with information that gets updated frequently. By adding some cache information to the HTTP header that you send out from the server, you can tell the WAP device that the following deck should never be stored in the cache.

NOTE This requires you to be able to produce HTTP headers on the server side, using a server scripting language such as PHP, ASP, JSP, or Perl. The lines cannot be included in the deck code as they are HTTP header information, not WML elements.

With the following lines added to the HTTP header, the deck will expire immediately:

```
Expires: Sat, 03 Jan 1970 00:00:00 GMT
Last-Modified: DD month YYYY HH:MM:SS GMT
Cache-Control: no-cache, must-revalidate
Pragma: no-cache
```

The first line tells the WAP device that the deck should have expired some time in the past, ensuring it will be immediately expired. The second line tells the browser when the deck was last modified, and `DD` should be replaced by the current day of the month (e.g., 7), `month` by the current month (e.g., Jun), `YYYY` by the current year (e.g., 2001), and `HH:MM:SS` by the current time (e.g., 10:34:21). The third and the fourth lines tell the browser that the deck should not be cached; line three is HTTP 1.1, and line four is HTTP 1.0 (for older clients).

The following examples show how server scripting languages can be used to produce the above header each time the deck is accessed. If you do not have a PHP, VB, or ASP background, you may choose to skip these examples. Note that all these examples, while written in different server side languages, produce the same HTTP header output.

PHP Example The following example, written in PHP, prevents the deck from being cached by setting the response headers accordingly. The `Expires` header indicates that the response should have been removed from the cache some time ago and is thus not cached, the `Last-modified` header is defined as the current time, and the `Pragma` and `Cache-control` headers explicitly prevent caching for HTTP 1.0 and HTTP 1.1 clients respectively. The exception is the `Content-type` header, which informs the client to expect a WML deck.

```php
<?php

  // Set correct MIME type.
  header("Content-type: text/vnd.wap.wml");

  // Prevent deck from being cached.
  header("Expires: Sat, 03 Jan 1970 00:00:00 GMT");
  header("Last-modified: " . gmdate("D, d M Y H:i:s") . " GMT");
  header("Cache-control: no-cache, must-revalidate");
  header("Pragma: no-cache");
```

```
// Write the XML prologue.
echo "<?xml version=\"1.0\"?>\n";
echo "<!DOCTYPE wml PUBLIC \"-//WAPFORUM//DTD WML 1.1//EN\" ";
echo "   \"http://www.wapforum.org/DTD/wml_1.1.xml\">\n";
?>
```

> **NOTE** Prevent the PHP parser from wrongly interpreting the XML prologue <?xml version="1.0"?> by writing the prologue using PHP's `echo` or `print` commands.

VB Web Classes Example   In the following VB example, the Response.Expires method allows -1 to be used as an "old" date to prevent caching.

```
Private Sub WebClass_Start()

    'Set correct MIME type
    Response.ContentType = "text/vnd.wap.wml"

    'Prevent deck from being cached
    Response.Expires = -1
    Response.AddHeader "Pragma", "no-cache"
    Response.AddHeader "Cache-Control", "no-cache, must-revalidate"

End Sub
```

ASP Example   The following ASP example, which is similar to the VB example, also uses -1 as a value for Response.Expires to prevent caching.

```
<%
    'Set correct MIME type
    Response.ContentType = "text/vnd.wap.wml"

    'Prevent deck from being cached
    Response.Expires = -1
    Response.AddHeader "Pragma", "no-cache"
    Response.AddHeader "Cache-Control", "no-cache, must-revalidate"
%>
```

Data Quantities Using *GET* and *POST*

The amount of data you can send back using a GET request or POST request is device dependent. A GET request sends variables on the URL, and the amount of data that can be sent is less than you can send using a POST request. For example, the Nokia 7110 has a GET limit of around 512 bytes, while it handles POST requests up to the maximum size of a compiled deck, which is about 1300 bytes. The UP.SDK 4.0 has a limit of 970 bytes using a GET request and up to the maximum size of a compiled deck for POST requests.

Often the card holds the contents of the variables that are sent to the server, and since there is a compiled deck size limit, this will influence the total amount of data that can be transferred.

There's not much difference between performing a POST request or a GET request. The following is a GET request, but with <postfield> to set the variables that make for much more elegant code. Since it's almost identical to a POST request, it's easy to change from a GET request to a POST.

```
<input type="text" name="var1" format="*N"/>
<p>
  <anchor>Send it
  <go href="somescript.cgi" method="get">
    <postfield name="variable" value="$(var1)"/>
  </go>
  </anchor>
</p>
```

For a straight POST, see the following.

```
<input type="text" name="var1" format="*N"/>
<p>
  <anchor>Send it
  <go href="somescript.cgi" method="post">
    <postfield name="variable" value="$(var1)"/>
  </go>
  </anchor>
</p>
```

You will need to do some careful device testing to find out exactly how much data you can transfer using your development tools and target WAP devices.

The WML *<meta>* Element

The <meta> element is designed to allow you to set response header values from within static and dynamic documents. It is used to overcome the problem of controlling HTTP headers that are included in responses sent from your content back to a WAP device. Servers automatically place whatever headers they are designed to think are appropriate at the beginning of a response.

Using the http-equiv attribute of the <meta> element gives you a direct way to control headers in a response. When a server returns a document, the WAP gateway scans the message body looking for sequences of characters like the following:

```
<meta http-equiv="Cache-control" content="no-cache" />
```

Upon finding such a sequence, the WAP gateway extracts the http-equiv content and converts it to the WAP equivalent of an HTTP Cache-control header. This then gets passed on to the WAP device to tell it not to cache the response.

Following are some examples of headers and their <meta> equivalents:

```
Cache-Control: no-cache
Cache-Control: max-age=600
Expires: Sat, 3 Jan 1970 00:00:00 GMT
```

```
<meta http-equiv="Cache-Control" content="no-cache"/>
<meta http-equiv="Cache-Control" content="max-age=600"/>
<meta http-equiv="Cache-Control" content="Sat, 3 Jan 1970 00:00:00"/>
```

NOTE Not all WAP devices and servers support <meta> elements. You may therefore use HTTP headers from the server side to control WAP device caching if possible.

Using Multipart Messages to Enhance Responses

When you create a graphic for your application, you need to store it on a content server and use a series of requests to serve up the graphic. However, when the response deck returns to the WAP device, it issues a request for the same graphic every time a deck URL points to the image. This is a very inefficient use of the limited bandwidth available to WAP devices and causes poor response times for the user.

Multipart messages can be used to mitigate this problem. MIME (Multipurpose Internet Mail Extension) multipart messages, as defined in RFC 2046, allow you to define a single MIME-compatible message containing many parts of differing formats.

Consider the following example:

```
Content-type: multipart/mixed;boundary="aaaaaa"
```

In this example, boundary is any string you care to use. This tells the receiving wireless device to expect a message body with multiple parts, each with its own `Content-type` header. The boundary string is preceded by two hyphens (–), as follows:

```
--aaaaaa

Content-type: first

message 1

--aaaaaa

Content-type: second

message 2

--aaaaaa--
```

As you can see, the `message 1` and `message 2` message bodies are separated by the boundary string and terminated with a final set of two hyphens (–), and the message part uses a `Content-type` header. So the MIME multipart message is a series of MIME messages, each with its own message header. This is all the information that the receiving WAP device requires to understand the message.

Minimizing WML Security Risks

A number of techniques can be employed to minimize security risks when developing WML applications.

The most common type of security breach occurs when a user unknowingly accesses an illegitimate service. In this way, someone can gain access to your WML service illicitly. For example, the illegitimate service might directly access a card containing sensitive transactions relating to personal or financial data, or may corrupt variable settings in your service.

You can use the WML `sendreferer` attribute of the `<go>` element to control security risks from illegitimate services. This attribute specifies that the current deck's URL should be provided when a user requests a specific service. If `sendreferer` is set to `true`:

```
<go href="deck.wml#card_id" sendreferer="true">
```

the device specifies the URL address in the HTTP `Referer` request (the `GET` or `POST`) header.

Although the WAP specification tells us that the default setting of `sendreferer` is `false`, some WAP devices usually set `sendreferer="true"` as the default setting to ensure maximum security. However, there are instances when this must not be taken for granted. For example, if a service you are creating provides URL addresses performing operations that require security, you should design it to check the HTTP `Referer` header set by the Web server to ensure that requests do not come from a suspicious source.

As WML decks are public, a URL's variables are accessible by default, creating a security risk. You can define *access control* rules to control this on a deck-by-deck basis:

```
<wml>
  <head>
    <access domain="myserver.dom" path="path/to/decks"/>
  </head>
  <card>
    <!-- rest of card -->
  </card>
</wml>
```

where `domain` specifies the URL domain of other decks that can access your service and `path` specifies the URL root of other decks that can access your service.

By default, access control settings allow all URLs in the same domain to access your WML deck. This is fine unless you want to restrict access to your deck to URLs in a particular domain/path or you want to navigate between decks in different domains. You may also wish to set an entry point like `home/index`. When attributes are assigned to the domain and path attributes, the WAP device compares the values to the URL of the requesting deck. The requesting deck must match both values to access the deck.

WAP and Java

WAP applications can be written with existing Web technologies. Dynamic WML documents can be generated by CGI scripts, Java servlets, JSP, ASP, PHP, Perl, ColdFusion, and so forth. In other words, you can implement your own dynamic WAP service in Java (for example). This section briefly outlines how WAP applications can be developed in Java using servlets and JSP. If you are unfamiliar with Java, you may want to just skip this section.

WAP and Java Servlets

Dynamic WML documents for WAP devices can be easily developed using Java servlets. Once you know the WML syntax, building WAP applications using Java servlets is a relatively simple task.

The following code shows an example of a simple servlet that displays the current date and time on a WAP device when invoked.

```
import java.io.*;
import javax.servlet.*;
import javax.servlet.http.*;

/**
 * This is a simple servlet that will run on a server
 * to display the current date and time on a WAP device.
 **/

public class MobileDate extends HttpServlet {

  public void doGet (

    HttpServletRequest request,
    HttpServletResponse response)

    throws ServletException, IOException {
```

```java
            // Set content type for wireless data.
            response.setContentType("text/vnd.wap.wml");

            // Get the communication channel with the requesting client.
            PrintWriter out = response.getWriter();

            // Write the data.
            out.println("<?xml version=\"1.0\"?>");
            out.println("<!DOCTYPE wml PUBLIC");
            out.println("  \"-//WAPFORUM//DTD WML 1.1//EN\"");
            out.println("  \"http://www.wapforum.org/DTD/wml_1.1.xml\">");
            out.println("<wml>");
            out.println("  <card title=\"MobileDate\">");
            out.println("    <p align=\"center\">");
            out.println("      Date and Time Service<br/>");
            out.println("      Date is: "+ new java.util.Date());
            out.println("    </p>");
            out.println("  </card>");
            out.println("</wml>");
    }
}
```

WAP and JSP

Java Server Pages let you embed Java statements within HTML documents. When JSP is invoked, it is compiled into a Java servlet and executed by the server to create a dynamic HTML document. In the case of WAP, however, the creation of dynamic WML documents is required. Therefore, developing WAP applications using JSP can be easily done once you know the syntax of WML.

The following example is similar to the preceding servlet example; it displays the current date and time on a WAP device.

```jsp
<%
response.setContentType("text/vnd.wap.wml");
%>
<?xml version="1.0"?>
<!DOCTYPE wml PUBLIC "-//WAPFORUM//DTD WML 1.1//EN"
  "http://www.wapforum.org/DTD/wml_1.1.xml">

<wml>
  <card title="MobileDate">
```

```
    <p align="center">
    Date and Time Service<br/>
<%
out.println("Date is: "+ new java.util.Date());
%>
    </p>
   </card>
</wml>
```

Once this JSP document is invoked, a deck is returned that will display the server's current date and time.

In this chapter, we provided an overview of HTTP and introduced the similar methods of caching in WAP. You should now be able to determine the lifetime of each deck and other resources, and thus increase performance of WAP sites by specifying HTTP headers. In the next chapter, we will look into making our service more dynamic.

Chapter 7

Making Your Service Dynamic

So far in this book, we've looked at using static WML files to create content and WMLScript to add some client side processing. However, the real power in using WML lies in being able to generate dynamic pages, whose content depends on the needs of the user.

To generate dynamic WML decks, we're going to use some form of a server side programming language. You have a number of choices in the language and technologies that you can use to generate dynamic WML pages, including the following:

- Java servlets
- Active Server Pages
- PHP
- Perl
- CGI scripts
- Java Server Pages
- Tcl

In this chapter, we're going to show you how to create dynamic WML pages using Java servlets. We chose Java servlets for a number of reasons, including the following:

- The Java development environment is free (http://java.sun.com/).
- Using Java servlets is a very productive way of creating server side programs—you have access to all the programming ease and power provided by the Java classes.
- Java servlets perform better than many of the competing technologies.

We won't be looking at how to program using Java servlets in this chapter, as this is outside the scope of this book. What we will be looking at is how to use Java servlets to generate dynamic WML decks. In this chapter, we're going to almost totally rewrite our example application, using Java servlets, and turn it into a real WAP service that you can access using a WAP-enabled phone, or any other WAP-enabled device, from anywhere!

Basic Information about Java Servlets

Before we look at how the example application is going to change, we'll first take a brief tour of Java servlets, looking at the structure of Java applications and how certain general tasks are performed.

Importing the Classes

The first thing you have to do in any Java program is import the classes you're going to use in your application. Java is an object-oriented (OO) programming language. If you're new to Java programming, as we were when we started this book, you'll be wondering what *object-oriented* means.

Short Object-Oriented Primer

Although a full discussion of object-oriented programming is outside the scope of this book, we'll give you a brief overview of object-oriented programming to help you on your way. We'll use an analogy from the real world to describe object-oriented programming. Think of a house. It has certain characteristics that are shared by all houses: It has a roof, windows, and one or more doors. In object-oriented terminology, the description of this generic house is a *class*. The class *house* is a blueprint, which can be used for any house, of any size or shape. A house can have any number of rooms, all of which are generic parts of houses. For example, a house can have a bathroom, a bedroom, a kitchen, and a lounge.

To create a real house, you take the blueprint, and you add details to it. In this process, you create an instance of the class *house*, and the instance is called an *object*. The house may be made of red brick, and have 10 windows and one door. These details are *variables*, some of which are set at the time of creation (the number of windows and doors), and some of which may change over time (you might paint the house white in the future). A variable set at the time of creation will look something like the following:

```
windows = 10;
```

When using objects, you use *methods* to change the values held by the object's variables. Methods are routines, or processes, already included in the class. So, if the class we are using is called OurHouse, we may have a method named setColor to change the color of the house. To change the color of the house to white, the method we use will look something like the following:

```
OurHouse.setColor(white);
```

In this case, we're telling the class OurHouse to use the setColor method with the variable white.

There is plenty more to talk about on this subject, but a basic understanding of objects, methods, and classes will be enough for you to fully grasp what's going on in this chapter.

Back to Importing the Classes

So, the first thing we have to do in our application is import the classes we need. To do this we use the following command:

```
import class;
```

where *class* is the class or subclass you want to import into your application. The class import lines in our application are the following:

```
import java.io.*;
import java.util.*;
import javax.servlet.*;
import javax.servlet.http.*;
```

Declaring the Global Variables

Java servlets are *multithreaded*. This means that the same servlets can be executed simultaneously, with one instance of the variable running for each session between a user agent and the server that is currently active. Global variables can be used for the variables that are the same across all sessions. All other variables must be defined as local variables.

After importing the classes, the next task is to define the global variables that will be used in the servlet. The global variable declarations in our application are as follows:

- loginFileLoc, which is the directory location of the login files, the filenames of which are of the format /path/to/TELNO where TELNO is the WMLBrowser variable acquired in the Login card in account.wml. The format of the login files is as follows:

    ```
    UserID#1,UserID#2,UserID#3
    ```

- movieFileLoc, which is the location of the file containing the descriptions of the available movies, the content of which is in the following format:

    ```
    Title#1 % Category#1 % Certificate#1 % Star Rating#1
    Title#2 % Category#2 % Certificate#2 % Star Rating#2
    ```

- `priceFileLoc`, which is the location of the file containing the prices of the rows, the content of which is in the following format:

    Row A price × 100, *Row B price* × 100, *Row C price* × 100

and are declared by the following lines:

```
// Define file locations.
private static final String movieFileLoc = "/path/to/movies";
private static final String priceFileLoc = "/path/to/prices";
private static final String loginFileLoc = "/path/to/";
```

Handling User Agent Interaction

The heart of our program involves the following:

- Taking information sent from the user agent
- Performing a process on the server
- Returning a response to the user agent

When the user agent sends information (and as a result requests a process to be performed) to the server, our application builds a response to that request using the HTTP protocol, as with all Internet applications. The Java class for doing this is `javax.servlet.http`.

Every time our application is called by a user agent, it is called by the HTTP post request. Therefore, our entire program is nested within the routine for managing post requests. The main routine starts as follows:

```
public void doPost
    (HttpServletRequest request, HttpServletResponse response)
```

where *request* is the request stream and *response* is the response stream.

Outputting WML Code

Whatever our servlet is called to do, it will end up outputting a deck, containing at least one card. We know that the deck header will always be the same, whatever the card contents. Therefore, the first thing our servlet is going to do is output the WML prologue and ensure that the correct MIME type is set for the WML document:

```
// Get the communication channel with the requesting client.
PrintWriter out = response.getWriter();
```

```
// Set the MIME type to WML.
response.setContentType( "text/vnd.wap.wml" );

// Write prologue.
startDeck( out );
```

startDeck generates the WML prologue using the `println` method. The `println` method is called to output each line of the WML prologue, as well as the opening `<wml>` element for the deck. The `startDeck` method looks something like the following:

```
private void startDeck (PrintWriter out) {

    out.println("<?xml version=\"1.0\"?>");
    out.println("<!DOCTYPE wml PUBLIC \"-//WAPFORUM//DTD WML 1.1//EN\"");
    out.println("   \"http://www.wapforum.org/DTD/wml_1.1.xml\" >");
    out.println("<wml>");
}
```

Note the use of escaping with the backslash (\) character. WML uses a lot of quotation marks—these have to be escaped when they are included in the variable of the `println` method, as the method itself uses quotation marks to delimit the value to be output.

The servlet processes the necessary actions, for example, to extract local information such as movie details and prices, and displays the results in the deck. Once this is complete, we have to close the deck with a footer by calling `endDeck`, which looks like the following:

```
private void endDeck (PrintWriter out) {

    out.println( "</wml>" );
    out.close();
}
```

The Example Servlet

We're now going to take a look at our example servlet, and analyze what it does and how it does it. Before going any further, we recommend that you have your Web server software installed, configured, and running. You should also have your Java development environment installed and ready to use. We used Sun

Microsystem's JDK to develop these Java servlets, since it is free, and we found it easy to use.

However, before choosing your Java development environment, it's worth taking a look at what's around, downloading some trial software, and seeing which environment suits you.

The following paragraphs describe the various actions performed by our example Java servlet and show in detail how it performs these actions.

Logging On

The first thing a user is asked to do when they access our site is to log on. This part of our program is done using WML. This is the client side of the application. We will take our current `cinema.wml` file and modify it to reflect the use of a servlet. The user first sees the splash screen decks, which remain unchanged, then goes directly to the logon screen, which is a new deck. The WML code to do this looks like the following:

```
<?xml version="1.0"?>
<!DOCTYPE wml PUBLIC "-//WAPFORUM//DTD WML 1.1//EN"
  "http://www.wapforum.org/DTD/wml_1.1.xml" >

<wml>

  <card id="Splash">
    <onevent type="ontimer">
      <go href="#Splash1"/>
    </onevent>
    <timer value="10"/>
    <p align="center">
      <b><big>FirstUnwired.com</big></b>
      <br/>
      <br/>
      <br/>
      *
    </p>
  </card>

  <card id="Splash1">
    <onevent type="ontimer">
      <go href="#Splash2"/>
```

```
    </onevent>
    <timer value="10"/>
    <p align="center">
      <b><big>FirstUnwired.com</big></b>
      <br/>
      <br/>
      \ | /
      <br/>
      - -
      <br/>
      / | \
    </p>
  </card>

  <card id="Splash2">
    <onevent type="ontimer">
      <go href="#Login"/>
    </onevent>
    <timer value="10"/>
    <p align="center">
      <b><big>FirstUnwired.com</big></b>
      <br/>
      \   |   /
      <br/>
      <br/>
      -       -
      <br/>
      <br/>
      /   |   \
    </p>
  </card>

  <card id="Login">
    <do type="accept" label="Check">
      <go href="http://localhost/servlet/Cinema" method="post">
        <postfield name="Action" value="1"/>
        <postfield name="TELNO" value="$TELNO"/>
        <postfield name="UID" value="$UID"/>
      </go>
    </do>
    <do type="clear" label="Clear">
      <refresh>
```

```
            <setvar name="UID" value=""/>
            <setvar name="TELNO" value=""/>
          </refresh>
        </do>
        <p>
          Enter User ID:
          <input name="UID" format="AAAAA"/>
          Enter Phone No:
          <input name="TELNO" format="(NNN) NNN-NNNN"/>
        </p>
      </card>

</wml>
```

Once the user enters the logon details and presses the Accept button, the servlet Cinema is called, and the values Action, TELNO, and UID are passed to the servlet as postfield names. The first thing our servlet does is get the parameters entered in the client side: the user ID (UID) and telephone number (TELNO). To do this, the servlet uses the method getParameter, as follows:

```
String slUID = (String) request.getParameter( "UID" );
String slTELNO = (String) request.getParameter( "TELNO" );
```

Our site stores logon details in flat files—each user has a file whose name is their phone number. That file contains their user ID. When a user tries to log on to our site, the servlet tries to find a file with the same name as the telephone number; if it finds one, it reads the content of the file and compares each user ID in the file to that entered on the client side. If any two values are the same, the user is allowed to enter the site. Let's look at how this works:

```
// Open login file (/path/to/TELNO) for reading.
try {
  logonFile = new RandomAccessFile( loginFileLoc + slTELNO , "r" );
} catch (IOException e ) {
  logonFile = null;
  // Could not open login file, proceed no further.
  break;
}
```

This first bit of code provides exception handling. Java is very safety conscious. Any method that can produce a fatal error is protected by Java's exception-handling method, IOException. You must include exception-handling code in your Java servlets, and this code must define what to do when an exception is caught. In the above code, we try to open a file made up of the global variable `loginFileLoc`, which is the path to the directory where all the logon files are stored, and the variable `slTELNO`, which is the telephone number entered by the user on the client side. If this file doesn't exist, we set the logon file value to `null`.

In the following lines, we're going to read the contents of the file we opened above using the method `readLine`, then use the `StringTokenizer` method to order the read contents into an array, using commas as the array element separator:

```
// Assume UID is incorrect.
boolean validId = false;

// Read the one line from the (/path/to/TELNO) login file.
String logId = logonFile.readLine();

// Each TELNO has at least one UID.
StringTokenizer stContents = new StringTokenizer( logId, "," );
```

We know that each entry in the file is a valid user ID, so we're going to place each of these in the variable `logId` and compare that variable to the value sent by the user agent using the post method (`slUID`). If the values are the same, the code falls through to the next deck to display the choice of movies:

```
// Loop through all login UIDs.
while (stContents.hasMoreTokens()) {
  String slLogId = stContents.nextToken();
  // Determine if the file UID matches the user agent UID.
  if (slLogId.equalsIgnoreCase( slUID )) {
    validId = true;
  }
}

if (!validId) {
  // Login failed, inform user, proceed no further.
} else {
  // Write the deck.
}
```

If the variables `slLogId` and `slUID` are not the same, the user is told so, then prompted to press the Accept button. By doing so, they will reopen the file `cinema.wml`, which will prompt them to log in again:

```java
if (!validId) {

  // Login failed, inform user.
  startDeck( out );
  out.println( "<do type=\"accept\" label=\"Cont\">");
  out.println( "<go href=\"http://localhost/cinema.wml\">");
  out.println( "</go>");
  out.println( "</do>");
  out.println( "<p>");
  out.println( "Access Denied");
  out.println( "</p>");
  endDeck( out );

  // Proceed no further.
  break;
}
```

Now that we've introduced the code to read the contents of the login file and determine whether the user is valid, the Java servlet code for accessing the service should look like the following:

```java
// User authentication
String slUID = (String) request.getParameter( "UID" );
String slTELNO = (String) request.getParameter( "TELNO" );

// Open login file (/path/to/TELNO) for reading.
try {
  logonFile = new RandomAccessFile( loginFileLoc + slTELNO , "r" );
} catch (IOException e ) {
  logonFile = null;

  // Could not open login file, inform client.
  startDeck( out );
  out.println( "<p>Failed to open Access File</p>" );
  endDeck( out );

  // Proceed no further.
  break;
}

// Assume UID is incorrect.
boolean validId = false;

// Read the one line from the (/path/to/TELNO) login file.
String logId = logonFile.readLine();
```

```java
// Each TELNO has at least one UID.
StringTokenizer stContents = new StringTokenizer( logId, "," );

// Loop through all login UIDs.
while (stContents.hasMoreTokens()) {

  String slLogId = stContents.nextToken();

  // Determine if the file UID matches the user agent UID.
  if (slLogId.equalsIgnoreCase( slUID )) {
    validId = true;
  }
}

// Close the (/path/to/TELNO) login file.
logonFile.close();

if (!validId) {

  // Login failed, inform user.
  startDeck( out );
  out.println( "<do type=\"accept\" label=\"Cont\">");
  out.println( "<go href=\"http://localhost/cinema.wml\">");
  out.println( "</go>");
  out.println( "</do>");
  out.println( "<p>");
  out.println( "Access Denied");
  out.println( "</p>");
  endDeck( out );

  // Proceed no further.
  break;

} else {

  // Fall through to next case.
}
```

This gives you an example of how to generate WML code according to values entered by a user agent and the results of some simple processing: comparing the entered value with that stored in a file.

Of course, in a real-world application, accessing simple text files would be far too clumsy and inefficient. Instead, you would use a database, such as mySQL, Oracle, or SQL Server.

Listing the Movies

Once a user has logged on to the site, the movies that are currently showing are displayed. This list of movies is taken from a file described by the variable `movieFileLoc`. The contents of this file have the following format:

```
Movie name%Description%Certification%Star rating.
Movie name%Description%Certification%Star rating.
    // And so on.
```

A selection list is built from the movie names listed in this file. The following lines:

```
out.println("<select title=\"Choose Movie\" name=\"line\">");
while (filePos < movieFile.length()) {

    line ++;
    String slMovieInfo = movieFile.readLine();
    StringTokenizer slMovieDetails =
        new StringTokenizer( slMovieInfo, "%" );
    String slMovieTitle = slMovieDetails.nextToken();
    out.println(
        "<option value=\"" + line + "\">" + slMovieTitle + "</option>");
    filePos = movieFile.getFilePointer();
}
out.println("</select>");
```

read full lines from the file, taking the first token (as delimited by the value %), and display them in an option list, as in the following example:

```
<option value="1">Hello, Mary Lou</option>
<option value="2">The Long Goodbye</option>
```

Note that when the Accept button is pressed, the Java servlet variable `line` is used to set the WML variable `viewMovieNum`. The value `line` is set to the currently selected movie title in the list, enabling us to know which line was accepted.

Now that we've introduced the code to read the contents of the movies file and display the movie information in WML, the Java servlet code for listing the movies should look like the following:

```java
// Choosing a movie
try {
  // Open login file (/path/to/movies) for reading.
  movieFile = new RandomAccessFile( movieFileLoc , "r");

} catch (IOException e ) {
  movieFile = null;

  // Could not open movies file, inform client.
  startDeck( out );
  out.println( "<p>Failed to open Movie File</p>" );
  endDeck( out );

  // Proceed no further.
  break;
}

// Setting and initializing the variables
startDeck( out );
out.println("<do type=\"accept\" label=\"Details\">");
out.println("<go href=\"http://localhost/servlet/Cinema\"
   method=\"post\">");
out.println("<postfield name=\"viewMovieNum\" value=\"$(line)\"/>");
out.println("<postfield name=\"Action\" value=\"4\"/>");
out.println("</go>");
out.println("</do>");
out.println("<p>");
out.println("<select title=\"Choose Movie\" name=\"line\">");

// Build a list of movies from the movie file, index with
// the value of line, which is incremented on each loop.
int line = 0;
long filePos = 0;
movieFile.seek(0);
while (filePos < movieFile.length()) {

  line ++;
  String slMovieInfo = movieFile.readLine();
```

```
      StringTokenizer slMovieDetails =
        new StringTokenizer( slMovieInfo, "%" );
      String slMovieTitle = slMovieDetails.nextToken();
      out.println(
        "<option value=\"" + line + "\">" + slMovieTitle + "</option>");
      filePos = movieFile.getFilePointer();
    }
    // Close the (/path/to/movies) movies file.
    movieFile.close();

    out.println("</select>");
    out.println("</p>");
    endDeck( out );
```

Displaying the Movie Details

The movie has now been chosen by the user. The next stage is to extract the details of the selected movie from the file referenced by movieFileLoc and display them. The first step is to read the line corresponding to the chosen movie. This is done using the following lines:

```
// Loop through all movies until we find correct one.
for (int i = 0; i < movieNum; i ++){
  slMovieInfo = movieFile.readLine ();
}
```

Next, as the line is tokenized (by %), we will extract each token and display them on separate lines. This is done by the following lines:

```
// Build a list of details of the movie.
StringTokenizer stMovieDetails =
  new StringTokenizer( slMovieInfo, "%");

while (stMovieDetails.hasMoreTokens()) {
  String slMovieInfoItem = stMovieDetails.nextToken ();
  out.println( slMovieInfoItem );
  out.println("<br/>");
}
```

to produce the following example WML:

```
The Long Goodbye<br/>
Classic, romance<br/>
Cert. 13<br/>
Star Rating 2<br/>
```

We need to allow tickets for this movie to be reserved; we provide this with the use of an Accept button, as in the following code:

```
// Declaring and initializing all the required variables
out.println("<do type=\"accept\" label=\"Book\">");
out.println("<go href=\"http://localhost/servlet/Cinema\"
    method=\"post\">");
out.println("<postfield name=\"Action\" value=\"5\"/>");
out.println("</go>");
out.println("</do>");
```

Now that we've introduced the code to read the contents of the movies file and display the individual movie information in WML, the Java servlet code for detailing individual movies should look like the following:

```
// Displaying movie information
startDeck( out );

try {
  // Open login file (/path/to/movies) for reading.
  movieFile = new RandomAccessFile( movieFileLoc , "r");

} catch (IOException e ) {
  movieFile = null;

  // Could not open movies file, inform client.
  startDeck( out );
  out.println( "<p>Failed to open Movie File</p>" );
  endDeck( out );

  // Proceed no further.
  break;
}

// Determine chosen movie and convert to integer.
String slMovieInfo = "";
String viewMovieNum = (String) request.getParameter( "viewMovieNum" );
int movieNum = Integer.parseInt( viewMovieNum );

// Declaring and initializing all the required variables
out.println("<do type=\"accept\" label=\"Book\">");
out.println("<go href=\http://localhost/servlet/Cinema\"
    method=\"post\">");
out.println("<postfield name=\"Action\" value=\"5\"/>");
```

```
out.println("</go>");
out.println("</do>");
out.println("<p>");

// Loop through all movies until we find correct one.
for (int i = 0; i < movieNum; i ++){
  slMovieInfo = movieFile.readLine ();
}

// Build a list of details of the movie.
StringTokenizer stMovieDetails =
  new StringTokenizer( slMovieInfo, "%");

while (stMovieDetails.hasMoreTokens()) {

  String slMovieInfoItem = stMovieDetails.nextToken ();
  out.println( slMovieInfoItem );
  out.println("<br/>");
}
out.println("</p>");

endDeck( out );
```

Reserving the Tickets

The user has decided to reserve tickets for a movie. Now we have to let them choose the number of tickets they want to reserve in rows A, B, and C, then send that data back to the servlet to calculate the total cost of the reservation. This deck is very simple; the Java servlet code performs no processing, it just writes WML:

```
// Reserving tickets
startDeck (out);
out.println("<do type=\"accept\" label=\"Book\">");
out.println("<go href=\"http://localhost/servlet/Cinema\"
  method=\"post\">");
out.println("<postfield name=\"Action\" value=\"6\"/>");
out.println("<postfield name=\"ROWA\" value=\"$ROWA\"/>");
out.println("<postfield name=\"ROWB\" value=\"$ROWB\"/>");
out.println("<postfield name=\"ROWC\" value=\"$ROWC\"/>");
out.println("</go>");
out.println("</do>");
out.println("<p>");
out.println("Choose Tickets:<br/>");
```

```
out.println("Row A:");
out.println("<input title=\"Row A\" name=\"ROWA\" format=\"*N\"/>");
out.println("Row B:");
out.println("<input title=\"Row B\" name=\"ROWB\" format=\"*N\"/>");
out.println("Row C:");
out.println("<input title=\"Row C\" name=\"ROWC\" format=\"*N\"/>");
out.println("</p>");
endDeck (out);
```

Calculating the Cost of the Reserved Tickets

The next part is one of the most complicated. The user has entered the number of tickets they want to reserve in rows A, B, and C. We can now retrieve the ticket prices from a file and multiply the price of tickets in each row by the number of tickets reserved in that row.

Note that user agents always return values as strings. This means that if we want to carry out any mathematical calculations on the values returned by a user agent, we must first convert them to numbers—in this case, using the `parseInt` method:

```
// Convert strings returned by user agent to integers.
String rowA = (String) request.getParameter ( "ROWA" );
String rowB = (String) request.getParameter ( "ROWB" );
String rowC = (String) request.getParameter ( "ROWC" );
if (rowA.length() == 0) {
  rowA = "0"; // no value, use default of 0
}
if (rowB.length() == 0) {
  rowB = "0"; // no value, use default of 0
}
if (rowC.length() == 0) {
  rowC = "0"; // no value, use default of 0
}
int rowAnum = Integer.parseInt( rowA );
int rowBnum = Integer.parseInt( rowB );
int rowCnum = Integer.parseInt( rowC );
```

We then open the prices file referenced by the variable `priceFileLoc`, read the prices for each row, then calculate and display the total price:

```
// Open prices file (/path/to/prices) for reading.
try {
```

```
      priceFile = new RandomAccessFile( priceFileLoc , "r");
   } catch (IOException e ) {
      priceFile = null;
      // Could not open price file, proceed no further.
      break;
   }
```

The prices are stored in the prices file as integers separated by a comma (,); for this, we need to multiply each price by 100 before writing the prices file. The following is an example of the prices file:

```
525,600,675
```

We now read the single line of the prices file and tokenize the individual prices:

```
// Read the one line from the (/path/to/prices) prices file.
String tPrices = priceFile.readLine();

// Read the ticket prices from the file referred to by priceFile.
StringTokenizer tPriceRow = new StringTokenizer( tPrices, ",");
```

then convert those strings to integers and multiply each by the number of tickets booked per row:

```
rowAtot = (new Integer(tPriceRow.nextToken())).intValue() * rowAnum;
rowBtot = (new Integer(tPriceRow.nextToken())).intValue() * rowBnum;
rowCtot = (new Integer(tPriceRow.nextToken())).intValue() * rowCnum;
```

adding each to a total price, converting to a Float variable, which will be displayed:

```
int iPriceTotal = rowAtot + rowBtot + rowCtot;
Float fPriceTotal = new Float(iPriceTotal /100);
out.println(fPriceTotal);
```

Now that we've introduced the code to read the contents of the prices file, and calculate and display the total price in WML, the Java servlet code for booking tickets should look like the following:

```
// Booking tickets
// Convert strings returned by user agent to integers.
String rowA = (String) request.getParameter( "ROWA" );
String rowB = (String) request.getParameter( "ROWB" );
String rowC = (String) request.getParameter( "ROWC" );
if (rowA.length() == 0) {
   rowA = "0";
}
```

```java
    if (rowB.length() == 0) {
      rowB = "0";
    }
    if (rowC.length() == 0) {
      rowC = "0";
    }
    int rowAnum = Integer.parseInt( rowA );
    int rowBnum = Integer.parseInt( rowB );
    int rowCnum = Integer.parseInt( rowC );

    // priceFile contains the ticket prices.
    try {
      // Open prices file (/path/to/prices) for reading.
      priceFile = new RandomAccessFile( priceFileLoc , "r" );
    } catch (IOException e ) {
      priceFile = null;

      // Could not open prices file, inform client.
      startDeck( out );
      out.println( "<p>Failed to open Price File</p>" );
      endDeck( out );

      // Proceed no further.
      break;
    }

    // Read the one line from the (/path/to/prices) prices file.
    String tPrices = priceFile.readLine();

    // Read the ticket prices from the file referred to by priceFile.
    StringTokenizer tPriceRow = new StringTokenizer( tPrices, ",");
    priceFile.close();

    // The ticket prices are stored as integers and are separated
    // by commas in the file; e.g., 525,600,675.
    int rowAtot =
      (new Integer(tPriceRow.nextToken())).intValue() * rowAnum;
    int rowBtot =
      (new Integer(tPriceRow.nextToken())).intValue() * rowBnum;
    int rowCtot =
      (new Integer(tPriceRow.nextToken())).intValue() * rowCnum;
```

```
// Multiply the number of tickets in each row by the price of
// tickets in each row, then divide by 100.
int iPriceTotal = rowAtot + rowBtot + rowCtot;
Float fPriceTotal = new Float(iPriceTotal /100);

startDeck(out);
out.println("<do type=\"accept\" label=\"Confirm\">");
out.println("<go href=\"http://localhost/cinema.wml\"/>");
out.println("</do>");
out.println("<p>");

out.println("Tickets booked: <br/>");
out.println(rowA + " in row A<br/>");
out.println(rowB + " in row B<br/>");
out.println(rowC + " in row C<br/>");

out.println("Total price:");
out.println(fPriceTotal);
out.println("</p>");

endDeck(out);
break;
```

The Complete Servlet

Now that we've examined how the servlet works, let's take a look at the complete servlet. Note that all the individual processes are called depending on a number, using the switch...case commands. This enables us to include a number of options in the servlet, without having a heavy structure of ifs and elses.

```
// Imports
import java.util.*;
import java.math.*;
import javax.servlet.*;
import javax.servlet.http.*;
import java.io.*;

// Class definition
public class Cinema extends HttpServlet {
```

```java
        // Define file locations.
        private static final String movieFileLoc = "/path/to/movies";
        private static final String priceFileLoc = "/path/to/prices";
        private static final String loginFileLoc = "/path/to";

        // Define file handles.
        private RandomAccessFile movieFile;
        private RandomAccessFile priceFile;
        private RandomAccessFile logonFile;

        // The HTTP GET handler method
        public void doGet (
          HttpServletRequest request, HttpServletResponse response)
            throws ServletException, IOException  {
          doPost( request, response );
        }

        // The HTTP POST handler method
        public void doPost (
          HttpServletRequest request, HttpServletResponse response)
            throws ServletException, IOException  {

          // Get the communication channel with the requesting client.
          PrintWriter out = response.getWriter();

          // Set the MIME type to WML.
          response.setContentType( "text/vnd.wap.wml" );

          // Get the Action parameter sent by the user agent.
          String slAction = (String) request.getParameter( "Action" );

          // Convert String Action into an integer for use in switch.
          int servAction;
          try {
            servAction = Integer.parseInt( slAction );
          } catch (NumberFormatException e) {
            servAction = 1;
          }

          switch (servAction) {

            case 1:
              // User authentication
```

```java
String slUID = (String) request.getParameter( "UID" );
String slTELNO = (String) request.getParameter( "TELNO" );

// Open login file (/path/to/TELNO) for reading.
try {
  logonFile =
    new RandomAccessFile( loginFileLoc + slTELNO , "r" );
} catch (IOException e) {
  logonFile = null;

  // Could not open login file, inform client.
  startDeck( out );
  out.println( "<p>Failed to open Access File</p>" );
  endDeck( out );

  // Proceed no further.
  break;
}

// Assume UID is incorrect.
boolean validId = false;

// Read the one line from the (/path/to/TELNO) login file.
String logId = logonFile.readLine();

// Each TELNO has at least one UID.
StringTokenizer stContents =
  new StringTokenizer( logId, "," );

// Loop through all login UIDs.
while (stContents.hasMoreTokens()) {

  String slLogId = stContents.nextToken();

  // Determine if the file UID matches the user agent UID.
  if (slLogId.equalsIgnoreCase( slUID )) {
    validId = true;
  }
}

// Close the (/path/to/TELNO) login file.
logonFile.close();
```

```java
        if (!validId) {

          // Login failed, inform user.
          startDeck( out );
          out.println( "<do type=\"accept\" label=\"Cont\">" );
          out.println( "<go href=\"http://localhost/cinema.wml\">");
          out.println( "</go>" );
          out.println( "</do>" );
          out.println( "<p>" );
          out.println( "Access Denied" );
          out.println( "</p>" );
          endDeck( out );

          // Proceed no further.
          break;

        } else {

          // Fall through to next case.
        }

      case 3:
        // Choosing a movie
        try {
          // Open login file (/path/to/movies) for reading.
          movieFile = new RandomAccessFile( movieFileLoc , "r");

        } catch (IOException e) {
          movieFile = null;

          // Could not open movies file, inform client.
          startDeck( out );
          out.println( "<p>Failed to open Movie File</p>" );
          endDeck( out );

          // Proceed no further.
          break;
        }

        // Setting and initializing the variables
        startDeck( out );
        out.println( "<do type=\"accept\" label=\"Details\">" );
```

```
out.println( "<go href=\"http://localhost/servlet/Cinema\" ↲
    method=\"post\">" );
out.println( "<postfield name=\"viewMovieNum\" ↲
    value=\"$(line)\"/>" );
out.println( "<postfield name=\"Action\" value=\"4\"/>" );
out.println( "</go>" );
out.println( "</do>" );
out.println( "<p>" );
out.println( "<select title=\"Choose Movie\" name=\"line\">");

// Build a list of movies from the movie file, index with
// the value of line, which is incremented on each loop.
int line = 0;
long filePos = 0;
movieFile.seek(0);
while (filePos < movieFile.length()) {

    line ++;
    String slMovieInfo = movieFile.readLine();
    StringTokenizer slMovieDetails =
        new StringTokenizer( slMovieInfo, "%" );
    String slMovieTitle = slMovieDetails.nextToken();
    out.println( "<option value=\"" + line + "\">" + ↲
        slMovieTitle + "</option>");
    filePos = movieFile.getFilePointer();
}
// Close the (/path/to/movies) movies file.
movieFile.close();

out.println( "</select>" );
out.println( "</p>" );
endDeck( out );

break;

case 4:
    // Displaying movie information
    startDeck( out );

    try {
        // Open login file (/path/to/movies) for reading.
        movieFile = new RandomAccessFile( movieFileLoc , "r");
```

```java
      } catch (IOException e ) {
        movieFile = null;

        // Could not open movies file, inform client.
        startDeck( out );
        out.println( "<p>Failed to open Movie File</p>" );
        endDeck( out );

        // Proceed no further.
        break;
      }

      // Determine chosen movie and convert to integer.
      String slMovieInfo = "";
      String viewMovieNum =
          (String) request.getParameter( "viewMovieNum" );
      int movieNum = Integer.parseInt( viewMovieNum );

      // Declaring and initializing all the required variables
      out.println( "<do type=\"accept\" label=\"Book\">" );
      out.println( "<go href=\"http://localhost/servlet/Cinema\" ↵
        method=\"post\">" );
      out.println( "<postfield name=\"Action\" value=\"5\"/>" );
      out.println( "</go>" );
      out.println( "</do>" );
      out.println( "<p>" );

      // Loop through all movies until we find correct one.
      for (int i = 0; i < movieNum; i ++) {
        slMovieInfo = movieFile.readLine ();
      }

      // Build a list of details of the movie.
      StringTokenizer stMovieDetails =
        new StringTokenizer( slMovieInfo, "%");

      while (stMovieDetails.hasMoreTokens()) {

        String slMovieInfoItem = stMovieDetails.nextToken();
        out.println( slMovieInfoItem );
        out.println( "<br/>" );
      }
```

```
      out.println( "</p>" );

      endDeck( out );
      break;

    case 5:
      // Reserving tickets
      startDeck( out );

      out.println( "<do type=\"accept\" label=\"Book\">" );
      out.println( "<go href=\"http://localhost/servlet/Cinema\" ⏎
        method=\"post\">" );
      out.println( "<postfield name=\"Action\" value=\"6\"/>" );
      out.println( "<postfield name=\"ROWA\" value=\"$ROWA\"/>" );
      out.println( "<postfield name=\"ROWB\" value=\"$ROWB\"/>" );
      out.println( "<postfield name=\"ROWC\" value=\"$ROWC\"/>" );
      out.println( "</go>" );
      out.println( "</do>" );
      out.println( "<p>" );

      out.println( "Choose Tickets:<br/>" );
      out.println( "Row A:" );
      out.println(
        "<input title=\"Row A\" name=\"ROWA\" format=\"*N\"/>" );
      out.println( "Row B:" );
      out.println(
        "<input title=\"Row B\" name=\"ROWB\" format=\"*N\"/>" );
      out.println( "Row C:" );
      out.println(
        "<input title=\"Row C\" name=\"ROWC\" format=\"*N\"/>" );
      out.println( "</p>" );

      endDeck( out );
      break;

    case 6:
      // Booking tickets

      // Convert strings returned by user agent to integers.
      String rowA = (String) request.getParameter( "ROWA" );
      String rowB = (String) request.getParameter( "ROWB" );
      String rowC = (String) request.getParameter( "ROWC" );
```

```java
if (rowA.length() == 0) {
  rowA = "0";
}
if (rowB.length() == 0) {
  rowB = "0";
}
if (rowC.length() == 0) {
  rowC = "0";
}
int rowAnum = Integer.parseInt( rowA );
int rowBnum = Integer.parseInt( rowB );
int rowCnum = Integer.parseInt( rowC );


// priceFile contains the ticket prices.
try {
  // Open prices file (/path/to/prices) for reading.
  priceFile = new RandomAccessFile( priceFileLoc , "r" );

} catch (IOException e ) {
  priceFile = null;

  // Could not open prices file, inform client.
  startDeck( out );
  out.println( "<p>Failed to open Price File</p>" );
  endDeck( out );

  // Proceed no further.
  break;
}

// Read the one line from the (/path/to/prices) prices file.
String tPrices = priceFile.readLine();

// Read ticket prices from the priceFile.
StringTokenizer tPriceRow =
  new StringTokenizer( tPrices, ",");
priceFile.close();

// The ticket prices are stored as integers and are separated
// by commas in the file; e.g., 525,600,675.
int rowAtot =
```

```
            (new Integer(tPriceRow.nextToken())).intValue() * rowAnum;
        int rowBtot =
            (new Integer(tPriceRow.nextToken())).intValue() * rowBnum;
        int rowCtot =
            (new Integer(tPriceRow.nextToken())).intValue() * rowCnum;

        // Multiply the number of tickets in each row by the price of
        // tickets in each row, then divide by 100.
        int iPriceTotal = rowAtot + rowBtot + rowCtot;
        Float fPriceTotal = new Float( iPriceTotal /100 );

        startDeck( out );
        out.println( "<do type=\"accept\" label=\"Confirm\">" );
        out.println( "<go href=\"http://localhost/cinema.wml\"/>");
        out.println( "</do>" );
        out.println( "<p>" );

        out.println( "Tickets booked: <br/>" );
        out.println( rowA + " in row A<br/>" );
        out.println( rowB + " in row B<br/>" );
        out.println( rowC + " in row C<br/>" );

        out.println( "Total price:" );
        out.println( fPriceTotal );
        out.println( "</p>" );

        endDeck( out );
        break;
    }
}

private void startDeck (PrintWriter out) {

    out.println( "<?xml version=\"1.0\"?>" );
    out.println( "<!DOCTYPE wml PUBLIC \"-//WAPFORUM//DTD WML ↲
        1.1//EN\"" );
    out.println( "  \"http://www.wapforum.org/DTD/wml_1.1.xml\" >" );
    out.println( "<wml>" );
    out.println( "<card id=\"Login\">" );
}

private void endDeck (PrintWriter out) {
```

```
        out.println( "</card>" );
        out.println( "</wml>" );
        out.close();
    }

}
```

Now we've seen how to create a fully functional, dynamic WML site, using Java servlets. Creating dynamic WML sites in other server side technologies is very similar in concept; the main difference is just the syntax of the code that is produced to generate the WML output.

In the next chapter, we are going to look at how we can internationalize our service.

Chapter 8

Internationalizing Your WAP Service

WAP is a global specification. This means people all over the world can expect to access WAP content using WAP-enabled devices. More importantly, you should expect people all over the world to visit your WAP site! This chapter introduces you to the methods involved in *internationalizing* your WAP site.

Internationalization is important. Your WAP site will be accessible from all corners of the world, by users expecting content in their own language, with user agents expecting content in a particular format. You may lose a lot of potential visitors to your WAP site if you fail to internationalize it. Even if you consider your site to be irrelevant to people on the other side of the world, it may still be accessed by visitors bringing their WAP devices to your country, as in the case of, for example, a local amenities WAP site.

WAP device manufacturers produce devices for particular markets, especially in the case of cellular phones, which are determined by the prevailing local communication protocol—for example, GSM in Europe and CDMA/TDMA in Northern America. When a WAP device is produced for a particular market, the device is specialized with regard to natural-language support and transfer encodings (which are explained in this chapter). This is known as *localization*.

Where internationalization is the method of making your service generically applicable to all languages, localization is the method of tuning the internationalized service to a particular location. We will develop our cinema example to be internationalized by providing the means to implement language-specific content, and we will localize that content by specifying the natural-language alternatives. Note that localization isn't complete until you have considered all components of internationalization. Following is a list of some considerations we believe to be important:

- Natural-language translation
- Character-encoding translation
- Numerical and monetary formats
- Date and time formats
- Sorting algorithms
- Text direction

What happens if you don't internationalize your WAP site? You'll probably deliver content in English using the default transfer encoding, which may be suitable for most visitors you expect to view your site, but it's unreasonable to expect every user agent to be able to understand whatever you deliver. Localized user agents contain only enough fonts to display the relevant local natural languages and understand only a limited number of transfer encodings; at worst, without localization, the content delivered by your WAP site may not be displayed at all. If you think that your site may be viewed by users and user agents expecting content other than English (or your chosen primary language), then you should internationalize and localize your site.

Delivering Multilingual Content

It's easier than you may first think to deliver multilingual content using static WML, and it can produce great results on the WAP-enabled device. The user agent should do its best to present the data according to the specifics of the language. The different languages can be presented in the WML deck by the xml:lang attribute, which can be used with every element that can contain text. Nested elements can assume the parent's language, so if we consider a deck written as the following:

```
<wml xml:lang="language-identifier">
  <!-- rest of deck -->
</wml>
```

all the elements in the deck will assume the language identified by *language-identifier* unless they themselves have an xml:lang attribute. Where an element has both textual content and text-based attribute values that may be presented to the user, you should use the same language for both to avoid the following example of confusion:

```
<a xml:lang="fr" href="en.wml" title="English Version">anglais</a>
```

which should be written:

```
<a xml:lang="en" href="en.wml" title="English Version">English</a>
```

The user agent should present an element's language to the best of its ability according to the following rules, in order of preference:

1. Based on the element's xml:lang attribute
2. Based on the element's closest parent's xml:lang attribute
3. Based on any language information included in the deck's transport or metadata (see the following "HTTP Languages" section)
4. Based on user agent default properties, which may occur if the WAP device is intended solely for use in a particular language market

Let's put all this knowledge into an example. Say you're quite a linguist, and have converted your site to use not only English, but also several other languages. The following code, `language.wml`, could be used to invite a visitor to your WAP site to choose their preference of language:

```
<?xml version="1.0"?>
<!DOCTYPE wml PUBLIC "-//WAPFORUM//DTD WML 1.1//EN"
   "http://www.wapforum.org/DTD/wml_1.1.xml" >

<wml xml:lang="en">
  <card id="index">
    <p>
      Select a language:<br/>
      <a href="english.wml">english</a><br/>
      <a xml:lang="de" href="german.wml">deutsch</a><br/>
      <a xml:lang="es" href="spanish.wml">español</a><br/>
      <a xml:lang="fr" href="french.wml">français</a><br/>
      <a xml:lang="it" href="italian.wml">italiano</a><br/>
      <a xml:lang="no" href="norwegian.wml">norsk</a><br/>
      <a xml:lang="pt" href="portuguese.wml">português</a><br/>
      <a xml:lang="su" href="finnish.wml">suomi</a><br/>
      <a xml:lang="sv" href="swedish.wml">svensk</a><br/>
    </p>
  </card>
</wml>
```

If you view `language.wml` in your emulator, it should look something like Figure 8.1.

FIGURE 8.1:

Static multilingual content

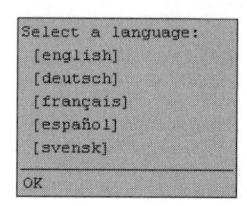

Allowing the visitors to your WAP site to choose their preferred language is great for static content, but if you can deliver dynamic content, then you can deliver the preferred language without the visitor needing to ask for it. We'll show you how to do this in the next section.

HTTP Languages

A natural language spoken, written, or otherwise conveyed in the communication of information between people is identified in HTTP by a language tag. Language tags are used in `Accept-Language` and `Content-Language` HTTP headers, and contain at least one natural-language identifier. The HTTP RFC 2616 contains the following example of the contents of an HTTP language tag:

```
en, en-US, en-cockney, i-cherokee, x-pig-latin
```

which indicates from left to right an order of language preference. The two-letter primary tag (`en` in both `en` and `en-US`) is an ISO 639 language abbreviation, and any two-letter initial subtag is an ISO 3166 country code. See Appendix C for the list of ISO 639 language codes and Appendix D for the list of ISO 3166 country codes.

The last three tags in the preceding example don't strictly conform to the language tag, but are used as examples of future tags. Some future tags are controlled—for example, you can't necessarily just make up your own tags beginning with `i`—as these are defined by the IANA (Internet Assigned Numbers Authority) registry of language codes. The following tags are examples of registered languages:

- `en-scouse` (an English regional dialect)
- `no-bok` (Norwegian bokmål)
- `zh-xiang` (a dialect of Hunanese)
- `i-navajo` (language of the Navajo Nation)
- `i-klingon` (as referenced by the Klingon dictionary)

You can use, for testing purposes, tags beginning with `x-`, which denote experimental codes, such as the following:

- `x-double-dutch`
- `x-gibberish`
- `x-pig-latin`
- `x-cardassian`

Quality Value

HTTP RFC 2616 informs us that each language may be given an associated quality value, which represents an estimate of the user agent's preference. The quality value defaults to q=1. The following example:

```
Accept-Language: da, en-gb;q=0.8, en;q=0.7
```

indicates the preference of Danish, but the user agent will accept British English and any other form of English, in that order. If the WAP site doesn't support any of the languages specified in the Accept-Language header, it may respond with content that the user agent and the user may not understand. You should ensure that your WAP site responds with some content—for example, defaulting to delivering content in your native language. The next section explains how you can do this.

Delivering Content Based on the *Accept-Language* Header

We'll now add user agent language determination to our cinema example. Let's say we want our WAP site to deliver content in a few Western European languages. The titles of the movies remain in English, but navigation will need to change dynamically in response to the user agent's Accept-Language header in the request.

Instead of the following lines of code in Cinema.java informing the user of a failed login:

```
out.println( "Access Denied" );
```

we can apply some logic determining which language to deliver:

```
String slLang = (String) request.getHeader("Accept-Language");
if (slLang.equals("de")) {
  out.println( "Zugriff verweigerte" );
} else {
  if (slLang.equals("es")) {
    out.println( "el acceso negó" );
  } else {
    if (slLang.equals("fr")) {
      out.println( "l'accès a nié" );
    } else {
      if (slLang.equals("it")) {
```

```
          out.println( "l'accesso ha negato" );
      } else {
        if (slLang.equals("pt")) {
          out.println( "o acesso negou" );
        } else {
          out.println( "Access Denied" );
        }
      }
    }
  }
}
```

which is far from perfect, as it attempts to match against the entire Accept-Language header regardless of how many languages have been indicated. If the user agent sends us the following Accept-Language header:

Accept-Language: sv, en

indicating a preference for Swedish, but accepting English, then we will respond with English, as the switch condition will fail to match sv, en and fall through to the default case. However, if the user agent had sent us an Accept-Language header indicating a preference for Spanish, accepting Portuguese, such as the following:

Accept-Language: es, pt

then the preceding code will also fail to match es, pt and will still respond with English.

Multiple *Accept-Language* Tags

A better solution is to parse the Accept-Language request language range for each tag, checking against a list of known supported languages. The following example shows how we do this. As with other development decisions, there are many different choices, possibly with no one perfect solution. We have decided to use a Hashtable object containing the supported languages to our servlet class. A Hashtable maps keys to values. In our example, language tags are the keys, and unique integers are the values:

```
Hashtable htSupportedLanguages = new Hashtable();
htSupportedLanguages.put( "en", new Integer(EN) );
htSupportedLanguages.put( "de", new Integer(DE) );
htSupportedLanguages.put( "es", new Integer(ES) );
htSupportedLanguages.put( "fr", new Integer(FR) );
htSupportedLanguages.put( "it", new Integer(IT) );
htSupportedLanguages.put( "pt", new Integer(PT) );
```

Instead of using cascaded `if` statements, we will use a `switch` statement, which makes the code more readable and maintainable. The `switch` statement requires constant integers for the case clauses:

```java
private static final int EN = 0;
private static final int DE = 1;
private static final int ES = 2;
private static final int FR = 3;
private static final int IT = 4;
private static final int PT = 5;
```

We also need to define a default language. It is likely that your service, like ours, will default to English. As the `Content-Language` response is a string, the default language tag is also a string:

```java
private static final String DEFAULT_LANGUAGE = "en";
```

To determine the most appropriate response language, we need to parse the `Accept-Language` request header. Thankfully, RFC 2616 defines the syntax for the header, and it is reasonable for us to assume that all `Accept-Language` headers will conform to this syntax. All language tags are separated by a comma (,), so to process each language tag, we need to split on comma boundaries. This is performed by the `StringTokenizer` class:

```java
String slAcceptLanguage =
  (String) request.getHeader( "Accept-Language" );
StringTokenizer stLanguage =
  new StringTokenizer( slAcceptLanguage, "," );
```

Each language tag separated by a comma is examined to determine if we support that language. However, just using `StringTokenizer` once isn't enough, as there may be a quality value for each tag, as in the following example (preferring Danish, then British English, then any English, finally accepting US English):

```
Accept-Language: da, en-gb;q=0.9, en;q=0.8, en-us;q=0.7
```

For our process to determine the most appropriate language, from left to right, each language tag on a comma boundary needs to discard text from a semicolon (;) onward, if one exists. We can do this by simply applying the `StringTokenizer` class once more, this time separating on a semicolon:

```java
StringTokenizer stTag =
  new StringTokenizer( stLanguage.nextToken(), ";" );
```

Once each language tag (the `stTag` variable) has been tidied by removing leading and trailing spaces, and converting to lowercase, we can determine whether the language is supported by simply looking to see if the language is a key in the `Hashtable`. If so, the language tag string is used in the subsequent response:

```
if ( htSupportedLanguages.containsKey( slTag ) ) {
  return slTag;
}
```

Using our previous example, by taking each language tag in the Accept-Language header, the calls to the `Hashtable.containsKey()` method will take the arguments of `"da"`, then `"en-gb"`, then `"en"`. The fourth language is not reached, as `"en"` is a key in our `Hashtable` object `htSupportedLanguages`.

If we apply this code to write a method `getAppropriateLanguage`, it would look like the following:

```
private String getAppropriateLanguage (HttpServletRequest request) {
  // Obtain the accept-language range.
  String slAcceptLanguage =
    (String) request.getHeader( "Accept-Language" );
  // Process the accept-language only if the header was sent.
  if ( slAcceptLanguage != null ) {
    // Language tags are separated by comma, RFC2616 ss14.4.
    StringTokenizer stLanguage =
      new StringTokenizer( slAcceptLanguage, "," );
    // Loop through all language tags.
    while (stLanguage.hasMoreTokens()) {
      // Obtain the significant characters of the language tag.
      StringTokenizer stTag =
        new StringTokenizer( stLanguage.nextToken(), ";" );
      // Convert to lowercase characters.
      String slTag = stTag.nextToken().trim().toLowerCase();
      // Does the tag appear in our supported languages hashtable?
      if ( htSupportedLanguages.containsKey( slTag ) ) {
        // Language supported, return the language code.
        return slTag;
      }
    }
  }
  return DEFAULT_LANGUAGE;
}
```

Now that we've determined the most appropriate language (or used the default language), we can deliver content based on that language. The return value from our new method getAppropriateLanguage can be used to obtain the constant integer for use in a switch statement:

```
String slLang = getAppropriateLanguage( request );
Integer iLang = (Integer) htSupportedLanguages.get( slLang );

switch (iLang.intValue()) {
  case DE:
    // Deliver content in German.
    out.println( "Zugriff verweigerte" );
    break;
  case ES:
    // Deliver content in Spanish.
    out.println( "el acceso negó" );
    break;
  case FR:
    // Deliver content in French.
    out.println( "l'accès a nié" );
    break;
  case IT:
    // Deliver content in Italian.
    out.println( "l'accesso ha negato" );
    break;
  case PT:
    // Deliver content in Portuguese.
    out.println( "o acesso negou" );
    break;
  case EN:
  default:
    // Deliver content in English.
    out.println( "Access Denied" );
    break;
}
```

We can now replace our English content with a simple switch statement like that above. We used the Hashtable class not only to allow us to write elegant code, but to allow easy modification of supported languages. If a language is temporarily unsupported, then it can be commented out of the Hashtable as follows:

```
// htSupportedLanguages.put( "it", new Integer(IT) );
// htSupportedLanguages.put( "pt", new Integer(PT) );
```

Similarly, new languages can be added (remembering to add content in the `switch` statements also) by the following:

```
private static final int SV = 6;
private static final int ENGB = 7;
htSupportedLanguages.put( "sv", new Integer(SV) );
htSupportedLanguages.put( "en-gb", new Integer(ENGB) );
```

The *Content-Language* Header

The `Content-Language` header describes the natural language of the content. You may think that if we're delivering language-specific content based on the `Accept-Language` request header, then we need to set the corresponding `Content-Language` response header. The answer is yes, and no. It depends on the WAP gateway, which may or may not pass your `Content-Language` header to the user agent. At the start of this chapter, we told you that the user agent should present an element's language to the best of its ability according to certain prioritized criteria: the `xml:lang` attribute, the deck's transport or metadata, and the default properties of the WAP-enabled device.

There is no real requirement for you to stick to one method, when you can use as many as possible to cover all eventualities. We can add the `Content-Language` header to where we set the `Content-Type`, add the `xml:lang` attribute to the `wml` element, and also set the `meta` tag:

```
public void doPost ( /* arguments */) {

  // Method preamble ...

  String slLang = getAppropriateLanguage( request )
  response.setContentType( "text/vnd.wap.wml" );
  response.setHeader( "Content-Language", slLang );

  // Method completion ...
}

private void startDeck (PrintWriter out, String slLang) {
  out.println("<?xml version=\"1.0\"?>");
  out.println( "<!DOCTYPE wml PUBLIC" );
  out.println( " \"-//WAPFORUM//DTD WML 1.1//EN\"" );
  out.println( "  \"http://www.wapforum.org/DTD/wml_1.1.xml\" >" );
  out.println("<head>");
```

```
  out.println("<meta " +
    "http-equiv=\"Content-Language\"" +
    "content=\""+slLang+"\"/>");
  out.println("</head>");
  out.println("<wml xml:lang=\""+slLang+"\">");
  out.println("<card id=\"Login\">");
}
```

Text Direction

Another important consideration for your WAP service is that of *text direction*. Not all languages read from left to right, top to bottom (see Table 8.1 for examples of language text directions).

TABLE 8.1: Language Text Directions

Language Set	Example Languages	Scripts	Text Direction
European	Western European,	Latin	Left to right
	Central European,		
	Eastern European,		
	Turkish, Indonesian		
	Greek	Greek	
	Turkish	Turkish	
	Russian	Cyrillic	
Middle Eastern	Arabic	Arabic, Latin	Bi-directional
	Hebrew	Hebrew, Latin	
Far Eastern	Chinese	Ideograph	Horizontal and vertical
	Korean	hangul, hanja	
	Japanese	Kana	
Thai	Thai	Thai	Left to right

Text Direction

The June 2000 (WML 1.3) WAP specification implies that the user agent should look after text direction, but we can give it a helping hand with the use of the `align` attribute of the `<p>` element.

```
<p xml:lang="en" align="left">text should be left aligned</p>
```

The preceding example aligns text to the left, whereas the following example aligns text to the right:

```
<p xml:lang="ar" align="right"> يجب أن يكون النص أيمن الصفحة </p>

<!-- or using entities -->

<p xml:lang="ar" align="right">
  &#xED;&#xCC;&#xC8;
  &#xC3;&#xE4;
  &#xED;&#xDF;&#xE6;&#xE4;
  &#xC7;&#xE1;&#xE4;&#xF8;&#xD5;&#xF8;
  &#xC3;&#xED;&#xE3;&#xE4;
  &#xC7;&#xD5;&#xD8;&#xDD;&#xF8;
</p>
```

The preceding code, if viewed in an internationalized emulator and assuming capable fonts are installed, should look something like Figure 8.2 and Figure 8.3.

FIGURE 8.2:

Static left-aligned English content

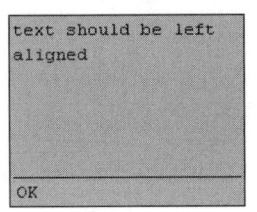

FIGURE 8.3:

Static right-aligned Arabic content

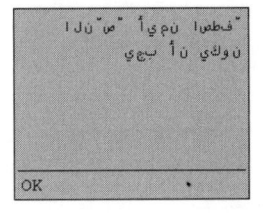

Note that in the preceding example, the Arabic for "text should be right aligned" will not be displayed in Arabic unless you specify the ISO 8859-6 character set and transfer encoding. We investigate character sets and transfer encodings in the following sections.

Character Sets

Computers deal with numbers. Strings are not recognized until they are converted to a stream of integers. A *character set* is a one-to-one mapping relating characters with a unique number. There are hundreds of character sets in use today. Some are 7-bit, some are 8-bit, and some use a mixture of single and double-byte codes. Each flavor of character set can cope with just enough characters required for a certain language or group of languages, and trying to deliver content between the sets can lead to ambiguities and errors.

The most popular character sets are the ISO Latin sets, ISO-8859-1 through ISO-8859-15, which are 8-bit, single-byte sets. In every ISO Latin character set, the first 128 characters match the US-ASCII character set, whereas the next 128 characters are different for each set, for use with different languages. See Table 8.2 for examples of character sets and their languages.

TABLE 8.2: Character Sets and Languages

Character Set	Example Languages
ISO-8859-1	English, German, French, Spanish, Swedish, Italian, Portuguese, Dutch, Norwegian, Finnish, Danish, Malay
ISO-8859-2	Croatian, Hungarian, Polish, Romanian, Slovak, Slovenian
ISO-8859-3	Maltese, Esperanto
ISO-8859-5	Bulgarian, Macedonian, Russian, Serbian, Ukrainian
ISO-8859-6	Arabic
ISO-8859-7	Greek
ISO-8859-8	Hebrew, Yiddish
ISO-8859-9	Turkish

Continued on next page

TABLE 8.2 CONTINUED: Character Sets and Languages

Character Set	Example Languages
ISO-8859-10	Nordic languages
ISO-8859-11	Thai
ISO-8859-13	Baltic Rim languages
ISO-8859-14	Celtic
ISO-8859-15	Estonian
koi-8-r	Russian
shift_jis	Japanese

Unicode is the standard WAP character set. It provides a unique identifier for every character, no matter what the language, and has been rapidly adopted by much of the Internet. The emergence of Unicode and the support it has received are quite significant. We will look at Unicode's transfer encodings in the next section.

Transfer Encodings

A *transfer encoding* defines the mapping of each character in a character set to actual bits including the byte ordering and is typically used when transporting content over a network. Unicode has seven transfer encodings: UTF-8, UTF-16, UTF-16BE, UTF-16LE, UTF-32, UTF-32BE, and UTF-32LE.

Why do we need transfer encodings? The early character sets—for example, ISO-8859-1—are transferred using the 8 bits of the character set. The purpose of transfer encodings is for those networks that do not support 8-bit encodings.

Character sets are space inefficient. To counteract that, Unicode's UTF-8 encoding is the most efficient as it employs a *variable* 1- to 4-byte sequence translation. The most likely used UTF-8 characters are represented by 1 byte, and those are the US-ASCII characters, just like the first 128 characters of all the ISO Latin character sets. The least likely used UTF-8 characters are represented by 4 bytes.

Some user agents expect content to be delivered in a specific transfer encoding, or would allow content in another or range of other encodings. When you deliver content to a user agent, you need to ensure that the user agent can properly understand and deal with the encoding. How can you tell when to send content using the correct encoding to a user agent accessing your WAP site? The answer is in the confusingly named HTTP header `Accept-charset`. It's confusing because `Accept-charset` is actually used to specify encodings.

As the WAP standard character set is Unicode, and the accepted default encoding is UTF-8, all WAP user agents must be able to understand Unicode and deal with the UTF-8 encoding. In the request to your WAP site, the user agent should send something like the following HTTP header:

```
Accept-charset: UTF-8, utf-8, *
```

This HTTP header informs your server that the user agent accepts, and expects, the UTF-8 encoding. The addition of the asterisk (*) means that the user agent will also accept any other encoding, as it will try to process the response, regardless of whether it is supported by the user agent.

If you know that the user agent accessing your WAP site supports the UTF-8 encoding, then you should be able to respond with any character set. However, what if the user agent doesn't support UTF-8 encoding? It sends a more restrictive `Accept-charset` HTTP header, like the following:

```
Accept-charset: iso-8859-5
```

which indicates that the user agent may be in a device intended for the Russian market. Responding with the content in the ISO-8859-5 character set would be the best course of action for your WAP site. You can do this by responding with the HTTP header `Content-type` including the particular encoding, as in the following example:

```
Content-type: text/vnd.wap.wml; charset=ISO-8859-5
```

If your WAP service delivers static (nondynamic) content, then you won't be able to set the `Content-type` HTTP header. You can still deliver the character set content, though—the trick is to use the `<meta http-equiv>` element and attribute combination. Most WAP gateways will convert, or *transcode*, the combination into the above HTTP `Content-type` header for delivery to the WAP device. The following code shows how to emulate the header for static WAP sites:

```
<wml>
  <head>
```

```
    <meta
      http-equiv="Content-type"
      content="text/vnd.wap.wml; charset=ISO-8859-5" />
  </head>
  <!-- rest of deck -->
</wml>
```

We'll now introduce a few static decks that will attempt to demonstrate the concept of delivering content with different character sets. We would like to keep it really simple by using just one deck of multiple cards, where each card uses a different character set. However, it's actually impossible to do this, as the character set applies to the deck as a whole, not individual cards.

This is the main deck, encoding.wml:

```
<?xml version="1.0"?>
<!DOCTYPE wml PUBLIC "-//WAPFORUM//DTD WML 1.1//EN"
   "http://www.wapforum.org/DTD/wml_1.1.xml" >

<wml>
  <card id="index">
    <p>
      Select a charset:<br/>
      <a href="iso-8859-1.wml">iso-8859-1</a><br/>
      <a href="iso-8859-2.wml">iso-8859-2</a><br/>
      <a href="iso-8859-3.wml">iso-8859-3</a><br/>
      <a href="iso-8859-4.wml">iso-8859-4</a><br/>
      <a href="iso-8859-5.wml">iso-8859-5</a><br/>
      <a href="iso-8859-6.wml">iso-8859-6</a><br/>
      <a href="iso-8859-7.wml">iso-8859-7</a><br/>
      <a href="iso-8859-8.wml">iso-8859-8</a><br/>
      <a href="iso-8859-9.wml">iso-8859-9</a><br/>
      <a href="iso-8859-10.wml">iso-8859-10</a><br/>
      <a href="iso-8859-11.wml">iso-8859-11</a><br/>
      <a href="iso-8859-13.wml">iso-8859-13</a><br/>
      <a href="iso-8859-14.wml">iso-8859-14</a><br/>
      <a href="iso-8859-15.wml">iso-8859-15</a><br/>
      <a href="shift_jis.wml">shift_jis</a><br/>
    </p>
  </card>
</wml>
```

The following is the `iso-8859-1.wml` file. The other files look similar to this, but with the `Content-type` and `charset` combination, and the card ID, altered to reflect the chosen character set:

```
<?xml version="1.0"?>
<!DOCTYPE wml PUBLIC "-//WAPFORUM//DTD WML 1.1//EN"
   "http://www.wapforum.org/DTD/wml_1.1.xml" >

<wml>
  <head>
    <meta
      http-equiv="Content-type"
      content="text/vnd.wap.wml; charset=iso-8859-1" />
  </head>
  <card id="iso-8859-1">
    <p>
      &#xc0; &#xc1; &#xc2; &#xc3; <br/>
      &#xc4; &#xc5; &#xc6; &#xc7; <br/>
      &#xc8; &#xc9; &#xca; &#xcb; <br/>
      &#xcc; &#xcd; &#xce; &#xcf; <br/>
    </p>
  </card>
</wml>
```

The following figures, from Figure 8.4 through Figure 8.19, show how the preceding example code would look on devices that accept and display content in the most popular encodings. Figure 8.4 is the indexer, which contains links to the other decks. Figure 8.5 shows sample characters in the ISO-8859-1 Latin 1 character set (for Western European languages). Figure 8.6 shows sample characters in the ISO-8859-2 Latin 2 character set (for Eastern European languages). Figure 8.7 shows sample characters in the ISO-8859-3 Latin 3 character set (for Southern European languages).

FIGURE 8.4:

Character set sample indexer

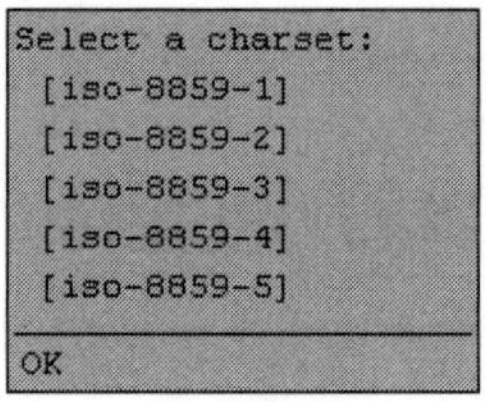

FIGURE 8.5:

Sample ISO-8859-1 characters

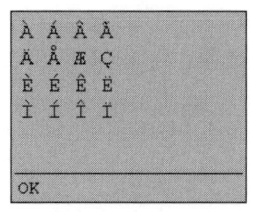

FIGURE 8.6:

Sample ISO-8859-2 characters

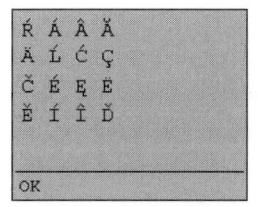

FIGURE 8.7:

Sample ISO-8859-3 characters

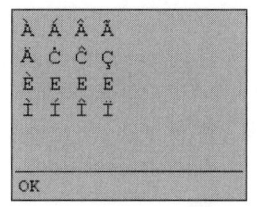

Figure 8.8 shows sample characters in the ISO-8859-4 Latin 4 character set (for Northern European languages). Figure 8.9 shows sample characters in the ISO-8859-5 Cyrillic character set (for languages such as Bulgarian, Byelorussian, Macedonian, Russian, Serbian and Ukrainian). Figure 8.10 shows sample characters in the ISO-8859-6 Arabic character set. Figure 8.11 shows sample characters in the ISO-8859-7 Greek character set.

FIGURE 8.8:

Sample ISO-8859-4 characters

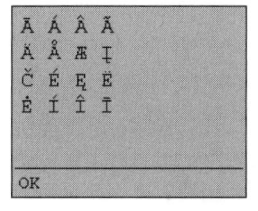

FIGURE 8.9:

Sample ISO-8859-5 characters

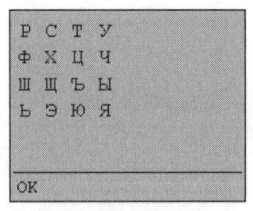

FIGURE 8.10:

Sample ISO-8859-6 characters

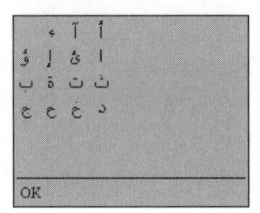

FIGURE 8.11:

Sample ISO-8859-7 characters

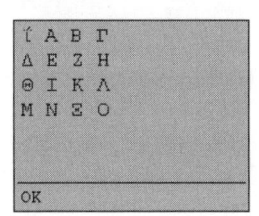

Figure 8.12 shows sample characters in the ISO-8859-8 Hebrew character set (for Hebrew and Yiddish). Figure 8.13 shows sample characters in the ISO-8859-9 Latin 5 character set (for Turkish). Figure 8.14 shows sample characters in the ISO-8859-10 Latin 6 character set (for Inuit and Nordic languages). Figure 8.15 shows sample characters in the ISO-8859-11 Thai character set.

FIGURE 8.12:

Sample ISO-8859-8 characters

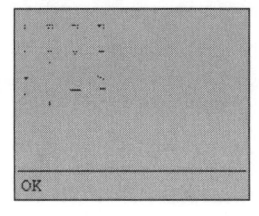

FIGURE 8.13:

Sample ISO-8859-9 characters

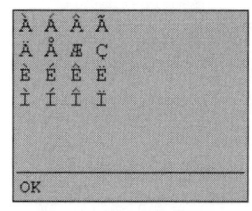

FIGURE 8.14:

Sample ISO-8859-10 characters

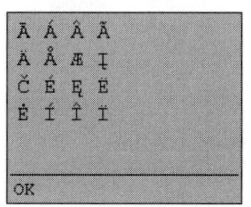

FIGURE 8.15:

Sample ISO-8859-11 characters

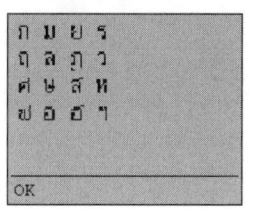

Figure 8.16 shows sample characters in the ISO-8859-13 Latin 7 character set (for Baltic Rim languages). Figure 8.17 shows sample characters in the ISO-8859-14 Latin 8 character set (for Celtic languages). Figure 8.18 shows sample characters in the ISO-8859-15 Latin 9 character set (an update to ISO-8859-1 Latin 1, replacing some less used characters with the Euro character and forgotten French and Finnish letters). Figure 8.19 shows sample characters in the shift_jis character set (for Japanese).

FIGURE 8.16:

Sample ISO-8859-13 characters

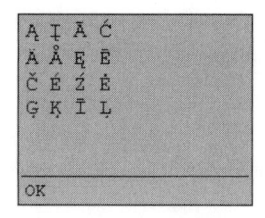

FIGURE 8.17:

Sample ISO-8859-14 characters

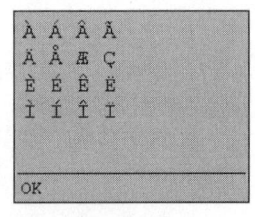

FIGURE 8.18:

Sample ISO-8859-15 characters

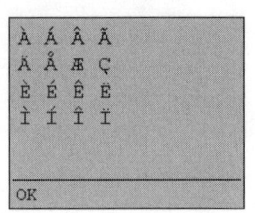

FIGURE 8.19:

Sample shift_jis characters

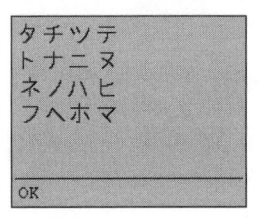

The preceding examples use character *entities*, which are used to specify characters that must be escaped in WML or that are difficult to enter in a text editor. Entities begin with an ampersand and end with a semicolon; for example, an ampersand (&) is represented by either the named entity & or the numeric entities & (decimal) or & (hexadecimal). The sample entities we've chosen are arbitrary values and are mostly letters in the respective character sets.

The preceding decks do actually *attempt* to demonstrate the concept, but it's very difficult to prove, as the WAP emulators and SDKs don't easily support different character sets, especially when using direct HTTP instead of a WAP gateway, as in the case of delivering content from your hard disk.

We will now gather all the information required and show you how to deliver tailored multilingual content depending on the request from the device.

Tailoring Multilingual Content

We can now apply the internationalization techniques to the cinema example. The languages we're supporting are defined in the following `Hashtable`:

```
Hashtable htSupportedLanguages = new Hashtable();
htSupportedLanguages.put( "en", new Integer(EN) );
htSupportedLanguages.put( "de", new Integer(DE) );
htSupportedLanguages.put( "es", new Integer(ES) );
htSupportedLanguages.put( "fr", new Integer(FR) );
htSupportedLanguages.put( "it", new Integer(IT) );
htSupportedLanguages.put( "pt", new Integer(PT) );
```

which are all available in the ISO-8859-1 transfer encoding. But the request charset is used in the response:

```
String slCharset = (String) request.getHeader( "Accept-Charset" );
if (slCharset != null) {
  if (slCharset.length() != 0) {
    response.setContentType( "text/vnd.wap.wml" +slCharset );
  }
}
```

as we must attempt to deliver content using a transfer encoding that the requesting user agent claims to support.

Here is the complete Cinema servlet class:

```
// Imports
import java.util.*;
import java.math.*;
import javax.servlet.*;
import javax.servlet.http.*;
import java.io.*;

// Class definition
public class Cinema extends HttpServlet {

  // Define file locations.
  private static final String movieFileLoc = "/path/to/movies";
  private static final String priceFileLoc = "/path/to/prices";
  private static final String loginFileLoc = "/path/to";

  // Define file handles.
```

```java
    private RandomAccessFile movieFile;
    private RandomAccessFile priceFile;
    private RandomAccessFile logonFile;

    // Define supported languages.
    private static final int EN = 0;
    private static final int DE = 1;
    private static final int ES = 2;
    private static final int FR = 3;
    private static final int IT = 4;
    private static final int PT = 5;
    private static final String DEFAULT_LANGUAGE = "en";
    private static Hashtable htSupportedLanguages;


    // The servlet class constructor
    public void init ( ServletConfig config ) throws ServletException {
        super.init( config );
        htSupportedLanguages = new Hashtable();
        htSupportedLanguages.put( "en", new Integer(EN) );
        htSupportedLanguages.put( "de", new Integer(DE) );
        htSupportedLanguages.put( "es", new Integer(ES) );
        htSupportedLanguages.put( "fr", new Integer(FR) );
        htSupportedLanguages.put( "it", new Integer(IT) );
        htSupportedLanguages.put( "pt", new Integer(PT) );
    }

    // The HTTP GET handler method
    public void doGet (
      HttpServletRequest request, HttpServletResponse response)
        throws ServletException, IOException  {
      doPost( request, response );
    }

    // The HTTP POST handler method
    public void doPost (
      HttpServletRequest request, HttpServletResponse response)
        throws ServletException, IOException  {

      // Get the communication channel with the requesting client.
      PrintWriter out = response.getWriter();
```

```java
// Get the appropriate charset.
String slCharset =
  (String) request.getHeader( "Accept-Charset" );

// Set the MIME type to WML.
response.setContentType( "text/vnd.wap.wml" );
if (slCharset != null) {
  if (slCharset.length() != 0) {
    response.setContentType(
    "text/vnd.wap.wml; charset=" +slCharset );
  }
}

// Set the appropriate Language.
String slLang = getAppropriateLanguage( request );
Integer iLang = (Integer) htSupportedLanguages.get( slLang );
response.setHeader( "Content-Language", slLang );

// Get the Action parameter sent by the User Agent.
String slAction = (String) request.getParameter( "Action" );

// Convert String Action into an integer for use in switch.
int servAction;
try {
  servAction = Integer.parseInt( slAction );
} catch (NumberFormatException e) {
  servAction = 1;
}

switch (servAction) {

  case 1:
    // User authentication
    String slUID = (String) request.getParameter( "UID" );
    String slTELNO = (String) request.getParameter( "TELNO" );

    // Open login file (/path/to/TELNO) for reading.
    try {
      logonFile =
        new RandomAccessFile( loginFileLoc + slTELNO , "r" );
    } catch (IOException e ) {
      logonFile = null;
```

```
      // Could not open login file, inform client.
      String sError = new String();
      switch (iLang.intValue()) {
        case DE:
          sError = "Konnte Zugriffsdatei öffnen nicht";
          break;
        case ES:
          sError = "No pudo abrir el fichero del acceso";
          break;
        case FR:
          sError = "N'a pas ouvert le fichier d'accès";
          break;
        case IT:
          sError ="Non è riuscito ad aprire l'archivio di accesso";
          break;
        case PT:
          sError = "Não abriu a lima do acesso";
          break;
        case EN:
        default:
          sError = "Failed to open Access File";
          break;
      }

      // Write the deck.
      startDeck( out, slLang, slCharset );
      out.println( "<p>" + sError + "</p>" );
      endDeck( out );

      // Proceed no further.
      break;
    }

    // Assume UID is incorrect.
    boolean validId = false;
    // Read the one line from the (/path/to/TELNO) login file.
    String logId = logonFile.readLine();
    // Each TELNO has at least one UID.
    StringTokenizer stContents = new StringTokenizer( logId, "," );
    // Loop through all login UIDs.
    while (stContents.hasMoreTokens()) {
      String slLogId = stContents.nextToken();
```

```
      // Determine if the file UID matches the user agent UID.
      if (slLogId.equalsIgnoreCase( slUID )) {
        validId = true;
      }
    }

    // Close the (/path/to/TELNO) login file.
    logonFile.close();

    if (!validId){

      // Login failed, inform user.
      String sError = new String();
      switch (iLang.intValue()) {
        case DE:
          sError = "Zugriff verweigerte";
          break;
        case ES:
          sError = "el acceso negó";
          break;
        case FR:
          sError = "accès nié";
          break;
        case IT:
          sError = "l'accesso ha negato";
          break;
        case PT:
          sError = "o acesso negou";
          break;
        case EN:
        default:
          sError = "Access Denied";
          break;
      }

      // Write the deck.
      startDeck( out, slLang, slCharset );
      out.println( "<do type=\"accept\" label=\"Cont\">");
      out.println( "<go href=\"http://localhost/wml/login.wml\">");
      out.println( "</go>");
      out.println( "</do>");
      out.println( "<p>" + sError + "</p>" );
      endDeck( out );
```

```java
          // Proceed no further.
          break;
      } else {
          // Fall through to next case.
      }

  case 3:
      // Choosing a movie
      try {
          // Open login file (/path/to/movies) for reading.
          movieFile = new RandomAccessFile( movieFileLoc , "r" );
      } catch (IOException e ) {
          movieFile = null;

          // Could not open movies file, inform client.
          String sError = new String();
          switch (iLang.intValue()) {
            case DE:
              sError = "konnte Filmdatei öffnen nicht";
              break;
            case ES:
              sError = "No pudo abrir el fichero de la película";
              break;
            case FR:
              sError = "N'a pas ouvert le fichier de film";
              break;
            case IT:
              sError = "Non è riuscito ad aprire l'archivio di movie";
              break;
            case PT:
              sError = "Não abriu a lima do filme";
              break;
            case EN:
            default:
              sError = "Failed to open Movie File";
              break;
          }

          // Write the deck.
          startDeck( out, slLang, slCharset );
          out.println( "<p>" + sError + "</p>" );
          endDeck( out );
```

Tailoring Multilingual Content

```
    // Proceed no further.
    break;
}

// Prompt user to choose movie.
String str = new String();
switch (iLang.intValue()) {

  case DE:
    str = "wählen Sie einen Film";
    break;
  case ES:
    str = "elija una película";
    break;
  case FR:
    str = "choisissez un film";
    break;
  case IT:
    str = "scelga un movie";
    break;
  case PT:
    str = "escolha um filme";
    break;
  case EN:
  default:
    str = "Choose Movie";
    break;
}

// Write the deck.
startDeck( out, slLang, slCharset );
out.println( "<do type=\"accept\" label=\"Details\">" );
out.println( "<go href=\"http://localhost/servlet/Cinema\" " +
  "method=\"post\">" );
out.println( "<postfield name=\"viewMovieNum\" " +
  "value=\"$(line)\"/>" );
out.println( "<postfield name=\"Action\" value=\"4\"/>" );
out.println( "</go>" );
out.println( "</do>" );
out.println( "<p>" );
out.println( "<select title=\"" + str + "\" name=\"line\">" );
```

```java
            // Build a list of movies from the movie file, index with
            // the value of line, which is incremented on each loop.
            int line = 0;
            long filePos = 0;
            movieFile.seek(0);
            while (filePos < movieFile.length()) {

              line ++;
              String slMovieInfo = movieFile.readLine();
              StringTokenizer slMovieDetails =
                new StringTokenizer( slMovieInfo, "%" );
              String slMovieTitle = slMovieDetails.nextToken();
              out.println("<option value=\"" + line + "\">" +
                slMovieTitle + "</option>");
              filePos = movieFile.getFilePointer();
            }
            // Close the (/path/to/movies) movies file.
            movieFile.close();

            out.println( "</select>" );
            out.println( "</p>" );
            endDeck (out);

            break;

          case 4:
            // Displaying movie information
            try {
              // Open login file (/path/to/movies) for reading.
              movieFile = new RandomAccessFile( movieFileLoc , "r" );
            } catch (IOException e ) {
              movieFile = null;

              // Could not open movies file, inform client.
              String sError = new String();
              switch (iLang.intValue()) {
                case DE:
                  sError = "konnte Filmdatei öffnen nicht";
                  break;
                case ES:
                  sError = "No pudo abrir el fichero de la película";
                  break;
```

```
      case FR:
        sError = "N'a pas ouvert le fichier de film";
        break;
      case IT:
        sError = "Non è riuscito ad aprire l'archivio di movie";
        break;
      case PT:
        sError = "Não abriu a lima do filme";
        break;
      case EN:
      default:
        sError = "Failed to open Movie File";
        break;
    }

    // Write the deck.
    startDeck( out, slLang, slCharset );
    out.println( "<p>" + sError + "</p>" );
    endDeck( out );

    // Proceed no further.
    break;
}

// Determine chosen movie and convert to integer.
String slMovieInfo = "";
String viewMovieNum =
  (String) request.getParameter( "viewMovieNum" );
int movieNum = Integer.parseInt( viewMovieNum );

// Declaring and initializing all the required variables
startDeck( out, slLang, slCharset );
out.println( "<do type=\"accept\" label=\"Book\">" );
out.println( "<go href=\"http://localhost/servlet/Cinema\" " +
  "method=\"post\">" );
out.println( "<postfield name=\"Action\" value=\"5\"/>" );
out.println( "</go>" );
out.println( "</do>" );
out.println( "<p>" );

// Loop through all movies until we find correct one.
for (int i = 0; i < movieNum; i ++){
```

```
        slMovieInfo = movieFile.readLine ();
      }

      // Build a list of details of the movie.
      StringTokenizer stMovieDetails =
        new StringTokenizer( slMovieInfo, "%" );

      while (stMovieDetails.hasMoreTokens()) {

        String slMovieInfoItem = stMovieDetails.nextToken();
        out.println( slMovieInfoItem );
        out.println( "<br/>" );
      }
      out.println( "</p>" );

      endDeck (out);
      break;

  case 5:
    // Reserving tickets
    switch (iLang.intValue()) {
      case DE:
        str = "wählen Sie Karten";
        break;
      case ES:
        str = "elija los boletos";
        break;
      case FR:
        str = "choisissez les billets";
        break;
      case IT:
        str = "scelga i biglietti";
        break;
      case PT:
        str = "escolha bilhetes";
        break;
      case EN:
      default:
        str = "Choose Tickets";
        break;
    }
```

Tailoring Multilingual Content

```java
        // Write the deck.
        startDeck (out, slLang, slCharset);

        out.println( "<do type=\"accept\" label=\"Book\">" );
        out.println( "<go href=\"http://localhost/servlet/Cinema\" " +
            "method=\"post\">");
        out.println( "<postfield name=\"Action\" value=\"6\"/>");
        out.println( "<postfield name=\"ROWA\" value=\"$ROWA\"/>");
        out.println( "<postfield name=\"ROWB\" value=\"$ROWB\"/>");
        out.println( "<postfield name=\"ROWC\" value=\"$ROWC\"/>");
        out.println( "</go>");
        out.println( "</do>");
        out.println( "<p>" + str + "<br/>" );
        out.println( "Row A:");
        out.println(
            "<input title=\"Row A\" name=\"ROWA\" format=\"*N\"/>");
        out.println( "Row B:");
        out.println(
            "<input title=\"Row B\" name=\"ROWB\" format=\"*N\"/>");
        out.println( "Row C:");
        out.println(
            "<input title=\"Row C\" name=\"ROWC\" format=\"*N\"/>");
        out.println( "</p>");

        endDeck( out );
        break;

    case 6:
        // Booking tickets

        // Convert strings returned by user agent to integers.
        String rowA = (String) request.getParameter( "ROWA" );
        String rowB = (String) request.getParameter( "ROWB" );
        String rowC = (String) request.getParameter( "ROWC" );
        if (rowA.length() == 0) {
            rowA = "0";
        }
        if (rowB.length() == 0) {
            rowB = "0";
        }
        if (rowC.length() == 0) {
            rowC = "0";
        }
```

```java
            int rowAnum = Integer.parseInt( rowA );
            int rowBnum = Integer.parseInt( rowB );
            int rowCnum = Integer.parseInt( rowC );

        // priceFile contains the ticket prices.
        try {
          // Open prices file (/path/to/prices) for reading.
          priceFile = new RandomAccessFile( priceFileLoc , "r" );

        } catch ( IOException e ) {
          priceFile = null;

          // Could not open price file, inform client.
          String sError = new String();
          switch (iLang.intValue()) {
            case DE:
              sError = "konnte Preisdatei öffnen nicht";
              break;
            case ES:
              sError = "no pudo abrir el fichero del precio";
              break;
            case FR:
              sError = "n'a pas ouvert le fichier des prix";
              break;
            case IT:
              sError = "non è riuscito ad aprire l'archivio di prezzi";
              break;
            case PT:
              sError = "não abriu a lima do preço";
              break;
            case EN:
            default:
              sError = "Failed to open Price File";
              break;
          }

          // Write the deck.
          startDeck( out, slLang, slCharset );
          out.println( "<p>" + sError + "</p>" );
          endDeck( out );

          // Proceed no further.
```

```
      break;
}

// Read the one line from the (/path/to/prices) file.
String tPrices = priceFile.readLine();

// Read the ticket prices from the (/path/to/prices) file.
StringTokenizer tPriceRow = new StringTokenizer(tPrices, ",");
priceFile.close();

// The ticket prices are stored as integers and are separated
// by commas in the file; e.g., 525,600,675.
int rowAtot =
   (new Integer(tPriceRow.nextToken ())).intValue() * rowAnum;
int rowBtot =
   (new Integer(tPriceRow.nextToken ())).intValue() * rowBnum;
int rowCtot =
   (new Integer(tPriceRow.nextToken ())).intValue() * rowCnum;

// Multiply the number of tickets in each row by the price of
// tickets in each row, then divide by 100.
int iPriceTotal = rowAtot + rowBtot + rowCtot;
Float fPriceTotal = new Float(iPriceTotal /100);

String sTicket,sPrice = new String();
switch (iLang.intValue()) {
   case DE:
     sTicket = "Karten angemeldet";
     sPrice  = "Gesamtpreis";
     break;
   case ES:
     sTicket = "boletos reservados";
     sPrice  = "precio total";
     break;
   case FR:
     sTicket = "billets réservés";
     sPrice  = "prix total";
     break;
   case IT:
     sTicket = "i biglietti hanno prenotato";
     sPrice  = "prezzo totale";
     break;
```

```
            case PT:
              sTicket = "os bilhetes registraram";
              sPrice  = "preço total";
              break;
            case EN:
            default:
              sTicket = "Tickets booked";
              sPrice  = "Total price";
              break;
          }

          startDeck (out, slLang, slCharset);
          out.println( "<do type=\"accept\" label=\"Confirm\">" );
          out.println( "<go href=\"http://localhost/wml/login.wml\"/>" );
          out.println( "</do>" );
          out.println( "<p>" + sTicket + "<br/>" );
          out.println( rowA + " row A<br/>" );
          out.println( rowB + " row B<br/>" );
          out.println( rowC + " row C<br/>" );
          out.println( sPrice + ":" + fPriceTotal );
          out.println( "</p>" );
          endDeck (out);
          break;
      }
    }

    private String getAppropriateLanguage (HttpServletRequest request) {
      // Obtain the accept-language range.
      String slAcceptLanguage =
        (String) request.getHeader( "Accept-Language" );
      // Process the accept-language only if the header was sent.
      if ( slAcceptLanguage != null ) {
        // Language tags are separated by comma, RFC2616 ss14.4.
        StringTokenizer stLanguage =
          new StringTokenizer( slAcceptLanguage, "," );
        // Loop through all language tags.
        while (stLanguage.hasMoreTokens()) {
          // Obtain the significant characters of the language tag.
          StringTokenizer stTag =
            new StringTokenizer( stLanguage.nextToken(), ";" );
```

```java
        // Convert to lowercase characters.
        String slTag = stTag.nextToken().trim().toLowerCase();
        // Does the tag appear in our supported languages hashtable?
        if ( htSupportedLanguages.containsKey( slTag ) ) {
          // Language supported, return the language code.
          return slTag;
        }
      }
    }
    return DEFAULT_LANGUAGE;
  }

  private void startDeck (
    PrintWriter out, String slLang, String slCharset) {
    out.println( "<?xml version=\"1.0\"?>" );
    out.println( "<!DOCTYPE wml PUBLIC" );
    out.println( "  \"-//WAPFORUM//DTD WML 1.1//EN\"" );
    out.println( "  \"http://www.wapforum.org/DTD/wml_1.1.xml\" >" );
    out.println( "<wml xml:lang=\""+slLang+"\">" );
    out.println( "<head>" );
    out.println( "<meta " +
       "http-equiv=\"Content-Language\" " +
       "content=\""+slLang+"\"/>" );
    if (slCharset != null) {
      if (slCharset.length() != 0) {
        out.println( "<meta " +
           "http-equiv=\"Content-Type\" " +
           "content=\"text/vnd.wap.wml; charset="+slCharset+"\"/>" );
      }
    }
    out.println( "</head>" );
    out.println( "<card id=\"Login\">" );
  }

  private void endDeck (PrintWriter out) {
    out.println( "</card>" );
    out.println( "</wml>" );
    out.close();
  }
}
```

There is more to internationalization than what's been presented in this chapter, such as paying attention to different date and time formats (and numerical and monetary formats) and sorting algorithms. We've demonstrated how to internationalize and localize your WAP site, concentrating specifically on natural-language and transfer encodings, which has provided enough information for you to understand the importance of a good foundation in internationalization. You can now apply this knowledge to develop great localized WAP sites!

Appendix A

WML Elements

This appendix lists all valid WML elements. WML elements follow the following syntax rules:

- WML tags (the WML element's start tag, end tag, or stand-alone tag) are enclosed in angle brackets: <...>. The tag has to follow the open bracket directly without space. WML is case sensitive, and all WML tags are lowercase.
- Tabs, blanks, carriage returns, and line feeds are treated as spaces. Spaces directly before or after a tag are ignored, with consecutive spaces being treated as one single space.
- Stand-alone tags such as <tag/> can appear anywhere in the text, while paired tags such as <tag> and </tag> enclose text and have the form <tag>...</tag>.

There are two core attributes that are applicable to all the WML elements:

- id="*valid XML name*" specifies a name to be associated with the element. It must be unique within the deck.
- class="*valid XML name*" specifies that the element is assigned to one or more classes (categories). To assign the element to more than one class, separate each class by a single space.

The xml:lang attribute is not a core attribute, as it does not apply to all elements, only those that may contain PCDATA (multiline text). We explained how to use the xml:lang attribute in Chapter 8, "Internationalizing Your WAP Service."

- xml:lang="*valid XML name*" specifies the natural language for the element and those elements nested within.

Where an element's attribute list contains "None," this indicates there are no extra attributes other than the preceding three attributes. Mandatory attributes appear in **boldface**, and default values are denoted by underlining.

<a>

Shortened form of the <anchor> element. It uses the <a> tag instead of the <anchor> tag and can be used only to define (implied) <go> tasks that require a URL specification. Unless you need to use the added functionality of the <anchor> element, you should instead use, and will often find yourself using, the <a> element. The following two lines are equivalent:

```
<a href ="deck.wml">Link</a>
<anchor>Link<go href="deck.wml"/></anchor>
```

The title and accesskey (from WML 1.2) attributes of the <a> element are identical to those of the <anchor> element.

Valid in

<p>, <fieldset>, <td>, <pre> (from WML 1.3)

Can contain

PCDATA, <br>, <img>

Attributes

- **href**="*absolute or relative URL, or variable references*" specifies the URL of the card or deck that is the target of the link.
- **title**="*string or variable reference*" specifies a brief description of this element, often ignored by small-device user agents.
- **accesskey**="*softkey identifier*" specifies a user agent soft key binding for this action (from WML 1.2).

Example

```
<p>
  <a href="deck.wml">Link</a>
  <a href="weather.wml"><img src="weather.wbmp"></a>
  <a href="purchase.wml" accesskey="1">Purchase</a>
</p>
```

<access>

This describes access control information for a WML deck. The deck's domain and path attributes specify what other decks can access it. The <access> element is placed in the <head> declaration. Each deck can have only one <access> element. All WML decks are publicly accessible by default; therefore, to allow everyone access to the "front door" of your WAP site, you should not use an <access> element at the main point of entry unless you wish to restrict access to known visitors—for example, to your extranet WAP site.

The domain attribute allows access to be limited to the current deck from a particular domain. If you do not specify the domain attribute, the default domain is your site, so only decks from the same site would be able to access the current deck.

The path attribute allows access to be limited to the current deck from a particular path prefix. Note that when using the path attribute, if you fail to specify the domain attribute, it defaults to the current domain.

Valid in

<head>

Can contain

Nothing

Attributes

- domain="*string*" limits access to this deck from a particular domain.
- path="*string*" limits access to decks residing in a particular path prefix.

Example

The following example restricts access to the current deck (which is hosted at http://wap.mydomain.com/private/example.wml) to only those decks hosted in the default domain (wap.mydomain.com) with a path prefix of /private/:

```
<head>
  <access path="/private/"/>
</head>
```

So, the following decks would be able to access the current deck:

- `http://wap.mydomain.com/private/index.wml`
- `http://wap.mydomain.com/private/main.wml`
- `http://wap.mydomain.com/private/user/home.wml`

but the following decks would be unable to access the current deck:

- `http://www.mydomain.com/private/index.wml`
- `http://wap.mydomain.com/index.wml`
- `http://wap.mydomain.com/priv/index.wml`
- `http://wap.mydomain.com/privateer/index.wml`
- `http://wap.yourdomain.com/private/index.wml`

`<anchor>`

This specifies the head of a link. It has a specified task: `go`, `prev`, or `refresh`. The `<anchor>` element anchors a task to a string of formatted text, known as a *link*. You can specify a link within any formatted text or image. When a user selects the link, the device executes the task.

The `title` attribute allows a text string to be associated with the element, which the user agent may or may not display. Even though the `title` attribute is often ignored by small-device user agents, you should use it to give a descriptive meaning to the anchor.

The `accesskey` attribute (from WML 1.2) specifies that the user agent should attempt to assign a key, which may be a soft key or a particular button, to this action. Not all user agents support access keys.

Valid in

`<p>`, `<fieldset>`, `<td>`, `<pre>` (from WML 1.3)

Can contain

PCDATA, <br>, <img>; one of <go>, <prev>, or <refresh>

Attributes

- title="*string or variable reference*" specifies a brief description of this element, often ignored by small-device user agents.
- accesskey="*softkey identifier*" specifies a user agent soft key binding for this action (from WML 1.2).

Example

```
<anchor> Link <go href="page.wml"/> </anchor>
<anchor> Back <prev/> </anchor>
<anchor> Refresh <refresh/> </anchor>
```

<b>

Text formatting rendered with boldface font. The <b>, <big>, <em>, <i>, <small>, <strong>, and <u> elements are used to display different rendered text, but are not supported on all browsers. Although these elements are valid, nesting them may produce unexpected results. They are all optional in WML 1.2, but it is recommended that <em> and <strong> be used in preference.

Valid in

<p>, <td>, <fieldset>, <br>, emphasis elements

Can contain

PCDATA, <br>, emphasis elements, <a>, <anchor>, <table>

Attributes

None

Example

```
<p>
  <b>Sample text</b>
</p>
```

`<big>`

The `<big>` element specifies large-font text. The `<b>`, `<big>`, `<em>`, `<i>`, `<small>`, `<strong>`, and `<u>` elements are used to display different rendered text, but are not supported on all browsers. Although these elements are valid, nesting them may produce unexpected results. They are all optional in WML 1.2, but it is recommended that `<em>` and `<strong>` be used in preference.

Valid in

`<p>`, `<td>`, `<fieldset>`, `<br>`, emphasis elements

Can contain

PCDATA, `<br>`, emphasis elements, `<a>`, `<anchor>`, `<table>`

Attributes

None

Example

```
<p>
  <big>Sample text</big>
</p>
```

`<br>`

The `<br>` break element is used to end a current line and begin a new one.

Valid in

<p>, <a>, <anchor>, <fieldset>, <td>

Can contain

Nothing

Attributes

None

Example

```
<p>
  + $$12.50<br/>
  + $$37.25<br/>
  + $$42.50<br/>
  = $$92.25
</p>
```

<card>

A card makes up the contents of a deck. A WML deck consists of one or more <card> elements, each specifying a single interaction between the user and the WAP device. WAP devices display a maximum of one card at a time—in some cases, however, a single card may appear as a series of screens.

Valid in

<wml>

Can contain

<p>, <do>, <onevent>, <timer>, <pre> (from WML 1.3)

Attributes

- `title="string"` specifies a label for the card.
- `newcontext="true|false"` reinitializes the card's browser context.
- `ordered="true|false"` is an indication to the user agent on card ordering.
- `onenterforward="url"` loads the URL when this card is entered on a forward navigation including by bookmark or direct entry.
- `onenterbackward="url"` loads the URL when this card is entered on a backward navigation.
- `ontimer="url"` loads the URL when the timer expires.
- `id="string"` provides a name for this card, unique within the deck.

Example

```
<card id="FirstCard" title="Welcome" newcontext=true" ordered="true">
  <p>
    <!-- content -->
  </p>
</card>
```

CDATA

The CDATA section enables you to provide literal text that will not be treated as markup. This keeps you from having to escape certain characters, such as dollar ($) and ampersand (&), with just one restriction—your literal text cannot contain the CDATA terminating sequence (]]>).

Valid in

PCDATA, emphasis elements, `<br>`, `<img>`, `<a>`, `<anchor>`, `<table>`, `<input>`, `<select>`, `<fieldset>`, `<do>`

Can contain

Literal text

Attributes

This is not a WML element and possesses no attributes.

Example

```
<p>
  <![CDATA[This literal text will not be treated as markup
  We can use special WML characters here like $, &, < and >
  without us having to escape them, as we need to below ]]>
  $$, &amp; &lt; &;gt
</p>
```

<do>

The <do> element enables you to perform actions on both cards and decks. The user agent will bind the <do> element to some soft key or button, or perhaps add an item to a menu. Note that the implementation of the <do> element is diverse across all user agents. You should not develop your <do> elements for one specific user agent, unless there is a compelling reason.

The mandatory type attribute suggests to the user agent how to bind the <do> element, which is likely to be different across user agents.

The label attribute allows a text string to be associated with the element, which the user agent may or may not display.

Valid in

<template>, <card>, <p>, <fieldset>, <pre> (from WML 1.3)

Can contain

One of <go>, <prev>, <noop>, or <refresh>

Attributes

- **type**="accept|prev|help|reset|options|delete|unknown" specifies the type of task binding.

- accept defines a positive acceptance (an OK) providing forward navigation.
- prev defines a negative response (a Cancel) providing backward navigation.
- help defines a help request.
- reset defines a state (variables) resetting task.
- options defines a request for context-sensitive options.
- delete deletes a context-sensitive item or choice.
- unknown defines a generic task.

- label="*string or variable reference*" specifies a label for the task binding.
- name="*valid XML name*" specifies a name for the task binding.
- optional="true|<u>false</u>" specifies whether the user agent may ignore the binding.

Example

When Next is selected, the user is taken to the card next.wml.

```
<card>
  <do type="accept" label="Next">
    <go href="next.wml"/>
  </do>
</card>
```

<em>

The <em> element specifies emphasized text. The <b>, <big>, <em>, <i>, <small>, <strong>, and <u> elements are used to display different rendered text, but are not supported on all browsers. Although these elements are valid, nesting them may produce unexpected results. They are all optional in WML 1.2, but it is recommended that <em> and <strong> be used in preference.

Valid in

<template>, <card>, <p>, <fieldset>, <pre> (from WML 1.3)

Can contain

PCDATA, <br>, emphasis elements, <a>, <anchor>, <table>

Attributes

None

Example

```
<p>
  <em>Sample text</em>
</p>
```

<fieldset>

The <fieldset> element allows you to group multiple text or input elements within a card. This allows easy control over card navigation. Specifying one or more <fieldset> elements lets you suggest to the device how it should present card content to simplify user navigation.

The title attribute allows a text string to be associated with the element, which the user agent may display.

Valid in

<p>, <fieldset>

Can contain

PCDATA, emphasis elements, <br>, <img>, <a>, <anchor>, <table>, <input>, <select>, <fieldset>, <do>

Attributes

- title="*string*" specifies a brief description of this element, often ignored by small-device user agents.

Example

```
<fieldset title="name">
  Insert Name
  <input type="text" name="Name" maxlength="15"/>
</fieldset>
<fieldset title="title">
  Insert Title
  <input type="text" name="Title" maxlength="10"/>
</fieldset>
```

<go>

The <go> task defines forward navigation to a URL, which may be another card, another deck, a particular card in another deck, or a WMLScript function.

The href attribute specifies the URL to load when the task is activated. The current location is pushed to the stack, unless the location is a WMLScript function.

The sendreferer attribute specifies whether the location of the current deck is sent with the forthcoming request in the HTTP header "Referer". You may wish to use this for dynamically created WML to enforce security over incoming requests (similar to the <access> element).

The method attribute specifies the HTTP request method to use for the forthcoming request, which may be get or post.

The accept-charset attribute informs the user agent (where the WML is currently being executed) how to encode the <go> data in the request to the server. The accept-charset attribute contains either one or more encodings (see Chapter 8, "Internationalizing Your WAP Service") that the server will accept, separated by a comma or a space. Note that the user agent may not support particular encodings.

The enctype attribute (from WML 1.2) informs the user agent of the Content-type of the request to be sent to the server. The default value of application/x-www-form-urlencoded is acceptable when the content of the <postfield> elements contains only US-ASCII characters; otherwise, you should use multipart/form-data, but you must combine this with method="post".

The cache-control attribute (from WML 1.3) allows the browser cache to be ignored. When cache-control="no-cache", the URL of the <go> element will always be retrieved from the server.

Valid in

<postfield>, <setvar>

Can contain

<do>, <onevent>, <anchor>

Attributes

- href="*absolute or relative URL, or variable references*" specifies the URL to load when the task is activated.
- sendreferer="true|<u>false</u>" specifies whether the current deck's URL is sent with the request.
- method="post|<u>get</u>" specifies the HTTP request method to use.
- accept-charset="*string*" specifies a list of acceptable charsets for the response.
- enctype="<u>application/x-www-form-urlencoded</u>| multipart/form-data" specifies the request content type (from WML 1.2). Note that multipart/form-data must use method="post".
- cache-control="no-cache" specifies whether the gateway and the browser shall ignore caches (from WML 1.3).

Example

```
<p>
  <go href="file.wml" method="post">
    <postfield name="a" value="1"/>
    <postfield name="b" value="2"/>
  </go>
</p>
```

> **NOTE** Specifying content for the `<go>` element is optional. If you don't specify any content, you must use the syntax `<go attributes/>` rather than `<go attributes>content</go>`.

`<head>`

This contains information relating to the deck as a whole, including metadata and access control information, and must include either an `<access>` or `<meta>` element.

Valid in

`<wml>`

Can contain

`<access>`, `<meta>`

Attributes

None

Example

```
<head>
  <access domain="mydomain.com" path="/private"/>
  <meta http-equiv="charset" content="UTF-8"/>
</head>
```

`<i>`

Specifies italics font text. The `<b>`, `<big>`, `<em>`, `<i>`, `<small>`, `<strong>`, and `<u>` elements are used to display different rendered text, but are not supported on all browsers. Although these elements are valid, nesting them may produce unexpected results. They are all optional in WML 1.2, but it is recommended that <em> and <strong> be used in preference.

Valid in

<p>, <td>, <fieldset>, <br>, emphasis elements

Can contain

PCDATA, emphasis elements

Attributes

None

Example

```
<p>
  <i>Italicized text</i>
</p>
```

<img>

This is used to place images in the card. They are not directly embedded into the card; instead, the <img> element contains a reference to an image file, which may be retrieved separately. All user agents that support graphics must support the monochrome bitmap format WBMP. As of WML 1.2, user agents that support color graphics must support the PNG format, though some user agents and SDKs support formats such as BMP, GIF, and JPG. If your WAP site uses images, you should restrict it to deliver WBMP images, unless there is some compelling reason otherwise.

The mandatory alt attribute specifies to the user agent alternative text should the image not be displayed (for example, if the user agent doesn't support graphics, the user has disabled images, or the image URL does not exist). If no alternative text is appropriate, the empty string " " or just a single space " " (depending on the user agent) should be used.

The mandatory src attribute specifies the URL of the image.

The `localsrc` attribute overrides the `src` attribute and specifies a user agent device-specific image that the browser can display immediately without having to perform a request from the server.

The `vspace` and `hspace` attributes inform the user agent to separate the image from the surrounding text.

The `height` and `width` attributes inform the user agent of the image's size, which may be used to display the deck, considering the size required for the image while accessing the server, with the image to be later displayed.

Valid in

<img>, <fieldset>, <td>

Can contain

Nothing

Attributes

- `alt="string or variable reference"` specifies the text to appear if the image cannot be displayed.
- `src="absolute or relative URL, or variable references"` specifies the URL of the image.
- `localsrc="string or variable reference"` identifies the local device's image, if available.
- `vspace="0|pixels|percentage"` specifies the amount of vertical padding around the image.
- `hspace="0|pixels|percentage"` specifies the amount of horizontal padding around the image.
- `align="top|middle|bottom"` specifies the alignment of the image relative to the surrounding text.
- `height="pixels|percentage"` specifies how much vertical space to allow for the image.
- `width="pixels|percentage"` specifies how much horizontal space to allow for the image.

Example

```
<p>
  Happiness
  <img alt=":-)" localsrc="face" src="smiley.wbmp"/>
</p>
```

`<input>`

The `<input>` element allows you to enter text that is assigned to a specified variable. This element is likely to be interpreted in the most varied ways by user agents. Typically, the user agent will display the initial value of the input field with some method of changing it.

The `name` attribute identifies a variable to which the contents of the input element will be assigned.

The `value` attribute specifies the default value of the `name` variable. It is used when the user's input is invalid.

Valid in

`<p>`, `<fieldset>`

Can contain

Nothing

Attributes

- `name="string"` specifies the name of the variable used to hold the input value.
- `title="string"` specifies a brief description of this element, often ignored by small-device user agents.
- `value="string"` specifies the default value of the named attribute.
- `type="text|password"` specifies whether the input field is displayed or hidden.

- `format="format"` specifies the format of the input field.
    - A: Uppercase alphabetic character or punctuation
    - a: Lowercase alphabetic character or punctuation
    - N: Numeric character
    - X: Symbolic, numeric, or uppercase alphabetic character (not changeable to lowercase)
    - x: Symbolic, numeric, or lowercase alphabetic character (not changeable to uppercase)
    - M: Symbolic, numeric, or uppercase alphabetic character (changeable to lowercase)
    - m: Symbolic, numeric, or lowercase alphabetic character (changeable to uppercase)
    - *f: Zero or more characters matching the format code f (for example, "*A")
    - nf: Up to n (1–9) characters matching the format code f (for example, "3A")
    - \c: Adds the literal character c to the value (for example, "\-")
- `emptyok="true|false"` specifies whether the field may be left blank.
- `size="numeric"` specifies the width in characters of the text input area.
- `maxlength="numeric"` specifies the maximum number of allowed inputted characters.
- `tabindex="numeric"` specifies the tabbing position of the current element.
- `accesskey="softkey identifier"` specifies a user agent soft key binding for this action (from WML 1.2).

Example

```
<p>
  Your name
  <input type="text" name="Name" maxlength="25"/><br/>
  Your job
  <input type="text" name="Job" maxlength="20" tabindex="4"/>
</p>
```

`<meta>`

Contains the meta information relating to the WML deck. It is specified within the deck header along with any access control information for the deck. It is often used for defining user agent–specific features or to assist the WAP gateway with HTTP headers.

The mandatory `name` or `http-equiv` attribute identifies the metadata's purpose. Metadata with a `name` attribute is usually stripped by the WAP gateway, and if not, is usually ignored by the user agent. Metadata with an `http-equiv` attribute may be used to generate HTTP response headers—for example, to control caching. However, even if you specify `forua="true"`, the meta element may reach the user agent—there is no guarantee that the WAP gateway will perform the translation.

The `forua` attribute specifies whether the meta element should not be stripped from the WML by the WAP gateway. Specifying `forua="true"` ensures that the user agent will see the element.

The `content` attribute specifies the value of the metadata.

Valid in

<head>

Can contain

Nothing

Attributes

- `name|http-equiv="string"` specifies the name of the metadata.
- `forua="true|false"` specifies whether the data is intended for the user agent.
- `content="string"` specifies the data.
- `scheme="string"` specifies additional information about the metadata.

Example

<head>

```
<meta http-equiv="charset" content="UTF-8"/>
</head>
```

\<noop\>

The <noop> element is a task element that instructs the device to do nothing.

Valid in

<do>, <onevent>

Can contain

Nothing

Attributes

None

Example

```
<wml>
  <template>
    <do type="options" name="do">
      <prev/>
    </do>
  </template>
  <card id="first">
    <!-- card information -->
  </card>
  <card id="second">
    <do type="options" name="do">
      <noop/> <!-- do not assume template level do action -->
    </do>
  </card>
</wml>
```

<onevent>

The <onevent> element associates a state transition or intrinsic event. Each transition is associated with a type and a task. When the intrinsic event occurs, the device performs the associated <onevent> task.

The mandatory type attribute specifies the type of event binding.

- The onenterforward and onenterbackward event bindings are used to define effects other than those normally associated with navigation (most likely to be used to create or reset a certain variable state).
- The onpick event binding allows a task such as input validation to be specified that will be executed when the user selects an option from a select list.
- The ontimer event binding allows a task to be specified that will be executed when a timer expires.

Valid in

<template>, <card> (onpick type valid only in <option>)

Can contain

One of <go>, <prev>, <noop>, or <refresh>

Attributes

- type="onenterforward|onenterbackward|onpick|ontimer" specifies the type of intrinsic event option binding.
    - onenterforward events occur when a card is entered as a result of forward navigation.
    - onenterbackward events occur when a card is entered as a result of a backward navigation.
    - onpick events occur when a user selects or deselects an option in a list.
    - ontimer events occur when a timer expires.

Example

```
<!-- navigating back to a url -->
<card>
  <onevent type="onenterbackward">
    <go href="mydomain.com/page.wml"/>
  </onevent>
</card>
```

`<optgroup>`

The `<optgroup>` element allows the grouping of multiple or nested options within a card. Creating option groups lets you specify control information about how the device should present the card content.

Valid in

`<select>`, `<optgroup>`

Can contain

`<option>`, `<optgroup>` (`<optgroup>` elements must contain at least one `<option>` or `<optgroup>` element)

Attributes

- `title="string"` specifies a brief description of this element, often ignored by small-device user agents.

Example

See `<option>` element for example.

`<option>`

The `<option>` element specifies a particular choice within the `<select>` element.

Valid in

`<select>`, `<optgroup>`

Can contain

PCDATA, `<onevent type="onpick">` (the `<option>` element cannot possess both an `onpick` attribute and an `<onevent type="onpick">` element)

Attributes

- `title="string"` specifies a brief description of this element, often ignored by small-device user agents.

- `value="string"` specifies the value to assign to the variable defined in the `<select name="variable">` element.

- `onpick="url"` specifies the URL to open if selected.

Example

```
<wml>
  <!-- Selecting a Hotel -->
  <card id="main" title="Hotel">
    <p>
      Select a Hotel
      <select name="hotel" multiple="true">
        <optgroup title="London">
          <option value="1">The Hilton</option>
          <option value="2">The Ritz</option>
          <option value="3">The Royal</option>
        </optgroup>
      </select>
    </p>
  </card>
</wml>
```

`<p>`

Specifies a new paragraph, and its alignment and line-wrapping attributes.

Valid in

    <card>

Can contain

PCDATA, emphasis elements, `<br>`, `<img>`, `<a>`, `<anchor>`, `<table>`, `<input>`, `<select>`, `<fieldset>`, `<do>`

Attributes

- `align="left|center|right"` specifies the alignment of the paragraph.
- `mode="wrap|nowrap"` specifies whether long lines are wrapped to the device's screen width.

Example

```
<card id="main">
  <p align="left">
    Sample text is left aligned.
  </p>
  <p align="center">
    Sample text is centered.
  </p>
  <p align="right">
    Sample text is right aligned.
  </p>
  <p mode="wrap">
    A large amount of text is wrapped to the next line.
  </p>
</card>
```

`<postfield>`

Defines name and value pairs that are passed to the HTTP server receiving the `<go>` request. The `<postfield>` element may be used with either HTTP method, `"post"` or `"get"`.

Valid in

<go>

Can contain

Nothing

Attributes

- **name**=*"valid XML name"* identifies the variable sent to the server.
- **value**=*"string or variable reference"* identifies the content of the variable sent to the server.

Example

```
<p>
  <go href="file.wml" method="post">
    <postfield name="a" value="1"/>
    <postfield name="b" value="2"/>
  </go>
</p>
```

<pre>

Available from WML 1.2 onward. Specifies preformatted (fixed pitch) text.

Valid in

<card>

Can contain

PCDATA, <a>, <br>, <i>, <b>, <em>, <strong>, <input>, <select> (from WML 1.3 <anchor>, <do>, <u>)

Attributes

None

Example

```
<p>
  <pre>
    -A- -B- -C- Total
    1.5 2.5 3.5  7.5
    2.5 3.5 4.5 10.5
    3.5 4.5 5.5 13.5
  </pre>
</p>
```

`<prev>`

Used to navigate to the previous URL in the stack. It is a *task* element that instructs the device to remove the current URL from the history stack and open the previous URL. If no previous URL exists in the history stack, specifying `<prev>` has no effect.

Valid in

`<do>`, `<onevent>`, `<anchor>`

Can contain

`<setvar>`

Attributes

None

Example

```
<wml>
  <template>
```

```
        <do type="options" name="do" label="back">
          <prev/>
        </do>
      </template>
    </wml>
```

Prologue

The XML document prologue is used to define the WML deck. It is required at the start of every deck and contains the reference to the DTD (document type definition) of the particular version of WML.

Valid in

Only at the very start of the deck before <wml>

Can contain

Nothing, though the deck (starting with <wml>) follows

Attributes

None

Example

```
<?xml version="1.0"?>
<!DOCTYPE wml PUBLIC "-//WAPFORUM//DTD WML 1.1//EN"
  "http://www.wapforum.org/DTD/wml_1.1.xml" >
```

<refresh>

Used to refresh the specified card variables. The device also refreshes the display if any of those variables are currently shown.

Valid in

<do>, <onevent>, <anchor>

Can contain

<setvar>

Attributes

None

Example

```
<!-- refresh input variable field -->
<refresh>
  <setvar name="user" value=""/>
</refresh>
```

<select>

Specifies a list of options to select from. The options list can be either a single-select list or a multiple-select list. Each individual option in the list is defined by an <option> element. Hierarchical lists are defined using <optgroup> elements.

The `name` attribute identifies a variable to which the contents of the select element will be assigned.

The `iname` and `ivalue` attributes determine which options are selected when the select list is initially displayed. For multiple-select lists, `iname` accepts a semicolon-separated list of indices.

The `value` attribute specifies the default value of the `name` variable. It is used when the user's input is invalid.

Valid in

<p>, <fieldset>

Can contain

<option>, <optgroup>

Attributes

- name="*valid XML name*" specifies a name for the select list.
- value="*string or variable reference*" specifies the default value of the name variable.
- iname="*valid XML name*" indicates the name of the variable to be set with the index result of the selection. The index result is the position of the currently selected option in the select list. An index of zero indicates that no option is selected.
- ivalue="*string or variable reference*" specifies the initial selected option element.
- multiple="true|<u>false</u>" specifies that the select list should accept multiple selections.
- tabindex="*numeric*" specifies the tabbing position of the current element.

Example

```
<wml>
  <!-- Selecting a Hotel -->
  <card id="main" title="Hotel">
    <p>
      Select a Hotel
      <select name="hotel" multiple="true">
        <optgroup title="London">
          <option value="1">The Hilton</option>
          <option value="2">The Ritz</option>
          <option value="3">The Royal</option>
        </optgroup>
      </select>
    </p>
  </card>
</wml>
```

\<setvar\>

This sets a variable to a specified value when the device executes a \<go\>, \<prev\>, or \<refresh\> task.

Valid in

\<go\>, \<prev\>, \<refresh\>

Can contain

Nothing

Attributes

- **name**="*valid XML name*" specifies the variable name to be assigned.
- **value**="*string or variable reference*" specifies the new content of the variable.

Example

```
<setvar name="user" value=""/>
```

\<small\>

Text formatting rendered with small font. The \<b\>, \<big\>, \<em\>, \<i\>, \<small\>, \<strong\>, and \<u\> elements are used to display different rendered text, but are not supported on all browsers. Although these elements are valid, nesting them may produce unexpected results. They are all optional in WML 1.2, but it is recommended that \<em\> and \<strong\> be used in preference.

Valid in

\<p\>, \<td\>, \<fieldset\>, \<br\>, emphasis elements

Can contain

PCDATA, emphasis elements

Attributes

None

Example

```
<p>
  <small>Sample text</small>
</p>
```

`<strong>`

Specifies strongly emphasized text. The `<b>`, `<big>`, `<em>`, `<i>`, `<small>`, `<strong>`, and `<u>` elements are used to display different rendered text, but are not supported on all browsers. Although these elements are valid, nesting them may produce unexpected results. They are all optional in WML 1.2, but it is recommended that `<em>` and `<strong>` be used in preference.

Valid in

`<p>`, `<td>`, `<fieldset>`, `<br>`, emphasis elements

Can contain

PCDATA, emphasis elements

Attributes

None

Example

```
<p>
  <strong>Sample text</strong>
</p>
```

`<table>`

The `<table>` element is used with `<tr>` and `<td>` to define aligned columns for text or images.

Valid in

`<p>`, `<fieldset>`

Can contain

`<tr>`

Attributes

- `title="string"` specifies a table caption, often ignored by small-device user agents.
- `align="L|C|R"` specifies the alignment of the table (`"L|C|D|R"` from WML 1.2, the D indicating default alignment).
- `columns="number"` specifies the number of columns in the table.

Example

```
<table columns="2">
  <tr>
    <td> ..... </td><td> .... </td>
  </tr>
</table>
```

<td>

This is used to hold a single table cell within a table row. Table cells may be empty. The user agent should make its best effort to deal with multiple-line data cells that may result from using images or line breaks.

Valid in

<tr>

Can contain

PCDATA, emphasis elements, <br>, <img>, <a>, <anchor>

Attributes

None

Example

```
<table columns="2">
  <tr>
    <td> ..... </td><td> .... </td>
  </tr>
</table>
```

<template>

This element declares a template for cards in the deck. It is used in conjunction with types and can be seen as a procedural navigational method. A WML deck may contain a <template> element that defines deck-level event bindings or characteristics that apply to all cards in the deck. You can override these characteristics on a card-by-card basis by specifying the same event bindings within the <card> definition.

Valid in

<wml>

Can contain

<onevent>, <do>

Attributes

- `onenterforward="`*absolute or relative URL, or variable references*`"` specifies the URL to load when a card is entered by forward navigation, or by a bookmark or direct entry.

- `onenterbackward="`*absolute or relative URL, or variable references*`"` specifies the URL to load when a card is entered by backward navigation.

- `ontimer="`*absolute or relative URL, or variable references*`"` specifies the URL to load when a card's timer expires.

Example

```
<!-- Navigation to previous card -->
<template>
  <do type="prev" label="previous">
    <prev/>
  </do>
</template>
```

<timer>

The <timer> element is used to implement a process within a card (the standard unit process is one-tenth of a second). A timer event may expire even when the user is navigating within the card.

Valid in

<select>, <optgroup>

Can contain

Nothing

Attributes

- name="*valid XML name*" specifies a name to control the timer.
- value="*string or variable reference*" specifies the expiry time in tenths of a second.

Example

```
<!-- Displays welcome text message then goes next card -->
<wml>
  <card id="splash" ontimer="#main">
    <timer value="30"/>
    <p>
      Welcome to the site
    </p>
  </card>
  <card id="main">
    <!-- rest of card -->
  </card>
</wml>
```

<tr>

This is used to hold a single table row.

Valid in

<table>

Can contain

<td>

Attributes

None

Example

```
<table columns="2">
  <tr>
    <td> ..... </td><td> .... </td>
  </tr>
</table>
```

<u>

Underlines text.

Valid in

`<p>`, `<td>`, `<fieldset>`, `<br>`, emphasis elements

Can contain

PCDATA, emphasis elements

Attributes

None

Example

```
<p>
  <u>Sample text</u>
</p>
```

<wml>

Defines the WML deck, and encloses all information and cards in it.

Valid in

Nothing

Can contain

<head>, <template>, <card>

Attributes

None

Example

```
<wml>
  <head>
    <meta http-equiv="charset" content="UTF-8"/>
  </head>
  <template>
  <do type="prev" label="previous">
    <prev/>
  </do>
  </template>
  <card id="main">
    <!-- rest of card -->
  </card>
</wml>
```

Appendix B

WMLScript Reference

WMLScript uses standard logic syntax operators such as for, if, and while, together with an extensive suite of operators. However, WMLScript is constrained by the restrictions inherent in the wireless environment and is relatively limited in scope with restricted coding capabilities.

WMLScript consists of six standard libraries:

Dialogs library This consists of functions that direct the WAP device to display prompts and messages.

Float library This is the only optional library and consists of functions that perform mathematical procedures and determine numeric boundary information from the WAP device.

Lang library This consists of functions that perform operations on integer and floating point numbers, create absolute values, determine support parameters, create random numbers, and stop code execution.

String library This consists of functions used to manipulate strings.

URL library This consists of functions for the manipulation and validation of URLs (Uniform Resource Locators).

WMLBrowser library This consists of functions used to navigate the information and content associated with a WML card.

The Dialogs Library

The Dialogs library allows you to interact with the user.

Dialogs.alert

The alert() function displays a message, suspending program execution until the user presses a key.

Syntax

```
Dialogs.alert(message)
```

Arguments

- message: a string displayed by the user agent

Returns

An empty string

Exceptions

None

Example

```
Dialogs.alert("Your transaction number is 03074287971");
```

Dialogs.confirm

The confirm() function displays a message, suspending program execution until the user presses a key, interpreted as a positive acknowledgment or negative response. The user agent device may support soft key labeling, in which case, the labels specified in the arguments acceptlabel and rejectlabel are presented (try to limit the length of the labels). Otherwise, some other device-specific controls will be used.

Syntax

```
Dialogs.confirm(message, acceptlabel, rejectlabel)
```

Arguments

- String message: a string displayed by the user agent
- String acceptlabel: a positive response string the user agent may offer to the user
- String rejectlabel: a negative response string the user agent may offer to the user

Returns

- Boolean true: if the user gave a positive response
- Boolean false: if the user gave a negative response

Exceptions

None

Example

```
result = Dialogs.confirm("Book tickets?","Yes","No");
if (result) {
  // Process booking.
} else {
  // Back out.
}
```

Dialogs.prompt

The prompt() function displays a message, suspending program execution until the user provides some input. The value default contains the initial value of the input and is thus used as the default value should the user not enter a different value prior to accepting the prompt.

Syntax

```
Dialogs.prompt(message, default)
```

Arguments

- String message: a string displayed by the user agent
- String default: a string value, used as the initial value, and the default value of the input

Returns

- String: containing the user's input or the default value

Exceptions

None

Example

```
hours = Dialogs.confirm("Enter working hours per week","40");
```

The Float Library

The Float library contains common functions for the manipulation of floating point numbers. Not all user agent devices implement the Float library functions, and where that is the case, the return value is always invalid. You can use the Lang.float() function to determine whether the user agent's device supports the Float library.

Float.ceil

The ceil() function computes and returns the next integer value greater than the floating point value passed.

Syntax

```
Float.ceil(number)
```

Arguments

- Float number: a floating point value

Returns

- Integer: an integer greater than or equal to the argument number

Exceptions

Returns invalid if number is not a number or if Float library is unsupported

Example

```
a = Float.ceil(-2.5);          // a = -2
b = Float.ceil(0.0);           // b = 0
c = Float.ceil(3.14159265);    // c = 4
d = Float.ceil("pi");          // d = invalid
```

Float.floor

The floor() function computes and returns the next integer value less than the floating point value passed.

Syntax

```
Float.floor(number)
```

Arguments

- `Float number`: a floating point value

Returns

- `Integer`: an integer less than or equal to the argument `number`

Exceptions

Returns `invalid` if `number` is not a number or if Float library is unsupported

Example

```
a = Float.floor(-2.5);         // a = -3
b = Float.floor(0.0);          // b = 0
c = Float.floor(3.14159265);   // c = 3
d = Float.floor("pi");         // d = invalid
```

Float.int

The `int()` function returns the integer value part of the floating point value passed.

Syntax

```
Float.int(number)
```

Arguments

- `Float number`: a floating point value

Returns

- `Integer`: the integer part of the argument `number`

Exceptions

Returns invalid if number is not a number or if Float library is unsupported

Example

```
a = Float.int(-2.5);        // a = -2
b = Float.int(0.0);         // b = 0
c = Float.int(3.14159265);  // c = 3
d = Float.int("pi");        // d = invalid
```

Float.maxFloat

The maxFloat() function returns the largest positive floating point value that can be represented by the user agent device.

Syntax

```
Float.maxFloat()
```

Arguments

None

Returns

- Float: the largest positive floating point value that can be represented

Exceptions

Returns invalid if the Float library is unsupported

Example

```
a = Float.maxFloat();   // a = 3.40282347E+38
```

Float.minFloat

The minFloat() function returns the smallest positive floating point value that can be represented by the user agent device.

Syntax

    Float.minFloat()

Arguments

None

Returns

- Float: the smallest positive floating point value that can be represented

Exceptions

Returns invalid if the Float library is unsupported

Example

    a = Float.minFloat();   // a = 1.17549435E-38

Float.pow

The pow() function returns the calculation of raising one number to the power of another number.

Syntax

    Float.pow(mantissa, exponent)

Arguments

- Float mantissa: a floating point number to be raised to the power of the exponent
- Float|Integer exponent: a floating point number specifying the power by which the mantissa should be multiplied. If the mantissa is a negative number, the exponent must be an integer.

Returns

- Float: the result of the calculation mantissa raised to the power of exponent

Exceptions

Returns `invalid` if `mantissa` is 0.0 and exponent is negative; `mantissa` is negative and exponent is not an integer; or the Float library is unsupported

Example

```
a = Float.pow(2,3);      // a = 8.0
b = Float.pow(2.0, -2);  // b = 0.25
c = Float.pow(-5, 3.5);  // c = invalid
```

Float.round

The round() function returns the closest integer to the passed floating point number, rounding up as appropriate.

Syntax

`Float.round(number)`

Arguments

- `Float number`: a floating point number

Returns

- `Integer`: the closest integer to the passed floating point `number`, rounding up to the next integer if the fractional part of the floating point number is 0.5 or above

Exceptions

Returns `invalid` if the Float library is unsupported

Example

```
a = Float.round(5.0);   // a = 5
b = Float.round(5.5);   // b = 6
c = Float.round(-5.5);  // c = -6
d = Float.round(-5.0);  // d = -5
```

Float.sqrt

The sqrt() function returns the square root of the passed floating point number.

Syntax

```
Float.sqrt(number)
```

Arguments

- Integer|Float number: an integer or floating point number

Returns

- Float: the square root of the passed floating point number

Exceptions

Returns invalid if number is invalid or if the Float library is unsupported

Example

```
a = Float.sqrt(65536);   // a = 256
b = Float.sqrt(20.25);   // b = 4.5
c = Float.sqrt(-1.5);    // c = invalid
```

The Lang Library

The Lang library contains core WMLScript functions similar to those found in ECMAScript core language and Math and Number libraries.

Lang.abort

The abort() function stops processing of the current WMLScript and passes control back to the user agent. This function should be used only as a last resort when your WMLScript can progress no further.

Syntax

`Lang.abort(message)`

Arguments

- `String message`: a descriptive message string. `invalid` may be passed, which results in the string "invalid" being used by the user agent.

Returns

`Nothing`

Exceptions

None

Example

`Lang.abort("Software Error, processing failed");`

Lang.abs

The `abs()` function returns the absolute (positive integer) part of a number.

Syntax

`Lang.abs(number)`

Arguments

- `Integer|Float|String|Boolean number`: an integer, floating point number, string representation of a number, or Boolean value

Returns

- `Integer`: the absolute (positive integer) part of a `number`

Exceptions

Returns `invalid` if the argument passed cannot be converted to a number

Example

```
a = Lang.abs(-5);         // a = 5
b = Lang.abs(9.23);       // b = 9
c = Lang.abs("9.23");     // c = 9
d = Lang.abs(-9.23);      // d = 9 (not -9)
e = Lang.abs("-9.23");    // e = 9 (not -9)
f = Lang.abs(true);       // f = 1
g = Lang.abs("number");   // g = invalid
```

Lang.characterSet

The characterSet() function returns an integer that represents the current character set according to the MIBEnum value from IANA.

Syntax

```
Lang.characterSet()
```

Arguments

None

Returns

- Integer: an integer corresponding to the IANA MIBEnum value of the current character set. Table B.1 lists common MIBEnum values and their character sets.

TABLE B.1: Common IANA MIBEnum Character Set Values

MIBEnum	Character Set	Alias	Example Languages
4	ISO-8859-1	Latin 1	Western European
5	ISO-8859-2	Latin 2	Eastern European
6	ISO-8859-3	Latin 3	Southern European
7	ISO-8859-4	Latin 4	Northern European
8	ISO-8859-5	Cyrillic	Bulgarian, Russian, Serbian, Ukrainian
9	ISO-8859-6	Arabic	Arabic

Continued on next page

TABLE B.1 CONTINUED: Common IANA MIBEnum Character Set Values

MIBEnum	Character Set	Alias	Example Languages
10	ISO-8859-7	Greek	Greek
11	ISO-8859-8	Hebrew	Hebrew, Yiddish
12	ISO-8859-9	Latin 5	Turkish
13	ISO-8859-10	Latin 6	Inuit, Nordic
(unlisted)	ISO-8859-11	Thai	Thai
109	ISO-8859-13	Latin 7	Baltic Rim
110	ISO-8859-14	Latin 8	Celtic
111	ISO-8859-15	Latin 9	"Latin 1" languages
17	shift_jis	Kanji	Japanese
36	KS_C_5601-1987	Korean	Korean
37	ISO-2022-KR	Korean	Korean
2025	GB2312	Chinese	Simplified Chinese
2026	Big5	Chinese	Traditional Chinese
106	UTF-8	(None)	Unicode (all) languages
1015	UTF-16	(None)	Unicode (all) languages

Exceptions

None

Example

```
a = Lang.characterSet();   // a = 4
```

Lang.exit

The exit() function causes a normal processing exit from WMLScript.

Syntax

```
Lang.exit(returnvalue)
```

Arguments

- `Integer|Float|String|Boolean returnvalue`: any value, which the user agent is likely to ignore as it will not understand WMLScript data types

Returns

Nothing. Execution of WMLScript is terminated.

Exceptions

None

Example

```
Lang.exit("Result = " + result);
Lang.exit(returnvalue);
Lang.exit(invalid);
```

Lang.float

The `float()` function determines whether floating point is supported on the device.

Syntax

```
Lang.float()
```

Arguments

None

Returns

- `Boolean`: `true` if floating point support is available, `false` otherwise

Exceptions

None

Example

```
if (!Lang.float()) {
  if (Dialogs.confirm("No floating point ", "Accept", "Quit")) {
    // Perform approximations using integers.
  } else {
    // Quit application.
  }
}
```

Lang.isFloat

The isFloat() function determines whether a value can be represented as a floating point value.

Syntax

```
Lang.isFloat(number)
```

Arguments

- Integer|Float|String|Boolean number: any value

Returns

- Boolean: true if the value number can be represented as a floating point value using Lang.parseFloat(), false otherwise

Exceptions

Returns invalid if Float library is unsupported

Example

```
a = Lang.isFloat(" -100");        // a = true
b = Lang.isFloat("3.14");         // b = true
c = Lang.isFloat("  3.14e1 Hz");  // c = true
d = Lang.isFloat("  1.30pm  ");   // d = false
```

```
e = Lang.isFloat("1");              // e = true
f = Lang.isFloat("");               // f = false
g = Lang.isFloat("number");         // g = false
h = Lang.isFloat(true);             // h = false
i = Lang.isFloat(invalid);          // i = invalid
```

Lang.isInt

The `isInt()` function determines whether a value can be represented as an integer value.

Syntax

```
Lang.isInt(number)
```

Arguments

- `Integer|Float|String|Boolean number`: any value

Returns

- `Boolean`: true if the value number can be represented as an integer value using `Lang.parseInt()`, false otherwise

Exceptions

None

Example

```
a = Lang.isInt(" -100");            // a = true
b = Lang.isInt("3.14");             // b = false
c = Lang.isInt("  3.14e1 Hz");      // c = false
d = Lang.isInt("  1.30pm  ");       // d = false
e = Lang.isInt("1");                // e = true
f = Lang.isInt("");                 // f = false
g = Lang.isInt("number");           // g = false
h = Lang.isInt(true);               // h = false
i = Lang.isInt(invalid);            // i = invalid
```

Lang.max

The max() function returns the larger of the two numbers.

Syntax

```
Lang.max(number1, number2)
```

Arguments

- Integer|Float number1: an integer or floating point number
- Integer|Float number2: an integer or floating point number

Returns

- Integer|Float: the larger of the two arguments number1, number2

Exceptions

Returns invalid if either of the two arguments cannot be converted to a number, or if either of the two arguments is a floating point number and the Float library is unsupported

Example

```
a = Lang.max(10,-1);       // a = 10
b = Lang.max(5,2.5);       // b = 5
c = Lang.max(5,5.5);       // c = 5.5
d = Lang.max(1,1.0);       // d = 1 or 1.0 depending on user agent
e = Lang.max(0,true);      // e = 1
f = Lang.max(-1,false);    // f = 0
g = Lang.max(0,"number");  // g = invalid
```

Lang.maxInt

The maxInt() function returns the maximum integer that can be represented by the user agent.

Syntax

```
Lang.maxInt()
```

Arguments

None

Returns

- `Integer`: the largest integer that can be represented by the user agent

Exceptions

None

Example

```
a = Lang.maxInt();   // a = 2147483647
```

Lang.min

The `min()` function returns the smaller of two numbers.

Syntax

```
Lang.min(number1, number2)
```

Arguments

- `Integer|Float number1`: an integer or floating point number
- `Integer|Float number2`: an integer or floating point number

Returns

- `Integer|Float`: the smaller of the two arguments `number1, number2`

Exceptions

Returns `invalid` if either of the two arguments cannot be converted to a number, or if either of the two arguments is a floating point number and the Float library is unsupported

Example

```
a = Lang.min(10,-1);       // a = -1
b = Lang.min(5,2.5);       // b = 2.5
c = Lang.min(5,5.5);       // c = 5
d = Lang.min(1,1.0);       // d = 1 or 1.0 depending on user agent
e = Lang.min(0,true);      // e = 0
f = Lang.min(-1,false);    // f = -1
g = Lang.min(0,"number");  // g = invalid
```

Lang.minInt

The minInt() function returns the minimum number that can be represented by the user agent.

Syntax

```
Lang.minInt()
```

Arguments

None

Returns

- Integer: the largest integer that can be represented by the user agent

Exceptions

None

Example

```
a = Lang.minInt();   // a = -2147483648
```

Lang.parseFloat

The parseFloat() function returns a floating point numeric value converted from another data type.

Syntax

```
Lang.parseFloat(number)
```

Arguments

- Integer|Float|String|Boolean number: any value

Returns

- Float: the floating point conversion of the passed number

Exceptions

Returns invalid if the argument number cannot be converted to a floating point number or if the Float library is unsupported

Example

```
a = Lang.parseFloat(" -100");        // a = -100.0
b = Lang.parseFloat("3.14");         // b = 3.14
c = Lang.parseFloat("  3.14e1 Hz");  // c = 3.14
d = Lang.parseFloat("  1.30pm  ");   // d = 1.0
e = Lang.parseFloat("1");            // e = 1.0
f = Lang.parseFloat("");             // f = invalid
g = Lang.parseFloat("number");       // g = invalid
h = Lang.parseFloat(true);           // h = invalid
i = Lang.parseFloat(invalid);        // i = invalid
```

Lang.parseInt

The parseInt() function returns an integer numeric value converted from another data type.

Syntax

```
Lang.parseInt(number)
```

Arguments

- Integer|Float|String|Boolean number: any value

Returns

- Float: the integer conversion of the passed number

Exceptions

Returns invalid if the argument number cannot be converted to an integer

Example

```
a = Lang.parseInt(" -100");        // a = -100
b = Lang.parseInt("3.14");         // b = invalid
c = Lang.parseInt("  3.14e1 Hz");  // c = invalid
d = Lang.parseInt("  1.30pm  ");   // d = invalid
e = Lang.parseInt("1");            // e = 1
f = Lang.parseInt("");             // f = invalid
g = Lang.parseInt("number");       // g = invalid
h = Lang.parseInt(true);           // h = invalid
i = Lang.parseInt(invalid);        // i = invalid
```

Lang.random

The random() function returns a pseudo random integer number.

Syntax

```
Lang.random(upperlimit)
```

Arguments

- Integer upperlimit: an integer denoting the upper limit of the random range

Returns

- Integer: a pseudo random integer between 0 and the argument upperlimit inclusive

Exceptions

Returns 0 if the argument upperlimit is zero, or returns invalid if the argument upperlimit is negative. If a floating point value is specified for the argument upperlimit, it is automatically converted to an integer.

Example

```
a = Lang.random(0);       // a = 0
b = Lang.random(100);     // b = integer between 0 and 100 inclusive
c = Lang.random(100.0);   // c = integer between 0 and 100 inclusive
d = Lang.random(-1);      // d = invalid
```

Lang.seed

The seed() function initializes the random number generator.

Syntax

`Lang.seed(number)`

Arguments

- Integer number: an integer seed for the random number generator. Reseeding with the same nonnegative value results in the same sequence of generated random numbers. Reseeding with a negative value produces device-specific results.

Returns

- String: an empty string

Exceptions

Returns invalid if the argument number cannot be converted to an integer

Example

```
s = 100;
Lang.seed(s);
a = Lang.random(s);    // a = 76 (for example)
b = Lang.random(s);    // b = 27 (for example)
c = Lang.random(s);    // c = 96 (for example)
d = Lang.random(s);    // d = 66 (for example)
Lang.seed(s);
e = Lang.random(s);    // e = 76 (for example)
f = Lang.random(s);    // f = 27 (for example)
g = Lang.random(s);    // g = 96 (for example)
h = Lang.random(s);    // h = 66 (for example)
```

The String Library

The String library contains string manipulation functions. Of those functions that take an index as an argument, the index is zero-based. Those functions that operate on *whitespace* use any of the space, tab, carriage return, linefeed, vertical tab, and form feed characters as delimiters.

String.charAt

The charAt() function obtains an indexed character from within a string.

Syntax

```
String.charAt(string, number)
```

Arguments

- String string: any string to obtain particular reference within
- Integer number: zero-based index into argument string

Returns

- String: a one-character string containing the character within argument string at zero-based index argument number, or an empty string if the argument number is equal to or greater than the length of the argument string

Exceptions

Returns invalid if the string argument string cannot be converted to a string or if the argument index cannot be converted to an integer

Example

```
a = String.charAt("WAP", 1);    // a = "A"
b = String.charAt("WAP", 10);   // b = ""
```

String.compare

The compare() function compares two strings.

Syntax

```
String.compare(string1, string2)
```

Arguments

- `String string1`: any string
- `String string2`: any string

Returns

- `Integer`: an indication, based on the current character set, of whether the argument `string1` precedes argument `string2` in a lexicographical sort. The return value is –1 if `string1` precedes `string2`, 0 if the strings are equal, and 1 if `string1` succeeds `string2`.

Exceptions

Returns `invalid` if any of the string arguments cannot be converted to a string

Example

```
s = Lang.characterSet();           // s = 4 (ISO-8859-1)
a = String.compare("WAP", "wap");  // a = -1
b = String.compare("WAP", "WAP");  // b = 0
c = String.compare("wap", "WAP");  // c = 1
```

String.elementAt

The `elementAt()` function returns an enumerated list element.

Syntax

```
String.elementAt(string, index, delimiter)
```

Arguments

- `String string`: any string, even the empty string
- `Integer index`: zero-based index into argument `string`
- `String delimiter`: a delimiter character, even the empty string

Returns

- String: the zero-based indexed element in argument string interpreted as a list when argument delimiter is applied as a separator. If index is negative, 0 is used; if index is equal to or greater than the number of elements in the list, the last element is returned. The empty string is returned if the list is empty.

Exceptions

Returns invalid if any of the string arguments cannot be converted to a string or if the argument index cannot be converted to an integer.

Example

```
u = "host.mydomain.com";
a = String.elementAt(u, -1, ".");   // a = "host"
b = String.elementAt(u, 0, ".");    // b = "host"
c = String.elementAt(u, 1, ".");    // c = "mydomain"
d = String.elementAt(u, 2, ".");    // d = "com"
e = String.elementAt(u, 3, ".");    // e = "com"
```

String.elements

The elements() function enumerates the elements in a list.

Syntax

```
String.elements(string, delimiter)
```

Arguments

- String string: any string, even the empty string
- String delimiter: a delimiter character

Returns

- Integer: the number of elements in argument string interpreted as a list when argument delimiter is applied as a separator

Exceptions

Returns `invalid` if any of the string arguments cannot be converted to a string or if the argument `delimiter` is the empty string

Example

```
a = String.elements("host.mydomain.com", ".");      // a = 3
b = String.elements("host.mydomain.com", ".com");   // b = 3
c = String.elements("host.mydomain.com/", "/");     // c = 2
d = String.elements("WAP", ".");                    // d = 1
e = String.elements("WAP", "");                     // e = 1
f = String.elements("/", "/");                      // f = 2
```

String.find

The `find()` function.

Syntax

```
String.find(string, substring)
```

Arguments

- `String string`: any string, even the empty string
- `String substring`: a string to find within argument `string`

Returns

- Integer: the zero-based index of the first character of the first occurrence (left to right) of the string `substring` within the argument `string`, or −1 if `substring` does not occur within argument `string`

Exceptions

Returns `invalid` if any of the string arguments cannot be converted to a string, or if the argument `substring` is the empty string

Example

```
a = String.find("host.mydomain.com", "host");       // a = 0
b = String.find("host.mydomain.com", "mydomain");   // b = 5
c = String.find("host.mydomain.com", "com");        // c = 14
d = String.find("host.mydomain.com", "www");        // d = -1
e = String.find("", "host.mydomain.com");           // e = -1
f = String.find("host.mydomain.com", "");           // f = invalid
```

String.format

The format() function formats a value to a string format template, very similar to the printf() function in the C programming language.

Syntax

```
String.format(format, value)
```

Arguments

- String format: any string. Format characters are presented in the following syntax (bracketed expressions are optional):

    - %[width][.precision]formattype

    surrounded by any other characters (as the percent character is already used in the format string, use two percent characters [%%] to represent one), where:

        - optional width is a positive integer specifying the minimum number of characters to hold the argument value. If the formatted value consists of fewer characters than width, it will be prepended (filled on the left) with spaces; however, if the formatted value consists of more characters than width, it will not be truncated.

        If typecode is d (decimal), the argument value will be formatted as an integer.

        If typecode is f (floating point), the argument value will be formatted as a floating point.

        If typecode is s (string), the argument value will be formatted as a string.

- optional `precision` is a positive integer specifying the number of decimal places to be used in formatting argument `value`. Its meaning (and default value) is variable depending on the `formattype` used:

  If `typecode` is d (decimal), `precision` is interpreted as the minimum number of digits to be used in formatting the whole of argument `value`, prepended with 0s should `precision` be larger than the number of digits in argument `value`.

  If `typecode` is f (floating point), `precision` is interpreted as the number of digits after the decimal point in argument `value` to format, appended with 0s should `precision` be larger than the number of digits after the decimal point in argument `value`.

  If `typecode` is s (string), `precision` is interpreted as the maximum number of characters for argument `value`, and no padding is performed.

- `Integer|Float value`: a number to be converted to a string using the formatting specified in argument `format`

Returns

- `String`: a string containing the results of formatting the argument `value` according to argument `format`

Exceptions

Returns `invalid` if the string argument `string` cannot be converted to a string or if the argument `format` is unsupported

Example

```
a = String.format("rate = %d%%", 100);      // a = "rate = 100%"
b = String.format("rate = %3d%%", 10);      // b = "rate =  10%"
c = String.format("rate = %d%%", 10);       // c = "rate = 10%"
d = String.format("rate = %.1f%%", 10.0) ;  // d = "rate = 10.0%"
e = String.format("rate = %5.1f%%", 10.0);  // e = "rate =  10.0%"
f = String.format("%s", true);              // e = "true"
g = String.format("%3f", 3.14159265);       // e = "3.141593"
h = String.format("%6d", 3.14159265);       // e = "3"
```

String.insertAt

The `insertAt()` function inserts a replacement element at a specified index of an enumerated list.

Syntax

```
String.insertAt(string, substring, index, delimiter)
```

Arguments

- `String string`: any string, even the empty string
- `String substring`: a string to replace the current element
- `Integer index`: zero-based index into argument `string`
- `String delimiter`: a delimiter character, even the empty string

Returns

- `String`: a copy of the argument `string` with the argument `substring` inserted before the zero-based indexed element, appended with the `delimiter`. If the argument `index` is negative, `substring` is inserted at the start of the returned string. If `index` is greater than the number of elements in `string`, then `substring` will be appended to the returned string. If argument `string` is empty, a new string will be returned containing just `substring`.

Exceptions

Returns `invalid` if any of the string arguments cannot be converted to a string or if the argument `index` cannot be converted to an integer

Example

```
a = String.insertAt("1 2 3 4", "0", 0, " ");   // a = "0 1 2 3 4"
b = String.insertAt("", "new", 5, " ");        // b = "new"
```

String.isEmpty

The `isEmpty()` function determines whether a string has zero length.

Syntax

```
String.isEmpty(string)
```

Arguments

- String string: any string, even the empty string

Returns

- Boolean: true if the number of characters in argument string is zero, false otherwise

Exceptions

Returns invalid if the string argument string cannot be converted to a string

Example

```
a = String.isEmpty("1234");      // a = false
b = String.isEmpty("");          // b = true
d = String.isEmpty(true);        // d = false
e = String.isEmpty(invalid);     // e = false
```

String.length

The length() function returns the length of a string.

Syntax

```
String.length(string)
```

Arguments

- String string: any string, even the empty string

Returns

- Integer: the number of characters in argument string

Exceptions

Returns invalid if the string argument string cannot be converted to a string

Example

```
a = String.length("1234");       // a = 4
b = String.length(1234);         // b = 4
c = String.length("");           // c = 0
d = String.length(true);         // d = 4
e = String.length(invalid);      // e = 7
```

String.removeAt

The removeAt() function removes an element at a specified index of an enumerated list.

Syntax

```
String.removeAt(string, index, delimiter)
```

Arguments

- String string: any string, even the empty string
- Integer index: zero-based index into argument string
- String delimiter: a delimiter character

Returns

- String: a copy of the argument string with the argument substring and its adjacent delimiter (if any) removed at the zero-based indexed element. If the argument index is negative, the first substring is removed. If index is greater than the number of elements in string, the last substring is removed. If argument string is empty, an empty string will be returned.

Exceptions

Returns invalid if any of the string arguments cannot be converted to a string or if the argument index cannot be converted to an integer

Example

```
a = String.removeAt("0 1 2 3 4", 0, " ");   // a = "1 2 3 4"
b = String.removeAt("0 1 2 3 4", 2, " ");   // b = "0 1 3 4"
c = String.removeAt("0 1 2 3 4", 9, " ");   // b = "0 1 2 3"
```

String.replace

The `replace()` function replaces every matched portion of a string with another portion.

Syntax

```
String.replace(string, oldsubstring, newsubstring)
```

Arguments

- String string: any string, even the empty string
- String oldsubstring: a string containing characters in argument string to be replaced with argument newsubstring
- String newsubstring: a string containing characters to replace those characters specified in argument oldsubstring, which are present in argument string

Returns

- String: a copy of the argument string with all the occurrences of argument oldsubstring replaced with corresponding contents of argument newsubstring

Exceptions

Returns `invalid` if any of the string arguments cannot be converted to a string or if the argument oldsubstring is the empty string

Example

```
s = "first-name_last-name@mydomain.com";
a = String.replace(s, "-", "");
b = String.replace(s, "_", ".");
//  b = "firstname.lastname@mydomain.com"
```

String.replaceAt

The `replaceAt()` function replaces an element at a specified index of an enumerated list.

Syntax

```
String.replaceAt(string, newsubstring, index, delimiter)
```

Arguments

- `String string`: any string, even the empty string
- `String newsubstring`: replacement string
- `Integer index`: zero-based index into argument `string`
- `String delimiter`: a delimiter character

Returns

- `String`: a copy of the argument `string` with the zero-based index element replaced with the argument `newsubstring`. If the argument `index` is negative, the first element is replaced. If `index` is greater than the number of elements in `string`, the last element is replaced. If argument `string` is empty, a string containing just `newsubstring` will be returned.

Exceptions

Returns `invalid` if any of the string arguments cannot be converted to a string or if the argument `index` cannot be converted to an integer

Example

```
a = String.replaceAt("0 1 2 3 4", 0, "X", " ");  // a = "X 1 2 3 4"
b = String.replaceAt("0 1 2 3 4", 2, "-", " ");  // b = "0 1 - 3 4"
c = String.replaceAt("0 1 2 3 4", 9, "X", " ");  // b = "0 1 2 3 X"
```

String.squeeze

The `squeeze()` function reduces all whitespace in a string to a single space.

Syntax

```
String.squeeze(string)
```

Arguments

- `String string`: any string, even the empty string

Returns

- String: a copy of the argument string with multiple consecutive sequences of whitespace characters reduced to just one space

Exceptions

None

Example

```
a = " Mary\r\n   had\r\n   a\r\n   little\r\n   lamb ";
a = String.squeeze(a);   // a = " Mary had a little lamb "
```

String.subString

The subString() function extracts a copy of a portion of a string.

Syntax

```
String.subString(string, index, length)
```

Arguments

- String string: any string, even the empty string
- Integer index: zero-based index into argument string
- Integer length: number of characters in portion to extract a copy of

Returns

- String: a copy of a portion of the argument string starting at zero-based index for length characters

Exceptions

If the argument index is negative, it is taken to be 0, indicating the start of argument string. If index is greater than the length of string, an empty string is returned. If index and length are such that the end of the portion would be greater than the length of string, just the end of string is returned; it is not padded.

Example

```
a = "mary had a little lamb";
length = String.length(a);            // length = 22
b = String.subString(a,0,length);     // b = "mary had a little lamb";
c = String.subString(a,-1,length));   // c = "mary had a little lamb";
d = String.subString(a,20,10);        // d = "mb";
```

String.toString

The `toString()` function returns a string representation of the passed argument regardless of type.

Syntax

```
String.toString(value)
```

Arguments

- `Integer|Float|String|Boolean value`: any value

Returns

- `String`: a string representation of the passed argument value with the additional conversion of `invalid` to `"invalid"`

Exceptions

None

Example

```
a = String.toString(0);          // a = "0"
b = String.toString("");         // b = ""
c = String.toString(true);       // c = "true"
d = String.toString("WAP");      // d = "WAP"
e = String.toString(invalid);    // e = "invalid"
```

String.trim

The `trim()` function removes all leading and trailing whitespace in a string.

Syntax

```
String.trim(string)
```

Arguments

- String string: any string, even the empty string

Returns

- String: a copy of the argument string with leading and trailing whitespace removed

Exceptions

None

Example

```
a = " Mary\r\n   had\r\n   a\r\n   little\r\n   lamb ";
a = String.trim(a);   // a = "Mary\r\n   had\r\n   a\r\n   little\r\n   lamb"
```

The URL Library

The URL library contains functions for the manipulation and validation of URLs (Uniform Resource Locators). The library does not contain an exhaustive list of functions required, but it does contain the most important functions. Note that except in the case of resolve(), the return values are relative URLs.

URL.escapeString

The escapeString() function converts a string replacing any occurrences of characters requiring *escaping* (as defined in RFC 2396) with the relevant hexadecimal escape sequence.

Syntax

```
URL.escapeString(string)
```

Arguments

- String string: any string, even the empty string

Returns

- String: a copy of the argument string with any occurrences of characters that require escaping replaced by the relevant hexadecimal escape sequence

Exceptions

Returns invalid if the argument string contains characters above 0xFF

Example

```
u = "host.mydomain.com";
p = "calculate price";
r = "checkout.wml";
a = "%00245/MED;+46/BL:DK";
b = "$24.50@1";
u =
    "http://" + URL.escapeString(u) +
    "/" + URL.escapeString(p) +
    "/" + URL.escapeString(r) +
    "?" + URL.escapeString("article") +
    "=" + URL.escapeString(a) +
    "&" + URL.escapeString("price") +
    "=" + URL.escapeString(b);

// u = "http://host.mydomain.com/calculate%20price/checkout.wml
     ➥?article=%2500245%2fMED%3b%2b46%2fBL%3aDK&price=%2424.50%401"
```

URL.getBase

The getBase() function returns a string containing the URL of the current WMLScript file.

Syntax

```
URL.getBase()
```

Arguments

None

Returns

- String: a string that contains the URL of the current WMLScript file without fragment (the part after the WMLScript filename), which comprises scheme, host, port, path, and script, as in the following:

    scheme://*host*:*port*/*path*/*script*;parameters?query#fragment

Exceptions

None

Example

```
// URL = "http://host.mydomain.com:80/path/script;x;y?x=1#frag";
a = URL.getBase();   // a = "http://host.mydomain.com:80/path/script"
```

URL.getFragment

The getFragment() function returns a string containing the fragment part of a URL.

Syntax

```
URL.getFragment(url)
```

Arguments

- String url: a string containing a well-formed URL

Returns

- String: a string that contains the fragment part of the url argument, as in the following:

    scheme://host:port/path/script;parameters?query#***fragment***

Exceptions

Returns invalid if the URL is not syntactically correct

Example

```
// URL = "http://host.mydomain.com:80/path/script;x;y?x=1#frag";
a = URL.getFragment();   // a = "frag"
```

URL.getHost

The getHost() function returns a string containing the host part of a URL.

Syntax

```
URL.getHost(url)
```

Arguments

- String url: a string containing a well-formed URL

Returns

- String: a string that contains the host part of the url argument, as in the following:

    scheme://**host**:port/path/script;parameters?query#fragment

Exceptions

Returns invalid if the URL is not syntactically correct

Example

```
// URL = "http://host.mydomain.com:80/path/script;x;y?x=1#frag";
a = URL.getHost();   // a = "host.mydomain.com"
```

URL.getParameters

The getParameters() function returns a string containing the parameters part of a URL.

Syntax

```
URL.getParameters(url)
```

Arguments

- String url: a string containing a well-formed URL

Returns

- String: a string that contains the parameters part of the url argument, as in the following:

    scheme://host:port/path/script;***parameters***?query#fragment

Exceptions

Returns invalid if the URL is not syntactically correct

Example

```
// URL = "http://host.mydomain.com:80/path/script;x;y?x=1#frag";
a = URL.getParameters();    // a = "x;y"
```

URL.getPath

The getPath() function returns a string containing the path part of a URL.

Syntax

```
URL.getPath(url)
```

Arguments

- String url: a string containing a well-formed URL

Returns

- String: a string that contains the path part of the url argument, as in the following:

    scheme://host:port/***path***/script;parameters?query#fragment

Exceptions

Returns invalid if the URL is not syntactically correct

Example

```
// URL = "http://host.mydomain.com:80/path/script;x;y?x=1#frag";
a = URL.getPath();   // a = "path"
```

URL.getPort

The getPort() function returns a string containing the port part of a URL.

Syntax

```
URL.getPort(url)
```

Arguments

- String url: a string containing a well-formed URL

Returns

- String: a string that contains the port part of the url argument, as in the following:

    scheme://host:**port**/path/script;parameters?query#fragment

Exceptions

Returns invalid if the URL is not syntactically correct

Example

```
// URL = "http://host.mydomain.com:80/path/script;x;y?x=1#frag";
a = URL.getPort();   // a = "80"
```

URL.getQuery

The getQuery() function returns a string containing the query string part of a URL.

Syntax

```
URL.getQuery(url)
```

Arguments

- String url: a string containing a well-formed URL

Returns

- String: a string that contains the query string part of the url argument, as in the following:

    scheme://host:port/path/script;parameters?*query*#fragment

Exceptions

Returns invalid if the URL is not syntactically correct

Example

```
// URL = "http://host.mydomain.com:80/path/script;x;y?x=1#frag";
a = URL.getQuery();   // a = "x=1"
```

URL.getReferer

The getReferer() function returns a string containing the contents of the HTTP Referer header on the request for this WMLScript file.

Syntax

```
URL.getReferer()
```

Arguments

None

Returns

- String: a string that contains the smallest possible relative URL to the resource that performed the request for the currently executing WMLScript file, as declared in the HTTP Referer header. If no such header exists, the empty string is returned.

Exceptions

None

Example

```
a = URL.getReferer();   // a = "index.wml#choice"
```

URL.getScheme

The getScheme() function returns a string containing the scheme part of a URL.

Syntax

```
URL.getScheme(url)
```

Arguments

- String url: a string containing a well-formed URL

Returns

- String: a string that contains the scheme part of the url argument, as in the following:

    scheme://host:port/path/script;parameters?query#fragment

Exceptions

Returns invalid if the URL is not syntactically correct

Example

```
// URL = "http://host.mydomain.com:80/path/script;x;y?x=1#frag";
a = URL.getScheme();   // a = "http"
```

URL.isValid

The isValid() function determines whether a string contains a well-formed URL.

Syntax

```
URL.isValid(url)
```

Arguments

- String url: a string containing a URL to be syntactically validated

Returns

- Boolean: true if the argument url contains a syntactically valid well-formed URL, false otherwise

Exceptions

None

Example

```
a = URL.isValid("http://w.hst.com/script#func()");      // a = true
b = URL.isValid("../common#test()");                    // b = true
c = URL.isValid("experimental?://www.host.com/cont>");  // c = false
```

URL.loadString

The loadString() function returns the content at a specified URL.

Syntax

```
URL.loadString(url, contenttype)
```

Arguments

- String url: a string containing a well-formed URL
- String contenttype: a string containing a MIME content type; the type must be *text*, but the subtype may be anything. For example, the following are valid contenttype arguments:
  - text/plain
  - text/html
  - text/vnd.wap.wml
  - text/x-vcard

  but the following are not valid contenttype arguments:
  - multipart/mixed
  - application/octet-stream
  - video/mpeg

Returns

- `Boolean`: `true` if the argument `url` contains a syntactically valid well-formed URL, `false` otherwise

Exceptions

Returns `invalid` if the argument `contenttype` is erroneous and an `Integer` error-code (which depends on the scheme used—e.g., HTTP, FTP) if the load fails

Example

```
u = "http://host.mydomain.com/vcards/manager.vcf";
s = URL.loadString(u, "text/x-vcard");

u = "http://host.yourdomain.com/news/headlines.html";
s = URL.loadString(u, "text/html");
```

URL.resolve

The `resolve()` function returns a relative URL resolved to its base.

Syntax

```
URL.resolve(base, relativeurl)
```

Arguments

- `String base`: a string containing a base hostname and optional path
- `String relativeurl`: a string representing a relative path to a file

Returns

- `String`: a string containing the absolute URL of the resolved base and relative URL

Exceptions

Returns `invalid` if either of the arguments contain malformed URLs

Example

```
a = URL.resolve("http://host.mydomain.com/path","index.wml");
// a = "http://host.mydomain.com/index.wml"

b = URL.resolve("http://host.mydomain.com/path/","index.wml");
// b = "http://host.mydomain.com/path/index.wml"

c = URL.resolve("http://host.mydomain.com/path/","/index.wml");
// c = "http://host.mydomain.com/index.wml"

d = URL.resolve("http://host.mydomain.com/path/","?a=1");
// d = "http://host.mydomain.com/path/?a=1"

e = URL.resolve("http://host.mydomain.com/path","?a=1");
// e = "http://host.mydomain.com/path?a=1"

f = URL.resolve("http://","index.wml"); // f = invalid
```

URL.unescapeString

The unescapeString() function converts a string replacing any occurrences of characters that have been *escaped* (as defined in RFC 2396) with the characters the hexadecimal sequences represent.

Syntax

```
URL.unescapeString(string)
```

Arguments

- String string: any string, even the empty string

Returns

- String: a copy of the argument string with any occurrences of characters that have been escaped replaced by the characters the hexadecimal sequences represent

Exceptions

Returns invalid if the argument string contains characters above 0xFF

Example

```
u = "http://host.mydomain.com/calculate%20price/checkout.wml
➥?article=%2500245%2fMED%3b%2b46%2fBL%3aDK&price=%2424.50%401"

u = URL.unescape(u);
// u = "http://host.mydomain.com/calculate price/checkout.wml
    ➥?article=%00245/MED;+46/BL:DK&price=$24.50@1"
```

The WMLBrowser Library

The WMLBrowser library contains functions for manipulating the WML browser (user agent). The functions take effect once the current WMLScript has completed execution.

WMLBrowser.getCurrentCard

The getCurrentCard() function returns a string containing the URL of the current WML card.

Syntax

```
WMLBrowser.getCurrentCard()
```

Arguments

None

Returns

- String: a string containing the URL of the browser's current WML card as the smallest relative URL to the current WMLScript file, or absolute URL should that not be possible

Exceptions

None

Example

```
u = WMLBrowser.getCurrentCard();
// u = "/wml/index.wml#choice"
```

WMLBrowser.getVar

The getVar() function returns a string containing the contents of a WML browser context variable.

Syntax

```
WMLBrowser.getVar(variable)
```

Arguments

- String variable: a string containing a legal WML browser context variable name

Returns

- String: a string containing the contents of the legal WML browser context variable, or the empty string if the variable does not have a value

Exceptions

Returns invalid if the argument variable is invalid in the WML browser context

Example

```
a = WMLBrowser.getVar("UID");   // a ="1234"
```

WMLBrowser.go

The go() function directs the WML browser to navigate to a new card.

Syntax

```
WMLBrowser.go(url)
```

Arguments

- `String url`: a string containing a well-formed URL

Returns

- `String`: an empty string

Exceptions

If the argument `url` is the empty string, no navigation is performed.

Example

```
// Reload current card.
WMLBrowser.go(WMLBrowser.getCurrentCard());
```

WMLBrowser.newContext

The `newContext()` function directs the WML browser to create a new context, similar to specifying `<go newcontext="true">` in WML, but without troubling the navigation history.

Syntax

```
WMLBrowser.newContext()
```

Arguments

None

Returns

- `String`: an empty string

Exceptions

None

Example

```
// Refresh current card's context.
WMLBrowser.newContext();
```

WMLBrowser.prev

The prev() function directs the WML browser to navigate to the previous (WMLScript-invoking) card, on completion of the current WMLScript file.

Syntax

```
WMLBrowser.prev()
```

Arguments

None

Returns

- String: an empty string

Exceptions

None

Example

```
// On completion, return to the calling WML card.
WMLBrowser.prev();
```

WMLBrowser.refresh

The refresh() function directs the WML browser to call the refresh task on completion of the current WMLScript file, causing the browser to refresh the display of the card, which is useful if WML variables have been altered within the current WMLScript.

Syntax

```
WMLBrowser.refresh()
```

Arguments

None

Returns

- String: an empty string

Exceptions

Returns invalid if immediate refresh unsupported

Example

```
// Refresh current card.
WMLBrowser.refresh();
```

WMLBrowser.setVar

The setVar() function directs the WML browser to set a WML browser context variable.

Syntax

```
WMLBrowser.setVar(variable, value)
```

Arguments

- String variable: a string containing a legal WML browser context variable name
- String value: a string containing the new value of the WML browser context variable name in argument variable

Returns

- Boolean: true if the assignment was successful, false otherwise

Exceptions

Returns invalid if the argument variable is invalid in the WML browser context

Example

```
a = WMLBrowser.setVar("UID", "1234");
```

Appendix C

ISO 639 Two-Letter Language Codes

Appendix C • ISO 639 Two-Letter Language Codes

TABLE C.1: ISO 639 Two-Letter Language Codes Ordered by Language

Language	Language Code
Abkhazian	ab
Afar	aa
Afrikaans	af
Albanian	sq
Amharic	am
Arabic	ar
Armenian	hy
Assamese	as
Avestan	ae
Aymara	ay
Azerbaijani	az
Bashkir	ba
Basque	eu
Belarusian	be
Bengali	bn
Bihari	bh
Bislama	bi
Bosnian	bs
Breton	br
Bulgarian	bg
Burmese	my
Catalan	ca
Chamorro	ch
Chechen	ce

Continued on next page

TABLE C.1 CONTINUED: ISO 639 Two-Letter Language Codes Ordered by Language

Language	Language Code
Chichewa; Nyanja	ny
Chinese	zh
Church Slavic	cu
Chuvash	cv
Cornish	kw
Corsican	co
Croatian	hr
Czech	cs
Danish	da
Dutch	nl
Dzongkha	dz
English	en
Esperanto	eo
Estonian	et
Faroese	fo
Fijian	fj
Finnish	fi
French	fr
Frisian	fy
Gaelic (Scots)	gd
Gallegan	gl
Georgian	ka
German	de
Greek, Modern (1453–)	el

Continued on next page

TABLE C.1 CONTINUED: ISO 639 Two-Letter Language Codes Ordered by Language

Language	Language Code
Guarani	gn
Gujarati	gu
Hausa	ha
Hebrew	he
Herero	hz
Hindi	hi
Hiri Motu	ho
Hungarian	hu
Icelandic	is
Indonesian	id
Interlingua (International Auxiliary Language Association)	ia
Interlingue	ie
Inuktitut	iu
Inupiaq	ik
Irish	ga
Italian	it
Japanese	ja
Javanese	jw
Kalaallisut	kl
Kannada	kn
Kashmiri	ks
Kazakh	kk
Khmer	km
Kikuyu	ki

Continued on next page

TABLE C.1 CONTINUED: ISO 639 Two-Letter Language Codes Ordered by Language

Language	Language Code
Kinyarwanda	rw
Kirghiz	ky
Komi	kv
Korean	ko
Kuanyama	kj
Kurdish	ku
Lao	lo
Latin	la
Latvian	lv
Letzeburgesch	lb
Lingala	ln
Lithuanian	lt
Macedonian	mk
Malagasy	mg
Malay	ms
Malayalam	ml
Maltese	mt
Manx	gv
Maori	mi
Marathi	mr
Marshall	mh
Moldavian	mo
Mongolian	mn
Nauru	na

Continued on next page

TABLE C.1 CONTINUED: ISO 639 Two-Letter Language Codes Ordered by Language

Language	Language Code
Navajo	nv
Ndebele, North	nd
Ndebele, South	nr
Ndonga	ng
Nepali	ne
Northern Sami	se
Norwegian	no
Norwegian Bokmål	nb
Norwegian Nynorsk	nn
Occitan (post 1500); Provençal	oc
Oriya	or
Oromo	om
Ossetian; Ossetic	os
Pali	pi
Panjabi	pa
Persian	fa
Polish	pl
Portuguese	pt
Pushto	ps
Quechua	qu
Raeto-Romance	rm
Romanian	ro
Rundi	rn
Russian	ru

Continued on next page

TABLE C.1 CONTINUED: ISO 639 Two-Letter Language Codes Ordered by Language

Language	Language Code
Samoan	sm
Sango	sg
Sanskrit	sa
Sardinian	sc
Serbian	sr
Shona	sn
Sindhi	sd
Sinhalese	si
Slovak	sk
Slovenian	sl
Somali	so
Sotho, Southern	st
Spanish	es
Sundanese	su
Swahili	sw
Swati	ss
Swedish	sv
Tagalog	tl
Tahitian	ty
Tajik	tg
Tamil	ta
Tatar	tt
Telugu	te
Thai	th

Continued on next page

TABLE C.1 CONTINUED: ISO 639 Two-Letter Language Codes Ordered by Language

Language	Language Code
Tibetan	bo
Tigrinya	ti
Tonga (Tonga Islands)	to
Tsonga	ts
Tswana	tn
Turkish	tr
Turkmen	tk
Twi	tw
Uighur	ug
Ukrainian	uk
Urdu	ur
Uzbek	uz
Vietnamese	vi
Volapük	vo
Welsh	cy
Wolof	wo
Xhosa	xh
Yiddish	yi
Yoruba	yo
Zhuang	za
Zulu	zu

TABLE C.2: ISO 639 Two-Letter Language Codes Ordered by Language Code

Language Code	Language
aa	Afar
ab	Abkhazian
ae	Avestan
af	Afrikaans
am	Amharic
ar	Arabic
as	Assamese
ay	Aymara
az	Azerbaijani
ba	Bashkir
be	Belarusian
bg	Bulgarian
bh	Bihari
bi	Bislama
bn	Bengali
bo	Tibetan
br	Breton
bs	Bosnian
ca	Catalan
ce	Chechen
ch	Chamorro
co	Corsican
cs	Czech
cu	Church Slavic

Continued on next page

TABLE C.2 CONTINUED: ISO 639 Two-Letter Language Codes Ordered by Language Code

Language Code	Language
cv	Chuvash
cy	Welsh
da	Danish
de	German
dz	Dzongkha
el	Greek, Modern (1453–)
en	English
eo	Esperanto
es	Spanish
et	Estonian
eu	Basque
fa	Persian
fi	Finnish
fj	Fijian
fo	Faroese
fr	French
fy	Frisian
ga	Irish
gd	Gaelic (Scots)
gl	Gallegan
gn	Guarani
gu	Gujarati
gv	Manx
ha	Hausa

Continued on next page

TABLE C.2 CONTINUED: ISO 639 Two-Letter Language Codes Ordered by Language Code

Language Code	Language
he	Hebrew
hi	Hindi
ho	Hiri Motu
hr	Croatian
hu	Hungarian
hy	Armenian
hz	Herero
ia	Interlingua (International Auxiliary Language Association)
id	Indonesian
ie	Interlingue
ik	Inupiaq
is	Icelandic
it	Italian
iu	Inuktitut
ja	Japanese
jw	Javanese
ka	Georgian
ki	Kikuyu
kj	Kuanyama
kk	Kazakh
kl	Kalaallisut
km	Khmer
kn	Kannada
ko	Korean

Continued on next page

TABLE C.2 CONTINUED: ISO 639 Two-Letter Language Codes Ordered by Language Code

Language Code	Language
ks	Kashmiri
ku	Kurdish
kv	Komi
kw	Cornish
ky	Kirghiz
la	Latin
lb	Letzeburgesch
ln	Lingala
lo	Lao
lt	Lithuanian
lv	Latvian
mg	Malagasy
mh	Marshall
mi	Maori
mk	Macedonian
ml	Malayalam
mn	Mongolian
mo	Moldavian
mr	Marathi
ms	Malay
mt	Maltese
my	Burmese
na	Nauru
nb	Norwegian Bokmål

Continued on next page

TABLE C.2 CONTINUED: ISO 639 Two-Letter Language Codes Ordered by Language Code

Language Code	Language
nd	Ndebele, North
ne	Nepali
ng	Ndonga
nl	Dutch
nn	Norwegian Nynorsk
no	Norwegian
nr	Ndebele, South
nv	Navajo
ny	Chichewa; Nyanja
oc	Occitan (post 1500); Provençal
om	Oromo
or	Oriya
os	Ossetian; Ossetic
pa	Panjabi
pi	Pali
pl	Polish
ps	Pushto
pt	Portuguese
qu	Quechua
rm	Raeto-Romance
rn	Rundi
ro	Romanian
ru	Russian
rw	Kinyarwanda

Continued on next page

TABLE C.2 CONTINUED: ISO 639 Two-Letter Language Codes Ordered by Language Code

Language Code	Language
sa	Sanskrit
sc	Sardinian
sd	Sindhi
se	Northern Sami
sg	Sango
si	Sinhalese
sk	Slovak
sl	Slovenian
sm	Samoan
sn	Shona
so	Somali
sq	Albanian
sr	Serbian
ss	Swati
st	Sotho, Southern
su	Sundanese
sv	Swedish
sw	Swahili
ta	Tamil
te	Telugu
tg	Tajik
th	Thai
ti	Tigrinya
tk	Turkmen

Continued on next page

TABLE C.2 CONTINUED: ISO 639 Two-Letter Language Codes Ordered by Language Code

Language Code	Language
tl	Tagalog
tn	Tswana
to	Tonga (Tonga Islands)
tr	Turkish
ts	Tsonga
tt	Tatar
tw	Twi
ty	Tahitian
ug	Uighur
uk	Ukrainian
ur	Urdu
uz	Uzbek
vi	Vietnamese
vo	Volapük
wo	Wolof
xh	Xhosa
yi	Yiddish
yo	Yoruba
za	Zhuang
zh	Chinese
zu	Zulu

Appendix D

ISO 3166 Two-Letter Country Codes

Appendix D • ISO 3166 Two-Letter Country Codes

TABLE D.1: ISO 3166 Two-Letter Country Codes Ordered by Country

Country	Country Code
Afghanistan	AF
Albania	AL
Algeria	DZ
American Samoa	AS
Andorra	AD
Angola	AO
Anguilla	AI
Antarctica	AQ
Antigua and Barbuda	AG
Argentina	AR
Armenia	AM
Aruba	AW
Australia	AU
Austria	AT
Azerbaijan	AZ
Bahamas	BS
Bahrain	BH
Bangladesh	BD
Barbados	BB
Belarus	BY
Belgium	BE
Belize	BZ
Benin	BJ
Bermuda	BM

Continued on next page

TABLE D.1 CONTINUED: ISO 3166 Two-Letter Country Codes Ordered by Country

Country	Country Code
Bhutan	BT
Bolivia	BO
Bosnia and Herzegovina	BA
Botswana	BW
Bouvet Island	BV
Brazil	BR
British Indian Ocean Territory	IO
Brunei Darussalam	BN
Bulgaria	BG
Burkina Faso	BF
Burundi	BI
Cambodia	KH
Cameroon	CM
Canada	CA
Cape Verde	CV
Cayman Islands	KY
Central African Republic	CF
Chad	TD
Chile	CL
China	CN
Christmas Island	CX
Cocos (Keeling) Islands	CC
Colombia	CO
Comoros	KM

Continued on next page

TABLE D.1 CONTINUED: ISO 3166 Two-Letter Country Codes Ordered by Country

Country	Country Code
Congo	CG
Congo, The Democratic Republic of the	CD
Cook Islands	CK
Costa Rica	CR
Cote D'Ivoire	CI
Croatia	HR
Cuba	CU
Cyprus	CY
Czech Republic	CZ
Denmark	DK
Djibouti	DJ
Dominica	DM
Dominican Republic	DO
East Timor	TP
Ecuador	EC
Egypt	EG
El Salvador	SV
Equatorial Guinea	GQ
Eritrea	ER
Estonia	EE
Ethiopia	ET
Falkland Islands (Malvinas)	FK
Faroe Islands	FO
Fiji	FJ

Continued on next page

TABLE D.1 CONTINUED: ISO 3166 Two-Letter Country Codes Ordered by Country

Country	Country Code
Finland	FI
France	FR
French Guiana	GF
French Polynesia	PF
French Southern Territories	TF
Gabon	GA
Gambia	GM
Georgia	GE
Germany	DE
Ghana	GH
Gibraltar	GI
Greece	GR
Greenland	GL
Grenada	GD
Guadeloupe	GP
Guam	GU
Guatemala	GT
Guinea	GN
Guinea-Bissau	GW
Guyana	GY
Haiti	HT
Heard Island and Mcdonald Islands	HM
Holy See (Vatican City State)	VA
Honduras	HN

Continued on next page

TABLE D.1 CONTINUED: ISO 3166 Two-Letter Country Codes Ordered by Country

Country	Country Code
Hong Kong	HK
Hungary	HU
Iceland	IS
India	IN
Indonesia	ID
Iran, Islamic Republic of	IR
Iraq	IQ
Ireland	IE
Israel	IL
Italy	IT
Jamaica	JM
Japan	JP
Jordan	JO
Kazakstan	KZ
Kenya	KE
Kiribati	KI
Korea, Democratic People's Republic of	KP
Korea, Republic of	KR
Kuwait	KW
Kyrgyzstan	KG
Lao People's Democratic Republic	LA
Latvia	LV
Lebanon	LB
Lesotho	LS

Continued on next page

TABLE D.1 CONTINUED: ISO 3166 Two-Letter Country Codes Ordered by Country

Country	Country Code
Liberia	LR
Libyan Arab Jamahiriya	LY
Liechtenstein	LI
Lithuania	LT
Luxembourg	LU
Macau	MO
Macedonia, The Former Yugoslav Republic of	MK
Madagascar	MG
Malawi	MW
Malaysia	MY
Maldives	MV
Mali	ML
Malta	MT
Marshall Islands	MH
Martinique	MQ
Mauritania	MR
Mauritius	MU
Mayotte	YT
Mexico	MX
Micronesia, Federated States of	FM
Moldova, Republic of	MD
Monaco	MC
Mongolia	MN
Montserrat	MS

Continued on next page

TABLE D.1 CONTINUED: ISO 3166 Two-Letter Country Codes Ordered by Country

Country	Country Code
Morocco	MA
Mozambique	MZ
Myanmar	MM
Namibia	NA
Nauru	NR
Nepal	NP
Netherlands	NL
Netherlands Antilles	AN
New Caledonia	NC
New Zealand	NZ
Nicaragua	NI
Niger	NE
Nigeria	NG
Niue	NU
Norfolk Island	NF
Northern Mariana Islands	MP
Norway	NO
Oman	OM
Pakistan	PK
Palau	PW
Palestinian Territory, Occupied	PS
Panama	PA
Papua New Guinea	PG
Paraguay	PY

Continued on next page

TABLE D.1 CONTINUED: ISO 3166 Two-Letter Country Codes Ordered by Country

Country	Country Code
Peru	PE
Philippines	PH
Pitcairn	PN
Poland	PL
Portugal	PT
Puerto Rico	PR
Qatar	QA
Réunion	RE
Romania	RO
Russian Federation	RU
Rwanda	RW
Saint Helena	SH
Saint Kitts and Nevis	KN
Saint Lucia	LC
Saint Pierre and Miquelon	PM
Saint Vincent and the Grenadines	VC
Samoa	WS
San Marino	SM
Sao Tome and Principe	ST
Saudi Arabia	SA
Senegal	SN
Seychelles	SC
Sierra Leone	SL
Singapore	SG

Continued on next page

TABLE D.1 CONTINUED: ISO 3166 Two-Letter Country Codes Ordered by Country

Country	Country Code
Slovakia	SK
Slovenia	SI
Solomon Islands	SB
Somalia	SO
South Africa	ZA
South Georgia and the South Sandwich Islands	GS
Spain	ES
Sri Lanka	LK
Sudan	SD
Suriname	SR
Svalbard and Jan Mayen	SJ
Swaziland	SZ
Sweden	SE
Switzerland	CH
Syrian Arab Republic	SY
Taiwan, Province of China	TW
Tajikistan	TJ
Tanzania, United Republic of	TZ
Thailand	TH
Togo	TG
Tokelau	TK
Tonga	TO
Trinidad and Tobago	TT
Tunisia	TN

Continued on next page

TABLE D.1 CONTINUED: ISO 3166 Two-Letter Country Codes Ordered by Country

Country	Country Code
Turkey	TR
Turkmenistan	TM
Turks and Caicos Islands	TC
Tuvalu	TV
Uganda	UG
Ukraine	UA
United Arab Emirates	AE
United Kingdom	GB
United States	US
United States Minor Outlying Islands	UM
Uruguay	UY
Uzbekistan	UZ
Vanuatu	VU
Venezuela	VE
Vietnam	VN
Virgin Islands, British	VG
Virgin Islands, U.S.	VI
Wallis and Futuna	WF
Western Sahara	EH
Yemen	YE
Yugoslavia	YU
Zambia	ZM
Zimbabwe	ZW

Appendix D • ISO 3166 Two-Letter Country Codes

TABLE D.2: ISO 3166 Two-Letter Country Codes Ordered by Country Code

Country Code	Country
AD	Andorra
AE	United Arab Emirates
AF	Afghanistan
AG	Antigua and Barbuda
AI	Anguilla
AL	Albania
AM	Armenia
AN	Netherlands Antilles
AO	Angola
AQ	Antarctica
AR	Argentina
AS	American Samoa
AT	Austria
AU	Australia
AW	Aruba
AZ	Azerbaijan
BA	Bosnia and Herzegovina
BB	Barbados
BD	Bangladesh
BE	Belgium
BF	Burkina Faso
BG	Bulgaria
BH	Bahrain
BI	Burundi

Continued on next page

TABLE D.2 CONTINUED: ISO 3166 Two-Letter Country Codes Ordered by Country Code

Country Code	Country
BJ	Benin
BM	Bermuda
BN	Brunei Darussalam
BO	Bolivia
BR	Brazil
BS	Bahamas
BT	Bhutan
BV	Bouvet Island
BW	Botswana
BY	Belarus
BZ	Belize
CA	Canada
CC	Cocos (Keeling) Islands
CD	Congo, The Democratic Republic of the
CF	Central African Republic
CG	Congo
CH	Switzerland
CI	Cote D'Ivoire
CK	Cook Islands
CL	Chile
CM	Cameroon
CN	China
CO	Colombia
CR	Costa Rica

Continued on next page

TABLE D.2 CONTINUED: ISO 3166 Two-Letter Country Codes Ordered by Country Code

Country Code	Country
CU	Cuba
CV	Cape Verde
CX	Christmas Island
CY	Cyprus
CZ	Czech Republic
DE	Germany
DJ	Djibouti
DK	Denmark
DM	Dominica
DO	Dominican Republic
DZ	Algeria
EC	Ecuador
EE	Estonia
EG	Egypt
EH	Western Sahara
ER	Eritrea
ES	Spain
ET	Ethiopia
FI	Finland
FJ	Fiji
FK	Falkland Islands (Malvinas)
FM	Micronesia, Federated States of
FO	Faroe Islands
FR	France

Continued on next page

TABLE D.2 CONTINUED: ISO 3166 Two-Letter Country Codes Ordered by Country Code

Country Code	Country
GA	Gabon
GB	United Kingdom
GD	Grenada
GE	Georgia
GF	French Guiana
GH	Ghana
GI	Gibraltar
GL	Greenland
GM	Gambia
GN	Guinea
GP	Guadeloupe
GQ	Equatorial Guinea
GR	Greece
GS	South Georgia and the South Sandwich Islands
GT	Guatemala
GU	Guam
GW	Guinea-Bissau
GY	Guyana
HK	Hong Kong
HM	Heard Island and Mcdonald Islands
HN	Honduras
HR	Croatia
HT	Haiti
HU	Hungary

Continued on next page

TABLE D.2 CONTINUED: ISO 3166 Two-Letter Country Codes Ordered by Country Code

Country Code	Country
ID	Indonesia
IE	Ireland
IL	Israel
IN	India
IO	British Indian Ocean Territory
IQ	Iraq
IR	Iran, Islamic Republic of
IS	Iceland
IT	Italy
JM	Jamaica
JO	Jordan
JP	Japan
KE	Kenya
KG	Kyrgyzstan
KH	Cambodia
KI	Kiribati
KM	Comoros
KN	Saint Kitts and Nevis
KP	Korea, Democratic People's Republic of
KR	Korea, Republic of
KW	Kuwait
KY	Cayman Islands
KZ	Kazakhstan
LA	Lao People's Democratic Republic

Continued on next page

TABLE D.2 CONTINUED: ISO 3166 Two-Letter Country Codes Ordered by Country Code

Country Code	Country
LB	Lebanon
LC	Saint Lucia
LI	Liechtenstein
LK	Sri Lanka
LR	Liberia
LS	Lesotho
LT	Lithuania
LU	Luxembourg
LV	Latvia
LY	Libyan Arab Jamahiriya
MA	Morocco
MC	Monaco
MD	Moldova, Republic of
MG	Madagascar
MH	Marshall Islands
MK	Macedonia, The Former Yugoslav Republic of
ML	Mali
MM	Myanmar
MN	Mongolia
MO	Macau
MP	Northern Mariana Islands
MQ	Martinique
MR	Mauritania
MS	Montserrat

Continued on next page

TABLE D.2 CONTINUED: ISO 3166 Two-Letter Country Codes Ordered by Country Code

Country Code	Country
MT	Malta
MU	Mauritius
MV	Maldives
MW	Malawi
MX	Mexico
MY	Malaysia
MZ	Mozambique
NA	Namibia
NC	New Caledonia
NE	Niger
NF	Norfolk Island
NG	Nigeria
NI	Nicaragua
NL	Netherlands
NO	Norway
NP	Nepal
NR	Nauru
NU	Niue
NZ	New Zealand
OM	Oman
PA	Panama
PE	Peru
PF	French Polynesia
PG	Papua New Guinea

Continued on next page

TABLE D.2 CONTINUED: ISO 3166 Two-Letter Country Codes Ordered by Country Code

Country Code	Country
PH	Philippines
PK	Pakistan
PL	Poland
PM	Saint Pierre and Miquelon
PN	Pitcairn
PR	Puerto Rico
PS	Palestinian Territory, Occupied
PT	Portugal
PW	Palau
PY	Paraguay
QA	Qatar
RE	Réunion
RO	Romania
RU	Russian Federation
RW	Rwanda
SA	Saudi Arabia
SB	Solomon Islands
SC	Seychelles
SD	Sudan
SE	Sweden
SG	Singapore
SH	Saint Helena
SI	Slovenia
SJ	Svalbard and Jan Mayen

Continued on next page

TABLE D.2 CONTINUED: ISO 3166 Two-Letter Country Codes Ordered by Country Code

Country Code	Country
SK	Slovakia
SL	Sierra Leone
SM	San Marino
SN	Senegal
SO	Somalia
SR	Suriname
ST	Sao Tome and Principe
SV	El Salvador
SY	Syrian Arab Republic
SZ	Swaziland
TC	Turks and Caicos Islands
TD	Chad
TF	French Southern Territories
TG	Togo
TH	Thailand
TJ	Tajikistan
TK	Tokelau
TM	Turkmenistan
TN	Tunisia
TO	Tonga
TP	East Timor
TR	Turkey
TT	Trinidad and Tobago
TV	Tuvalu

Continued on next page

TABLE D.2 CONTINUED: ISO 3166 Two-Letter Country Codes Ordered by Country Code

Country Code	Country
TW	Taiwan, Province of China
TZ	Tanzania, United Republic of
UA	Ukraine
UG	Uganda
UM	United States Minor Outlying Islands
US	United States
UY	Uruguay
UZ	Uzbekistan
VA	Holy See (Vatican City State)
VC	Saint Vincent and the Grenadines
VE	Venezuela
VG	Virgin Islands, British
VI	Virgin Islands, U.S.
VN	Vietnam
VU	Vanuatu
WF	Wallis and Futuna
WS	Samoa
YE	Yemen
YT	Mayotte
YU	Yugoslavia
ZA	South Africa
ZM	Zambia
ZW	Zimbabwe

INDEX

Note to the reader: Throughout this index **boldfaced** page numbers indicate primary discussions of a topic. *Italicized* page numbers indicate illustrations.

SYMBOLS AND NUMBERS

!= (not equal to operator), 98
& (AND bitwise operator), 97
&& (AND operator), 98
" (quotation marks)
    for attributes, **26**
    to enclose literal character string, 7
$ (dollar sign) to reference variables, 28, 70
% (remainder operator), 97
; (semicolon) to end WMLScript statement, 7, 91
< (less than operator), 98
< > (angle brackets for tags), 24–25
<< (left shift) bitwise operator, 97
== (equal to operator), 98
> (greater than operator), 98
>> (right shift) bitwise operator, 97
^ (XOR bitwise operator), 97
| (OR bitwise operator), 97
| | (OR operator), 98
// (slashes) for WMLScript comments, 91
/* and */ (slash-asterisk), for WMLScript comments, 91
{ } (braces) for block statements, 102
3G (third-generation) wireless networks, 15

A

<a> element, 26, **222–223**
abort() function, **268–269**
abs() function, **269–270**
accept-charset attribute of <go> element, 61, 233, 234
Accept-Language HTTP header, 187
    content delivery based on, **188–193**
accept user event, 82
access control rules for decks, 148
<access> element, 25, **223–225**
access pragmas, 106
accesskey attribute
    of <a> element, 223
    of <anchor> element, 225, 226
    of <input> element, 239
actions, <do> element to perform, **230–231**
alert() function, 8, 118, **260–261**
align attribute
    of <p> element, 49, 50, 245
    of <table> element, 253
alt attribute of <img> element, 51, 236, 237
<anchor> element, 26, **225–226**
    <a> tag as alternative, 222–223
    for lists, 54, 55–56
    syntax, 61
anchors, WML elements for, 26
AND bitwise operator (&), 97
AND operator (&&), 98
angle brackets for tags (< >), 24–25
AnywhereYouGo.com, 30
Apache server, configuring to deliver WAP content, 38
Apache Software, 32

apostrophe, escape character, 93
arithmetic operator (WMLScript), **97**
array operator (WMLScript), **99**
ASP for server-produced header, 144
assignment operator (WMLScript), **96–97**
attributes, **26**
    and elements, 28
    mandatory, 222
authentication, and caching, 137

B

<b> element, 49, **226–227**
backslash, escape character, 93
backspace, escape character, 93
bandwidth, 18
    cache impact on, 136
    constraints, 2
bearers, **14**
<big> element, 49, 226, 227
binary operators, complex, 97
block statement (WMLScript), **102**
Bluetooth, 18
BMP file format, 236
bold text, 49, 226–227
Boolean literal (WMLScript), **94**

 element, 25, **227–228**
braces ({ }) for block statements, 102
break in line, **227–228**
break statement (WMLScript), **104**
bridging 2.5G technologies, 20
"buttonsm" on WAP-compatible devices, **52–54**

C

cache
    features, **137–138**
    rules, 137
    in WAP, 130, **139–147**
        model, **139–144**
        preventing from reading WML deck, **142–144**
    Web, 136
cache-control attribute of <go> element, 234
Cache-control header, 138, 140
<card> element, 25, 48, 53, **228–229**
    syntax, 28–29
card-level event, 78
cards, 4, **22–24**, *23*
    adding images, **50–51**
    formatting text, **48–50**
    grouping elements within, **232–233**
    name for, 48
    navigating between, **52–63**
    templates for, 254–255
    WML elements for, 25
carriage return, escape character, 93
case sensitivity
    in WML, 28
        of variables, 70
    in WMLScript, 7, 91
CD-ROM. *See* companion CD
CDATA section, **229–230**
CDMA (Code Division Multiple Access), 14
CDPD (Cellular Digital Packet Data), 14
ceil() function, **263**
cells in tables, 254
Cellular Digital Packet Data (CDPD), 14
Cellular Telecommunications Industry Association (CTIA), 15
centered text, 49
CGI scripting, 4, 24
    passing variables for, 73
character sets, for internationalized WAP site, **196–197**, *201–204*
characters
    converting to number, 112, 278–279
    String library to manipulate, **113–114**. *See also* String library (WMLScript)
characterSet() function, **270–271**
charAt() function, 8, **281**

cinema application. *See* example program
class attribute, 222
classes, importing in Java, **155–156**
client/server architecture, 3
client side processing, passing variables for, **72–73**
Code Division Multiple Access (CDMA), 14
ColdFusion, 4
columns attribute of <table> element, 253
comma operator (WMLScript), **99**
comments
   in WML, **27**
   in WMLScript, 7, **91**
      for code clarity, 102
companion CD
   myfirst.wml, 36
   prologue.wml file, 46
compare() function, **281–282**
compilation unit, 88
complex binary operators, 97
computers, WAP phone emulator for, 16
concatenating strings, 97
conditional operations
   if statement, **102–103**
   for statement, **104**
   while statement, **104**
conditional operator (WMLScript), **99–100**
confirm() function, 8, **261–262**
content attribute of <meta> element, 240
Content-Language HTTP header, 187, **193–194**
Continue button, 69–70
continue statement (WMLScript), **105**
conversion mode for escaping, 77
CTIA (Cellular Telecommunications Industry Association), 15

D

data types in WMLScript, 7, **95–96**
database, 43
debugging in WMLScript, **90**
decimal integers, 92

deck-level event, 78
decks, 4, **22–24**, 23
   access by other decks, 223–225
   access control rules for, 148
   character sets applied to, 199
   <head> element for metadata and access control, **235**
   to invoke WMLScript, 107
   meta information, **240–241**
   structure, **28–29**
   templates for, 254–255
   WML elements for, 25
declaring variables in WMLScript, 94, 103
default value
   of attributes, 222
   of <select> element, 68
DELETE method (HTTP), 135
delete user event, 82
design issues, **34–35**
device sensing, 6
Dialogs library (WMLScript), 8, 107, **260–262**
   alert() function, 118, **260–261**
   confirm() function, **261–262**
   prompt() function, **262**
display on wireless devices, 34
<do> element, 25, 52, 53, **230–231**
   to bind user event to task, 82–85
Document Type Definition (DTD), WML 1.1, 5
documents in WML as decks, 4
doing nothing, instructions for, 241
dollar sign ($) to reference variables, 28, 70
domain attribute of <access> element, 224
DTD (Document Type Definition), WML 1.1, 5
Dynamic Systems Research Ltd., SDK (software development kit), 31
dynamic WML page, 43
   from JSP, 150
   programming language for, 154

E

ECMAScript, 6

EDGE (Enhanced Data Rate for GSM Evolution), 18
elementAt() function, 113, **282–283**
elements() function, **283–284**
elements in WML, **24–26**
   attributes, **26**, 28
   nesting, 49
   start and end tags, 47
   syntax, 222
   valid, 222
<em> element, 226, **231–232**
empty statement (WMLScript), **102**
emptyok attribute of <input> element, 67, 239
emulator, WAP, 5, *5*, **32–34**
enctype attribute of <go> element, 233, 234
end tag, 24
Enhanced Data Rate for GSM Evolution (EDGE), 18
equal to operator (==), 98
Ericsson, 8
   R380 emulator, 33
   WapIDE SDK 2, 30, 32
error handling in WMLScript, **90**
escape characters
   CDATA section to avoid, **229–230**
   replacing characters in variable with, 77
escapeString() function, **294–295**
ETSI (European Telecommunications Standards Institute), 15
events, **78–85**
   binding, 242
   intrinsic, **78–81**
   user, **82–85**
   WML elements for, 25
example program, **39–43**
   account.wml file, 69–70, 73–74
      <refresh> element, 83–84
   CalculatePrice function, 114–118, 125
   Cinema servlet class, 205–219
   content based on Accept-language header, **188–193**
   Details deck, 125
   first steps, 39–40, *40*

index card, *59*
Java servlet, **159–173**
   complete servlet code, **173–182**
   cost calculation for tickets, **170–173**
   logon, **159–165**
   movie details, **167–169**
   movie listing, **165–167**
   ticket reservations, **169–170**
logon screen, 41, 69–70, *70*, 124–125
   script, 108–111
movie card, 60–63, *63*
multilingual content, **205–220**
password screen, *70*
Phone Number screen, *70*
Prices screen, *76*
Problem card, 125
referencing variables in, **73–74**
script.wmls file, 109, 110
   full compilation unit, **121–127**
selection lists, 57, 58–59
server side programming, **41–43**
validations with WMLScript, **40–41**
exception handling in Java, 161
exit() function, **271–272**
expiration
   immediate, 143
   information for cache, 138
Expires header, 140–141
expression statement (WMLScript), **102**
eXtensible Markup Language (XML), 4, 15
   prologue, 28, 46
external functions, 110, **119–120**
ExWAP, 33
EZOS, 33

F

<fieldset> element, 25, **232–233**
file format for WAP graphics, 51
file name extension, 36

files, decks as WML, 22
financial transactions, security for, 41
find() function, 8, **284–285**
float() function, **272–273**
Float library (WMLScript), 8, 107, **263–268**
    ceil() function, **263**
    floor() function, **263–264**
    int() function, **264–265**
    maxFloat() function, 95, **265**
    minFloat() function, 95, **265–266**
    pow() function, **266–267**
    round() function, **267**
    sqrt() function, **268**
floating point literal (WMLScript), **92**
floating point numbers in WMLScript, 95
floor() function, **263–264**
fonts
    big, 49, **227**
    bold, 49, **226–227**
    emphasized, 252–253
    italics, **235–236**
    small, 251–252
for statement (WMLScript), **104**, 115, 117
form feed, escape character, 93
format attribute of <input> element, 67, 239
    mask, 69
format() function, **285–286**
formatting text, **48–50**
forua attribute of <meta> element, 240
freshness in caching, 136, 138
function call stack, 89
functions in WMLScript, 88, **119–121**
    calling, **108–111**
    exiting, 105
    external functions, **119–120**
    internal, **120–121**
    library, **120**. *See also* libraries in WMLScript

G

gateway server, 10, 14. *See also* WAP gateway

Gelon, 33
General Packet Radio System (GPRS), 18
GET method (HTTP), 131, **133**
    data quantities using, **145**
    passing name/value pairs, 245–246
getBase() function, **295–296**
getCurrentCard() function, 8, **305–306**
getFragment() function, **296–297**
getHost() function, 8, **297**
getParameters() function, 161, **297–298**
getPath() function, 8, **298–299**
getPort() function, **299**
getQuery() function, **299–300**
getReferer() function, 8, **300–301**
getScheme() function, **301**
getVar() function, 110, **306**
GIF file format, 236
global variable declaration in Java, **156–157**
<go> element, 26, 52, 108, **233–235**
    as intrinsic event task, 79
    for lists, 54, 55–56
    post method, **72–73**
    sendreferer attribute, 148
    syntax, 61
    syntax to call WMLScript function, 89
go() function, 8, 107, **306–307**
GPRS (General Packet Radio System), 18
graphics. *See also* images; <img> element
    low-resolution, 6
greater than operator (>), 98
grouping elements within card, **232–233**
grouping options, 243

H

Hashtable, 189, 205
HDML (Handheld Device Markup Language), 8
<head> element, 25, **235**
    <access> element in, 224
HEAD method (HTTP), **133–134**
header information in client request, 131

height attribute of <img> element, 237
help user event, 82
hexadecimal integers, 92
High Speed Circuit Switched Data (HSCSD), 18
horizontal tab, escape character, 93
hosts
    function to return string containing for URL, 297
    for WAP site, 37
href attribute
    of <a> element, 223
    of <go> element, 52, 61, 233, 234
HSCSD (High Speed Circuit Switched Data), 18
hspace attribute of <img> element, 237
.htaccess file, 38
HTML (Hypertext Markup Language), 10
HTTP (Hypertext Transport Protocol), 10, **130–135**
    methods, **132–135**
        GET method, **133**
        HEAD method, **133–134**
        POST method, **134–135**
    and WML access, 4
http-equiv attribute of <meta> element, 146, 240
httpd.conf file, ResourceConfig variable, 38
Hypertext Markup Language (HTML), 10

I

<i> element, 226, **235–236**
id attribute, 222
    of <card> element, 48, 229
IETF (Internet Engineering Task Force), 15
if statement (WMLScript), **102–103**
images
    adding to cards, **50–51**
    WML elements for, 26
<img> element, 26, 51, **236–238**
importing classes in Java, **155–156**
iname attribute of <select> element, 249, 250
indexes for array elements, 99, 281

Inetis, DotWAP SDK, 31
infrared links, 18
initializing variable, 103
input by users, **66–71**
<input> element, 25, 27, 66–67, 145, **238–249**
input validation, 90
insertAt() function, **287**
Instruction Pointer, 89
int() function, **264–265**
integer literal (WMLScript), **92**
integers in WMLScript, 95
Intelligent Terminal Transfer Protocol (ITTP), 8
internal functions, **120–121**
internationalizing WAP site
    character sets, **196–197**
    delivering multilingual content, **185–186**
    HTTP languages, **187–194**
        accept-language header, **188–193**
        content-language header, **193–194**
        quality value, **188**
    importance, 184
    multilingual content customization, **205–220**
    text direction, **194–196**
    transfer encodings, **197–205**
Internet Engineering Task Force (IETF), 15
Internet Information Server (Microsoft), configuring to deliver WAP content, 39
Internet Protocol (IP), 15
Internet protocol stacks, WAP (Wireless Application Protocol) and, *12*
interpreter architecture in WMLScript, **89–90**
intranets, 16
intrinsic events, **78–81**
invalid literal (WMLScript), **94**
IOException method, 161
IP (Internet Protocol), 15
isEmpty() function, **287–288**
isFloat() function, **273–274**
isInt() function, **274**
ISO 639 language codes, 187
    ordered by language, 312–318
    ordered by language code, 319–325

ISO 3166 country codes, 187
    ordered by country, 328–337
    ordered by country code, 338–347
ISO Latin character sets, 196–197
isValid() function, **301–302**
isvalid operator (WMLScript), **101**
italics font, **235–236**
ITTP (Intelligent Terminal Transfer Protocol), 8
ivalue attribute, of <select> element, 249, 250

J

Java
    advantages for dynamic page development, 154
    basics, **155–158**
        global variable declaration, **156–157**
        importing classes, **155–156**
        user agent interaction, **157**
        WML code output, **157–158**
    example servlet, **159–173**
        complete servlet code, **173–182**
        cost calculation for tickets, **170–173**
        logon, **159–165**
        movie details, **167–169**
        movie listing, **165–167**
        ticket reservations, **169–170**
    exception handling in, 161–162
    for Nokia WAP Toolkit, 31
    and WAP, **149–151**
Java Server Pages, **150–151**
JPG file format, 236

K

Klondike WAP Browser, 32

L

label attribute, of <do> element, 230, 231
Lang library (WMLScript), 8, 106, **268–280**
    abort() function, **268–269**
    abs() function, **269–270**
    characterSet() function, **270–271**
    converting values with, **112–113**
    exit() function, **271–272**
    float() function, **272–273**
    isFloat() function, **273–274**
    isInt() function, **274**
    max() function, **275**
    maxInt() function, **275–276**
    min() function, **276–277**
    minInt() function, **277**
    parseFloat() function, **277–278**
    parseInt() function, 112, **278–279**
    random() function, **279–280**
    seed() function, **280**
language tags, 187
left shift (<<) bitwise operator, 97
length() function, 8, **288–289**
less than operator (<), 98
lexical structure for WMLScript, **91**
libraries in WMLScript, 7, 8, **106–107**
    calling, 107
    Dialogs library, **260–262**
    Float library (WMLScript), **263–268**
    functions, **120**
    Lang library (WMLScript), **268–280**
    String library (WMLScript), **113–114**, **281–294**
    URL library (WMLScript), **294–305**
    WMLBrowser library (WMLScript), **305–308**
lines of text, break for, **227–228**
link, 225. *See also* <anchor> element
LINK method (HTTP), 135
lists
    for navigating, **54–63**, *55*
    of user entry options, **68–71**

literal character string, " (quotation marks) to enclose, 7
literal text, CDATA section for, **229–230**
literals in WMLScript, **92–94**
    Boolean, **94**
    floating point, **92**
    integer, **92**
    invalid, **94**
    string, **93**
loadString() function, **302–303**
localization, 184. *See also* internationalizing WAP site
localsrc attribute of <img> element, 51, 237
logical operator (WMLScript), **98**
logon screen, 41, 69–70, *70*
loops, 104

M

M3Gate, 32
mandatory attributes, 222
market growth, 3
max-age cache control, 140
max() function, **275**
maxFloat() function, 95, **265**
maxInt() function, 95, **275–276**
maxlength attribute of <input> element, 67, 239
memory cache in microbrowsers, **139–147**
message
    alert() function to display, 118, 260
    confirm() function to display, 261–262
    prompt() function to display, 262
<meta> element, 25, **146**, **240–241**
meta pragmas, 106
method attribute of <go> element, 61, 233, 234
methods
    in HTTP, 130, **132–135**
        GET method, **133**
        HEAD method, **133–134**
        POST method, **134–135**
    in object-oriented programming, 155

microbrowsers, 3, 5
    environment in WAE, 13
Microsoft Internet Information Server, configuring to deliver WAP content, 39
MIME (Multipurpose Internet Mail Extension)
    multipart messages, 147
    support for WML files, 37–38
min() function, **276–277**
minFloat() function, 95, **265–266**
minInt() function, 95, **277**
Mitsubishi, Trium Geo, 17
mobile phones, 2
mode attribute of <p> element, 49, 245
Motorola, 8
    Mobile ADK, 30
    Timeport P7389, 17
movie tickets application. *See* example program
multilingual content, delivering, **185–186**
multiple attribute of <select> element, 250
multithreaded servlet, 156
must-revalidate cache control, 140, 141

N

name attribute
    of <do> element, 231
    of <input> element, 238
    of <meta> element, 240
    of <postfield> element, 246
    of <select> element, 68, 249, 250
    of <setvar> element, 251
    of <timer> element, 256
name for card, 48
navigating between cards, **52–63**
    with anchored lists, **59–63**
    <go> element to define, **233–235**, 306–307
    with lists, **54–63**
    <prev> element for, 247–248
    using user agent buttons, **52–54**
negative zero, 95
nesting elements, 49

new line
    escape character, 93
    forcing, **227–228**
newcontext attribute of <card> element, 229
newContext() function, **307**
next() function, 8
no-cache cache control, 140
noesc mode, 77
Nokia, 8
    WAP phones, 17
    WAP Toolkit, 31
<noop> element, 26, **241**
    as intrinsic event task, 79
not equal to operator (!=), 98
Numeric Algorithm Laboratories, 32
numeric values, converting characters to, 112, 278–279

O

object-oriented programming, **155–156**
octal integers, 92
Omnipoint, 9
onenterbackward attribute
    of <card> element, 229
    for intrinsic events, 78
    of <template> element, 255
<onenterbackward> element, 25
onenterforward attribute
    of <card> element, 229
    of <template> element, 255
<onenterforward> element, 25
    for intrinsic events, 78
<onevent> element, 25, **242–243**
    syntax, 78
onpick attribute
    to call script, 109
    for intrinsic events, 78
    of <option> element, 57–58, 244

<onpick> element, 25
ontimer attribute
    of <card> element, 229
    for intrinsic events, 78
    of <template> element, 255
<ontimer> element, 25
open protocol, WAP as, 2
Openwave, 8
    UP.SDK, 31, 32
Opera, 34
operand stack, 89
operators in WMLScript, 8, **96–101**
    arithmetic, **97**
    array, **99**
    assignment, **96–97**
    comma, **99**
    conditional, **99–100**
    isvalid, **101**
    logical, **98**
    relational, **98–99**
    string, **97**
    typeof, **100**
<optgroup> element, 25, **243**
<option> element, 25, 68, **243–244**
    for lists, 54
        syntax, 57–58
optional attribute of <do> element, 231
OPTIONS method (HTTP), 135
options user event, 82
OR bitwise operator (|), 97
OR operator (||), 98
ordered attribute, of <card> element, 229
origin server, 10

P

<p> element, 26, 48–49, **244–245**
    <select> element inside, 54, 58
pagers, 2

parameters, function to return string containing for URL, 297–298
parseFloat() function, **277–278**
parseInt() function, 112, 170, **278–279**
password screen, 69–70, *70*
path attribute of <access> element, 224
path, function to return string containing for URL, 298–299
PDAs (personal digital assistants), 2
phone emulator, 16
Phone.com, 8
phones, 17
PHP, for server-produced header, 143–144
PNG file format, 236
port, function to return string containing for URL, 299
positive zero, 95
POST method (HTTP), **134–135**
    data quantities using, **145**
    passing name/value pairs, 245–246
<postfield> element, 25, 72–73, 145, **245–246**
pow() function, 8, **266–267**
pragmas in WMLScript, **106**
    use, 120
<pre> element, **246–247**
<prev> element, 26, 226, **247–248**
    as intrinsic event task, 79
prev() function, 8, **308**
prev user event, 82
prologue in deck, 28, 46, **248**
prompt() function, 8, **262**
protocol, stateless, 132
proxy server, 10
    as cache server, 136
PUT method (HTTP), 135

Q

query, function to return string containing for URL, 299–300

quotation marks (")
    for attributes, **26**
    to enclose literal character string, 7
    escape character, 93

R

random() function, **279–280**
<refresh> element, 26, 226, **248–249**
    as intrinsic event task, 79
    for user input, 83–84
refresh() function, 8, **308**
relational operator (WMLScript), **98–99**
relative URLs, 58
    function to return resolution to base URL, 303–304
remainder operator (%), 97
removeAt() function, **289**
replace() function, 8, 114, **290**
replaceAt() function, **290–291**
reserved words in WMLScript, **105–106**
reset user event, 82
resolve() function, **303–304**
ResourceConfig variable in httpd.conf file, 38
return statement (WMLScript), **105**
RFC 2616, 136, 187
    quality value, 188
right shift (>>) bitwise operator, 97
round() function, 8, **267**
row of table, 256–257

S

scheme, function to return string containing for URL, 301
script.wmls file, 109, 110
    full compilation unit, **121–127**
SDK (software development kit), **29–32**

security, 41
    and caching, 137
    minimizing risks in WML, **147–149**
seed() function, **280**
<select> element, 25, 68, **249–250**
    for lists, 54, 57–59
    to set variable, 74–77
semicolon (;) to end WMLScript statement, 7, 91
sendreferer attribute of <go> element, 61, 148, 233, 234
server side programming, **41–43**
servers
    HTTP header production on, 142
    reply to client request, 131–132
    for testing WML pages, 32
    types for World Wide Web, 10
    uploading file to, 37
<setvar> element, 26, 27, 72, 108, **251**
Short Message Service (SMS), 14
short-range radio links, specification for, 18
size attribute of <input> element, 67, 239
skins, 32
slashes (//)
    escape character, 93
    for WMLScript comments, 91
Slob-Trot Software Oy Ab, 33
<small> element, 226, **251–252**
Smart Messaging concept, 8
SMS (Short Message Service), 14
soft keys, mapping, 6
software development kits (SDK), **29–32**
    with WAP emulators, 16
Sony, CMD-Z5, 17
splash screen, 46, *49*
    animation with <timer> element, 79–81, *81*
    with redefined buttons, *54*
sqrt() function, 8, **268**
squeeze() function, **291–292**
src attribute of <img> element, 51, 236, 237
srm.conf file, 38
stateless protocol, 132

statements in WMLScript, **101–104**
    block, **102**
    break, **104**
    continue, **105**
    empty, **102**
    expression, **102**
    for, **104**, 115, 117
    if, **102–103**
    return, **105**
    switch...case statement, 173
        code example, 174–179
    variable, **103**
    while, **104**
static WML page, 43
String library (WMLScript), 8, 107, **113–114**, **281–294**
    charAt() function, **281**
    compare() function, **281–282**
    elementAt() function, 113, **282–283**
    elements() function, **283–284**
    find() function, **284–285**
    format() function, **285–286**
    insertAt() function, **287**
    isEmpty() function, **287–288**
    length() function, **288–289**
    removeAt() function, **289**
    replace() function, 114, **290**
    replaceAt() function, **290–291**
    squeeze() function, **291–292**
    subString() function, **292–293**
    toString() function, **293**
    trim() function, **293–294**
string literal (WMLScript), **93**
string operator (WMLScript), **97**
StringTokenizer class, 190
<strong> element, 226, **252–253**
subString() function, **292–293**
switch...case statement, 173
    code example, 174–179

T

tabindex attribute
  of <input> element, 239
  of <select> element, 250
<table> element, 26, **253**
tags, 24, 222. *See also* elements in WML
tasks, WML elements for, 26
<td> element, 26, **254**
<template> element, 25, 78, **254–255**
text. *See also* fonts
  direction in internationalized WAP site, **194–196**
  formatting, **48–50**
    WML elements for, 25–26
  preformatted, 246–247
  underlined, 257
text editor, 36
third-generation (3G) wireless networks, 15
<timer> element, 26, 79–81, **255–256**
title attribute
  of <a> element, 223
  of <anchor> element, 61, 225, 226
  of <card> element, 229
  of <fieldset> element, 232
  of <input> element, 67, 238
  of <optgroup> element, 243
  of <option> element, 57, 244
  of <select> element, 68
  of <table> element, 253
tokenized lines for display, 167
toString() function, **293**
<tr> element, 26, **256–257**
TRACE method (HTTP), 135
transfer encodings, **197–205**
trim() function, 8, **293–294**
truth value, 94
type attribute
  of <do> element, 230
  of <input> element, 238

  of <onevent> element, 242
type conversions in WMLScript, **101**
typeof operator (WMLScript), **100**

U

<u> element, 226, **257**
UDP (User Datagram Protocol), 15
UMTS (Universal Mobile Telecommunications System), 18
unary operators, 97
underlined text, 257
unesc mode, 77
unescapeString() function, **304–305**
Unicode character set, 197, 198
  escape character, 93
Uniform Resource Locator (URL), 10
  in HTTP method command, 131
Universal Mobile Telecommunications System (UMTS), 18
unknown user event, 82
UNLINK method (HTTP), 135
Unstructured Supplementary Service Data (USSD), 14
Unwired Planet, 8
URI Generic Syntax RFC 2396, 77
URL (Uniform Resource Locator), 10
  function to return content, 302–303
  header rule on caching, 140
  in HTTP method command, 131
  relative, 58
  validating, 301–302
  in WAP programming model, 11–12
URL library (WMLScript), 8, 107, **294–305**
  escapeString() function, **294–295**
  getBase() function, **295–296**
  getFragment() function, **296–297**
  getHost() function, **297**
  getParameters() function, 161, **297–298**

getPath() function, **298–299**
getPort() function, **299**
getQuery() function, **299–300**
getReferer() function, **300–301**
getScheme() function, **301**
isValid() function, **301–302**
loadString() function, **302–303**
resolve() function, **303–304**
unescapeString() function, **304–305**
url pragmas, 106
use pragma, 120
user agents
   interaction in Java, **157**
   support for graphics, 236
   understanding of transfer encoding by, 198
   warnings with cache use, 138
User Datagram Protocol (UDP), 15
user events, **82–85**
user input, **66–71**
   from list options, **68–71**
   text entry, **66–68**
   validating, 90
   variables to store, 108–109
   WML elements for, 25
user interface, 17–18
   for WML, 4
USSD (Unstructured Supplementary Service Data), 14

V

validation
   in caching, 136, 141
   of data, **118–119**
   of input, 90
   of URL, 301–302
   with WMLScript, **40–41**
value attribute
   of <input> element, 238
   of <option> element, 57, 244

of <postfield> element, 246
of <select> element, 68, 249, 250
of <setvar> element, 251
of <timer> element, 256
var keyword, 7, 94, 111–112
variable statement (WMLScript), **103**
variables
   declaring global in Java, **156–157**
   in object-oriented programming, 155
   in WML, **27–28**
variables in WMLScript, **71–78**, **94**
   acting on settings by user, **74–77**
   converting type, **112**
   displaying values, **71**
   escaping, **77**
   passing from browser to script, 110
   passing values to other applications, **72–73**
   referencing in example application, **73–74**
   refreshing, 248–249
   setting values, **72**
   WML elements for, 26
Visual Basic, for server-produced header, 144
vspace attribute of <img> element, 237

W

WAE (Wireless Application Environment), **13**
WAP (Wireless Application Protocol), **12–14**
   1997 Forum specification, 3
   architecture, **9–16**
     bearers, **14**
     programming model, 11, *11*
     standards, **15–16**
     WAE (Wireless Application Environment), **13**
     WDP (Wireless Datagram Protocol), **14**
     WSP (Wireless Session Protocol), **13**
     WTLS (Wireless Transport Layer Security), **14**
     WTP (Wireless Transaction Protocol), **14**

design issues, **34–35**
future, **18–20**
and Internet protocol stacks, *12*
Web server configuration to deliver content, **37–39**
what it is, **2–3**
WMLScript Virtual Machine in, 29
WAP devices, **16–18**. *See also* cache, in WAP
    multipart messages to enhance responses, **146–147**
WAP emulator, 5, *5*, 16, **32–34**
    displaying file in, 36
WAP Forum, **8–9**, 15
WAP gateway, 3, *3*, 4, 11
    translation by, 5, *5*
WAP-120 (WAP Caching Model Specification), 139
WAP-175 (WAP Cache Operation Specification), 139
WAPalizer, 33
WAPEmulator, 34
WAPman for Windows 95/98/NT, 33
Wapmore, 34
Wapnet, 31
Wappy, 34
WAPsilon, 34
WAR (Wireless Application Reader), 31
warnings, from cache, 138
WBMP (Wireless BitMap) format, 51, 236
WBMPs (low-resolution graphics), 6
WDP (Wireless Datagram Protocol), **14**
Web browsers, WML support, 34
Web cache, 136
Web servers, 4
    configuring to deliver WAP content, **37–39**
Web sites
    for Java development language, 154
    for WAP development tools, 30–31
    WML 1.1 DTD, 5
well-formed URL, function to determine, 301–302
while statement (WMLScript), **104**
whitespace, 281
    squeeze() function to reduce, 291–292

trim() function to remove, 293–294
width attribute of <img> element, 237
WinWAP, 33
Wireless Application Environment (WAE), **13**
Wireless Application Protocol (WAP), what it is, **2–3**
Wireless Application Reader (WAR), 31
Wireless Companion, 34
Wireless Datagram Protocol (WDP), **14**
Wireless Markup Language (WML), what it is, **4–6**
Wireless Session Protocol (WSP), **13**
    message conversion, 130
Wireless Telephony Application Interface (WTAI), 13
Wireless Transaction Protocol (WTP), **14**
Wireless Transport Layer Security (WTLS), **14**
WML (Wireless Markup Language)
    example program, **39–43**
        first steps, 39–40, *40*
        server side programming, **41–43**
        validations with WMLScript, **40–41**
    minimizing security risks, **147–149**
    returning processing from WMLScript to, 107
    SDK install, **29–32**
    simple program, *35*, **35–36**
        testing, **37**
    structure
        attributes, **26**
        cards and decks, 4, **22–24**, *23*
        comments, **27**
        deck structure, **28–29**
        elements, **24–26**
        variables, **27–28**
    syntax to call WMLScript function, 89
    what it is, **4–6**
WML code output, from Java, **157–158**
<wml> element, 28, 47, **258**
WML files, 22
    prologue, 46
    text editor to create, 36
WMLBrowser library (WMLScript), 8, 107, **305–308**
    getCurrentCard() function, **305–306**

getVar() function, 110, **306**
go() function, 107, **306–307**
newContext() function, **307**
prev() function, **308**
refresh() function, **308**
.WMLS file extension, 88
WMLScript
    characteristics, **88–91**
        debugging, **90**
        error handling, **90**
        interpreter architecture, **89–90**
    comments, **91**
    connecting with WML, **107–127**
        calling function, 107, **108–111**
    data types, **95–96**
    data validation, **118–119**
    full compilation unit, **121–127**
    functions, **119–121**
        external, **119–120**
        internal, **120–121**
        library, **120**
    lexical structure, **91**
    libraries, 89, **106–107**. *See also* libraries in WMLScript
    literals, **92–94**
        Boolean, **94**
        floating point, **92**
        integer, **92**
        invalid, **94**
        string, **93**
    operators, **96–101**
        arithmetic, **97**
        array, **99**
        assignment, **96–97**
        comma, **99**
        conditional, **99–100**
        isvalid, **101**
        logical, **98**
        relational, **98–99**
        string, **97**
        typeof, **100**

    passing variables to, **72–73**
    pragmas, **106**
    reserved words, **105–106**
    statements, **101–104**
        for, **104**
        block, **102**
        break, **104**
        continue, **105**
        empty, **102**
        expression, **102**
        if, **102–103**
        return, **105**
        variable, **103**
        while, **104**
    syntax rules, 7
    type conversions, **101**
    validations with, **40–41**
    variables, **94**, **111–118**
    virtual machine inclusion in WAP browser, 29
    what it is, **6–8**
word wrap, 49
Wordpad, 36
World Wide Web, programming model, *10*, 10
wrap mode, 49
WSP (Wireless Session Protocol), **13**
    message conversion, 130
WTAI (Wireless Telephony Application Interface), 13
WTLS (Wireless Transport Layer Security), **14**
WTP (Wireless Transaction Protocol), **14**

X

Xitami intranet Web server, 32
XML (eXtensible Markup Language), 4, 15
    prologue, 28, 46
xml:lang attribute, 185, 222
XOR bitwise operator (^), 97

Y

Yospace, 33
YOURWAP.com, 34

Z

zero, negative or positive, 95
zero-based index, 281

TAKE YOUR SKILLS TO THE NEXT LEVEL
with Visual Basic Developer's Guides
from Sybex

Noel Jerke
ISBN: 0-7821-2621-9 • 752pp
$49.99

Mike Gunderloy
ISBN: 0-7821-2745-2 • 432pp
$39.99

Dianne Siebold
ISBN: 0-7821-2679-0 • 608pp
$39.99

Yair Alan Griver
ISBN: 0-7821-2692-8 • 320pp
$39.99

Mike Gunderloy
ISBN: 0-7821-2556-5 • 480pp
$39.99

A. Russell Jones
ISBN: 0-7821-2557-3 • 416pp
$39.99

Wayne Freeze
ISBN: 0-7821-2558-1 • 496pp
$39.99

Steve Brown
ISBN: 0-7821-2559-X • 480p
$39.99

- Develop industrial-strength enterprise applications.
- Focus on real-world issues, with code examples you can use in your own work.
- Learn from authors who are experienced Visual Basic developers.

SYBEX®
www.sybex.com

What's on the CD-ROM

The accompanying CD-ROM contains the following products and programs, as well as the code from the book. For information on each item and for installation instructions, please see the readme file on the CD-ROM.

> **NOTE** This CD includes the Sybex CLICKME interface, an easy-to-use interface that makes it easy for you to install the programs you want from the CD. The CLICKME interface starts automatically and runs completely from the CD.

- EzWAP: A trial version of the first platform-independent WAP browser; enables you to use a standard Web browser to view WAP sites as easily as HTML sites

- WinWAP 3.0 Trial Version: WAP browser for Windows; incorporates all standard Windows capabilities, such as saving, printing, and copying

- SmartPhone Emulator Developer Edition: Test WAP content from your desktop with this stand-alone application

- Breeze XML Studio 2.2: Development environment for building XML-based business solutions

- Peter's XML Editor: Tool for XML editing

- Wapple: Simple Text Editor designed for creating and editing WML code, thus making all WML commands available

- M3Gate Emulator: Surf over WAP resources with this browser; WML and WMLScript are fully suuported